翻译讲堂

My Random Thoughts
with
My English Translation

雜感自譯

注释与解析

〔澳〕林巍 著

商务印书馆
The Commercial Press

图书在版编目（CIP）数据

杂感自译：注释与解析：汉、英/（澳）林巍著. —北京：商务印书馆，2020（2022.5 重印）
（翻译讲堂）
ISBN 978-7-100-18731-2

Ⅰ.①杂… Ⅱ.①林… Ⅲ.①英语—翻译—研究 Ⅳ.①H315.9

中国版本图书馆 CIP 数据核字（2020）第 122273 号

权利保留，侵权必究。

翻译讲堂
杂感自译：注释与解析
〔澳〕林巍 著

商 务 印 书 馆 出 版
（北京王府井大街 36 号 邮政编码 100710）
商 务 印 书 馆 发 行
北京虎彩文化传播有限公司印刷
ISBN 978 - 7 - 100 - 18731 - 2

2020 年 8 月第 1 版　　　开本 880×1230　1/32
2022 年 5 月北京第 2 次印刷　印张 10¾
定价：66.00 元

让思维具有立体性

——我学翻译的体会

（代序）

我学习外语、翻译的过程要追溯到上世纪 60 年代小学三年级在北京外国语学校（白堆子）的经历。那时贪玩，对英语没有特殊的兴趣，只是应付课程。能记起有趣的是外教，一个满头银发的英国老太太 Ms. Spink，每次由中国老师陪同，坐着小汽车来到教室门口，满脸慈祥的笑容，和我们每个小孩儿打招呼（小妞，十几个人）。之后，能和她简单对话了，便有了无上的成就感和优越感，特别是当着不懂英语的人。在思维上，当时得到的最大启示是：原来一种东西，如桌子、椅子、门窗、香蕉、苹果等的名称，并不是唯一、固定的，还可有其他的叫法，取决于不同的民族和语言，于是有了最初的观念启蒙。后来，又到录音机房，每人录下自己的英语讲话（那时算是一种奢侈的教学活动），再回到教室，与大家一起来听，有一种既熟悉又陌生的惊异感觉。回想起来，正是从那时开始，自己的思维乃至人生开始变得多面、立体起来。

改革开放后，有机会去国外学习、工作了十余年，并入了外籍。后又到北美、欧洲、日本等地以及回国在大陆和港澳台地区讲学或任教，眼界和思维自然都更加开阔。

人们问我，"开阔"了之后，最大的感觉是什么？回答：更好地认识了中文、中国文化及其与其他语言和文化的关系。为什么是"开阔"之后才有这种认识呢？因为有了比较和鉴别，即思维不再是平面的了。歌德（Goethe）说，只懂一种语言的人，其实不懂得语言。或许，可否将他的意思再推得更极端一点：只懂得一种文化的人，其实不懂得文化；只会一种思维方式的人，其实不会思维。翻译的实质是什么？从心理学上讲，就是不同语言和文化内容在不同思维表达方式上的相互转换。所以，关键还是思维模式的拓展和变化。

人们常说，学习了一门外语，等于又打开了一扇窗户。但是，一定是"又一扇"，而且不能失去自己原来的房子。现在学外语的人，往往追求的是更像老外，从语音、语调到表达方式等，然而我的体会是，如果真是把自己变成了一个"纯老外"（或"假洋鬼子"），自身的价值也就失去了。特别是对有志于翻译和跨文化的中国学子来讲，应该知道学习外语的最高境界，不是最终形成单一的外语思维模式，而是在深刻认识母语基础上所形成的可比较、转换的立体性思维。

这体现在从日常生活到文化交流及学术研究的各个方面。比如，20多年前我刚到澳大利亚时，听到"Thank you very much."的对应词不是"No, no, no thanks."之类的中国式谦辞，而是"You are welcome."，甚至是 Ta，起初感到有些新鲜，因为跟教科书上不一样，但习惯了，感到是一种"顺势而为"（而不是以拒绝形式来表达感谢）。再如，我们学院召开国际会议，学生做志愿者接待远道而来的外宾，本是一种中国式的体谅"您一路辛苦了"，但变成英文后成了"You must have suffered a lot on your journey!"，我看那外宾的脸上先是有些尴尬，后马上解释道："No, no, I didn't suffer at all."我对这学生讲，下次换个说法："How did you enjoy your journey?"果然得到的对应话语"正常"了很多："Yes, I enjoyed it very much!"又如，在珠海与澳门的过境大厅的验证台前，用中英文写着"请在黄线后排队"（Please queue up behind the yellow line），似乎合情合理；而我到美国的入境大厅时，却看到了"The line starts from here"。表面上是文字表达的不同，实际是思维上的差异，即前者是从执法者角度，而后者是从顾客角度来考虑问题的。

我在澳大利亚南昆士兰大学（University of Southern Queensland）读博士期间，一次国际会议上，一位中国学者发言后有句结束语"我的发言中一定有不少错误和不妥之处，请大家给予批评指正"，他不等口译员的翻译，便自告奋勇将其译成："There must be a lot of mistakes in my speech, so everyone now, please criticize me."我注意到台上台下老外的异样表情，有的相互会心地笑了。其实该句不妨译为："Now, the floor is open to you. Everyone is welcome to ask me questions, and any suggestions pointing out inappropriateness in my paper would be highly appreciated."这里与其说是措辞失当，不如说是一种思维方式的套用与转换的问题。而在此期间，我导师的一句口头语也让我琢磨了许久："Do you know what you are doing?"此语若直译成中文似乎很不中听："你知道自己在干什么吗？"但我知道这位极度和蔼的基督徒教授绝不是这个意思，于是我慢慢悟出了，他在问："你真的弄明白我跟你说的意思了吗？"原来是一句非常体贴的话。

　　在国外学习、生活、工作的十余年间，我体会到，即使在英语环境中，也要有意识地从点点滴滴中储存、积累这类的"可比材料"。回国后，我曾担任过几届韩素音青年翻译大奖赛的评委，遇到过许多值得推敲的翻译难点。譬如，第24届中有一句："我的英国朋友在澳大利亚时，其'英国腔'保持得更为明显，不知是否有意显出其身份。"对于其中的"身份"，绝大多数参赛者根据该篇题目（Language and Social Identity）顺理成章译成了identity，但分析起来并不确切，因这里主要应表达的是他的英国特性。于是，我自然联想到，我初到澳洲留学时，住在当地一老妇人家，有天我们一起看电视，当"007"中的 James Bond 出现时，她冒出一句"Very English."由此话题谈到了 Englishness，我便把它纳入了此处的"参考译文"："A friend of mine, native English, once he was in Australia, as I observed, he had an especially reserved speech manner prompting his Englishness, whether consciously or subconsciously."这句译文收到不错的效果。第26届中有一句："于是，我们年复一年不是真正地生活着，而是间接地生活着。"参赛者努力采取各种办法试图区分"真正地生活"和"间接地生活"，但都不尽如人意。较为典型的如："Thus, we are not, year after year, living a true life, but an indirect one.""So we never truly live, year in and year out. Instead, we are living an unfulfilled life.""Therefore, we don't live as our real self year after year. Instead, we live in an indirect way."若追问一下：什么是 indirect life? 与此对应的，direct life 的涵义是什么？似乎都经不起推敲。就 unfulfilled 而言，其原义为"not having fully utilized or exploited one's abilities or character"。unfulfilled life 一般译为"失落的生活"，如："There are other forces that can drive your life but all lead to the same dead end: unused potential, unnecessary stress, and an unfulfilled life."（其他还有许多动力会驾驭你的人生，但这些全部导向一个死胡同——埋没了的潜能、不必要的压力和失落的人生。）显然，用在此处有些言过其实了，特别是相对"真正地生活着"而言。作为一个音乐爱好者，我想不妨借鉴一下美国歌星迈克尔·杰克逊（Michael Jackson）在《拯救地球》（Heal the World）里的一句歌词："We stop existing / And start living."（我们不再苟活，而开始生活。）同时，在《圣经》里也有这样的话："If you haven't known the purpose of life, you aren't truly living; you're merely existing."（若没有生活目的，你就不是真正地生活，而只不过是活着而已。）于是参考译文选择了 living 和 existing 这一组对应词语，将其译为："Year in and year out, we are not really living in our cities but existing there, being alienated from human nature…"许多参赛者说，出乎意料，又在情理之中。

习近平总书记在文艺座谈会上讲道："低俗不是通俗，欲望不代表希望，单纯感官娱乐不等于精神快乐。"《中国日报》的译文是："Popularity should not necessitate vulgarity and hope should not entail covetousness, pure sensual entertainment does not equate to spiritual elation."其中的 spiritual 使我不自觉地联系到我在国外参加教会活动的经历,那里用得最多的就是 spirit、spiritual exercise 等,而有关词典的解释是:"Spiritual means relating to people's thoughts and beliefs, rather than to their bodies and physical surroundings; Relating to religion or religious belief."(COBUILD 英汉双解词典,2002)与此相关的如 a spiritual approach to life、spiritual fulfillment、spiritual values、spiritual healing 等。其实,还有两个词组可以表述:mental contentment 和 head trip。如:① If we look closely, we can see that there are two kinds of happiness. One is based more on physical comfort; the other is founded on a deeper, mental contentment.(探究起来,有两种快乐,一种偏重于感官上的舒适,另一种则更注重深层的精神愉悦。)② Man, this book is a head trip.(嘿,这本书读起来真是一种精神享受。)同时,以全篇主旨看,"低俗不是通俗,欲望不代表希望"是以交谈形式对全国文艺工作者说明的道理,而在此之前,许多人对此认识是模糊的,故可不必那么刻板,而不妨用 … should not be confused with… nor… with… 等句式。至于"单纯感官娱乐",可不必译得那么实,如"感官"不必要 pure,而是泛指与精神层面相对立的一种享受,对此英文表达中常用的有 sensual pleasure,如:① Both directors were Italian, both depicted their characters in a fruitless search for sensual pleasure, both films ended at dawn with emptiness and soul-sickness.(两人均为意大利人,两人镜头下的角色都深陷于对感官享受的徒劳探索,而两部影片都终以空虚与精神病态的黎明结尾。)

② We have made up our mind from now on to live a regular life, doing sport every day, not staying up, drinking, and indulging in sensual pleasure.（我们下了决心，今后生活要规律、要检点，每天做运动，绝不熬夜、喝酒、纵欲。）所以，我以为该文不妨改译为："Popularity should not be confused with vulgarity, nor hope with avarice, and we have to realize that sensual pleasure in fact has little to do with mental contentment."当然，这是一己之见。

类似的，"民族精神""时代精神""人民精神文化生活"，我们通常翻译成 national spirit、the spirit of the time、people's spiritual and cultural life 等，实际推敲起来，翻译成 national character、underlying the trend of the times、intellectual pursuit and cultural entertainment of people 似更为确切。至于将"精神家园"翻译成 spiritual garden，更会让海外赤子们感觉不到实际内容，尽管在字面上是贴近的，而其真实内涵应为 sense of belonging 等。

出国之前，我对于"中国人"这一概念的认识是单薄的，在与各种人群交往、比较之后，才意识到它原来是一个具有丰富内涵而又非常敏感的政治概念，涉及两岸问题、港澳问题、东南亚华人华侨问题、"一国两制"、移民融入、国家认同问题等，所以在国际场合，使用和翻译这一概念时须十分谨慎。从外国人的角度，对"中国人"这一概念的研究就有这样一些类别：the Chinese、ethnic Chinese、a foreigner of Chinese Ancestry、*Huaren*、Diaspora of Chinese、Chinese Diaspora、November 1st Chinese，等等。我也去过联合国的翻译现场，那里 People's

Republic of China、Republic of China 等翻译的差异，就足以引起重大的政治问题。

我们通常讲要与国际社会接轨，就翻译而言，有时表现为思维方式的表述在语言层面上的转换，典型的如"同志们"，我们历来翻译成 comrade，而到了西方社会才意识到，该词原来与苏联、东欧社会主义阵营、冷战时期等紧密相连，容易引起大众反感，故在翻译中可做灵活处理，以便读者和听众接受。如：习主席在党内和政府中讲话时，可译为 dear colleagues；在乡村对农民讲话时，可译为 my fellow countrymen；而在其他场合时，又不妨译为 friends 等。有意思的是，在最近杭州召开的 G20 会议上，习近平主席对所有外国元首的称谓，都被现场同声传译为 dear colleagues，没人感到意外，却很自然。类似的如"人民群众"，我们通常译成 the people，而西方则为 fellow citizens，前者是个政治概念，后者是个法律概念，对此在翻译时应做适当变通。

就所要表达内容的重要程度而言，我认为，中国人的思维模式是正三角，即上面的分量轻，下面的分量重；西方人的思维模式则是倒三角，即把重要的、议论或结论性的放上面（前面），其余的放下面（后面）。如我早前的一篇文章《如何理解日本人的"不道歉"》（《英语世界》2016年第5期）的第一段，可拿来做一对比：

原文：同是战败国，[1]德国和日本对于二战的反省态度截然不同，[2]常让世人拿来比较、评论。[3]

译文：People often compare and comment on[3] the contrasting attitudes to self-examination over World War II, of Germany and

Japan[2] as the two vanquished countries.[1]
可以看到，次序是完全相反的。

正如思维是有维度和层次的，毋庸讳言，翻译的质量也有档次之分。记得很清楚，我在外文局工作时，见证了杨宪益与戴乃迭的合作，有时一句很简单的话翻译成外文，即刻显出水平的高低。例如，王蒙的《组织部来了个年轻人》中有一句，"相信我的话吧，没错"，别人译成"Please believe in me, it wouldn't be wrong."，字面好似完美；可到了他们手里，改成了"Take it from me. I know what I'm talking about."，看似在语言上不着边际，但在实际内涵上却再地道不过。这是多年在两种语境转换中历练出的真功夫。

这种思维模式的转换实际运用的也是一种想象力，思维的立体性为想象力提供了施展的空间。作者、译者的功力，其实就在这里。王国维在《红楼梦评论》中说，"如谓书中种种境界、种种人物，非局中人不能道，则是《水浒传》之作者必为大盗，《三国演义》之作者必为兵家"，译成英文则是："If it is said that every kind of world in a book or every type of character in literary works can only be created by an author who has experienced the same personally, then the conclusion would be the author of *The Water Margin* was a great gangster and the author of *Historical Novel of the Three Kingdoms* was a military strategist..." 这里揭示出的是创造和翻译中的一种规律。

正如美国大文豪爱默生（Emerson）所说："Words are also actions, and actions are a kind of words."（语言也是行为，而行为

不过是语言的一种。）对于译者而言，若能将自己在不同文化、语境中的感受和认识，分门别类地融汇在思维模式里，经过想象力的加工，日益减少磕绊而愈加自由地行走于不同的语言之间，我想这便是一种应追求的佳境。

郭沫若说，译者不同于作者，作者只需要感受他所写的对象，而译者除此之外还要感受作者的感受。从这个意义上讲，译者的思维会更加多面，精神世界也会更加丰富。

前　言

写过《杂文自译》之后，觉得应该把"文"字改成"感"，因为前者强调的是文体，后者是感想；而就文学传统而言，我那些文章似乎又缺乏典型杂文的味道，更多的是个人的想法与思考，故不妨名正言顺地归结为《杂感自译》。

我的这些散见于有关英语、翻译杂志上的短文及英译文，曾受到读者的欢迎，现受商务印书馆之约，经过加工、充实，以期更具阅读价值。

比起长篇大论来，短文要灵活很多，涉及的面也可更广，如时事、政治、经济、文化、艺术、教育、心理、历史、医学、科技等等，但杂感写作并不轻松，要积攒很多材料，把问题想通透后，才敢下笔，所谓"厚积而薄发"。

由于本人长期从事翻译教学和研究，一向重视相关翻译的注释与解析，故将本书的文章和译文分为"注释篇"和"解析篇"两大部分：前者就原文的某些理解和翻译技巧做了解释，后者则涉及相关的翻译理论和历史背景等。

总之，此类文章和译文，都是作者所独创，力求思想性、知识性、可读性和翻译理念与技巧的结合，专业性与普及性的融汇，从而雅俗共赏。

目录

注释篇

热闹与孤独 ······ 3
Socializing and Solitude ······ 4
观念改变一切 ······ 7
It's All about Ideas ······ 9
碎片化与深思考 ······ 15
Fragmentary Reading and Thoughtful Reflection ······ 16
理论的胜利 ······ 19
A Victory for Theory ······ 20
自由成就了他——饶宗颐 ······ 24
Rao Zongyi: Freedom Made the Man ······ 26
当中医遇到西医 ······ 31
When Traditional Chinese Medicine Meets Western Medicine ··· 33
与细菌共生存 ······ 39
Living with Bacteria ······ 41

城市的温度	45
The Warmth of a City	47
找北	52
Finding the North	54
"道"与物理学	61
Dao and Physics	63
科学与哲学	68
Science and Philosophy	70
哲学的用处	74
Why Do We Study Philosophy?	76
无止境的认知	80
Thinking Infinity	82
李约瑟的疑惑	86
Needham's Puzzle	88
读史使人明智	92
Histories Make Men Wise	94
作者与读者	99
The Author and the Reader	100
简单容易快乐	105
The Simple Life, Happy Life	106
生活中不能没有音乐	110
Music: We Can't Live Without It	113
我的北京冬天	122
Beijing in Winter: It's So Dear to Me!	128

富与贵 ··· 141
 Wealth and Nobility ··· 143
老炮儿的讲究 ·· 151
 Mr. Six's Way ··· 152
从法制到法治 ·· 156
 From "Rule of Law" to "Rule by Law" ··············· 158
自由需要素质 ·· 165
 True Freedom Has to Be Based on Its Quality ······ 167

解析篇

启蒙的真谛 ··· 173
 The True Meaning of Enlightenment ·················· 175
隐私：现代社会的文明概念 ····································· 195
 Privacy: A Civilized Concept in Modern Society ··· 197
独处是一种能力 ··· 210
 Practising Solitude Requires Special Ability ········ 211
中医：一门人的系统医学 ······································· 228
 Traditional Chinese Medicine: Treating the Human System ····· 229
"革命"概念的中国化 ·· 243
 "Revolution": A Sinicized Concept ···················· 246
"西法东渐"的启示 ··· 268
 Some Revelations of the "Western Jurisprudence Moving towards the East" ·· 271

哲学意义上的中医 ……………………………………… 288
   Traditional Chinese Medicine: A Philosophical Aspect ………… 290

附录

家（节选） ………………………………………… 周国平 307
   The Family（By Zhou Guoping）……………………………… 308
古村落："我们的根性文化" …………………………… 魏青 312
   Ancient Villages: Our Indigenous Culture（By Wei Qing）…… 314
地名中的传统文化含量 ………………………………… 张国刚 320
   Traditional Chinese Culture Embodied in Place Names ………… 322
   （By Zhang Guogang）………………………………………… 322

注释篇

热闹与孤独

现代社会里,想热闹并不难,特别是在中国。譬如,朋友聚会、唱K、抱团旅游、聚餐、凑伙玩牌、打麻将等等。就是回到家里,在"朋友圈"中,仍可议论纷纷,热闹非凡。[1]

但是,热闹并不总能排解孤独。当年朱自清在清华感叹:"热闹是它们的,我什么也没有。"如今,当红的一首歌便是《越热闹越孤单》。参与社交,需要能力;单人独处,更求素质。[2]

现在,要想完全地静下心来,真正回归自我,并不是一件容易的事——需要更大的毅力、智慧和自制。爱因斯坦说:"一个人成功与否,不在其工作时间,而在其业余时间。"他指的"业余"可理解为个人的独处。[3]

孤独,可以是单调、无聊、乏味的,也可是丰富、有趣、精彩的,取决于个人的修养、志向和境界。[4]

正如身体需要不断摄取能量,人的智力、精神领域也需要不断补充新的信息;但信息不等于知识、思想和情感,它需要沉淀,慢慢地被转化和整合,而这些不是在乱哄哄的社交,而是在静静的独处中完成的。古今中外,许多成功人士的经历证明:灵魂在孤独中成长,才能在寂寞中升华。[5]

一定意义上,说"浅薄的热闹、深刻的孤独",不无道理。[6]

其实，人既需要热闹，更需要孤独。往往是，有丰富的孤独，才会有高质量的热闹。[7]

译 文

Socializing and Solitude

Nowadays, especially in China, everything seems to favor social intercourse, such as gatherings of friends, KTV, group travel, dining together, playing cards and Mahjong, among many other things. Back home, discussions can still be boisterously carried on within the "circle of friends" of WeChat. [1]

However, boisterous scenes cannot always ease a sense of solitude. Zhu Ziqing, a well-known professor of Tsinghua University, sighed with emotion: "The bustles and excitements are theirs, which have nothing to do with me." One popular song today is also called "A lonely man in crowds". Actually, engaging in social intercourse requires ability, while being alone involves the whole character. [2]

It is not easy those days to calm down totally and return to one's true self-tremendous willpower, intellect and discipline are required. Einstein said, "It is not your working time but your spare time that determines the possibility of whether you will be successful or not." The "spare time" he referred could be taken as "spending time by yourself". [3]

Solitary life could be either dull, boring and tasteless, or abundant, interesting and colorful, depending on one's qualities, ambition and inspiration. [4]

Just as the body constantly requires energy, the mind and soul also demand unceasing inputs. However, for information to be processed and integrated into knowledge, thoughts and feelings, serenity, instead of bustle seems to be the right condition. Successful careers in all walks of life worldwide have proved that "the soul grows in tranquility and talent is nurtured in solitude". [5]

In a sense, it may be reasonable to say that "Jollity tends to be shallow while solitude involves profoundity." [6]

Man, in fact, needs solitude more than jollity, and only abundant solitude can produce quality jollification. [7]

译 注

[1] 中的"不难"不一定是"It's not difficult to…",此处不妨"反说正译",如用 favor,作动词,类似的例子有:Companies now tend to favor someone with an oversea study background. (公司现在更倾向使用那些有海外留学背景的人。)

[2] 中,"热闹"译为两个词 bustles 和 excitements,以与作者的"孤独"形成鲜明的对比;而"我什么也没有",不是 I have nothing at all,而是表示与作者此时的心境格格不入,故宜译为"which

have nothing to do with me"。个人素质，包括生理和心理两个方面，决定着其日后的发展，似可译成 quality、diathesis、personality、making、stuff 等，但此处都不如 characters，其原义为 the inherent complex of attributes that determine a person's moral and ethical actions and reactions，更全面、确切。

［4］中的"孤独"，可以是 lonely、lonesome、single、reclusive、loneliness 等，但此处讲的是一种生活境界，故不妨用 solitary life。

观念改变一切

中外媒体,喜欢定期评选出最具影响力的人或发明。其实在我看来,真正改变世界的,是观念。古往今来,莫不如此。[1]

在西方,"观念"一词最早源于希腊文的"观看""理解",从14世纪起便用该概念表达事物和价值的思想类型。简单而言,观念是表达典型思想的关键词和基本要素。观念的社会化,便导致社会行动和变革。[2]

典型的,如15世纪的欧洲,正因为改变了对"人"的观念,才有了著名的文艺复兴运动;而后经过洛克、斯密、伏尔泰、卢梭、狄德罗等一批启蒙思想家对于相关概念的深刻分析和理性发挥,又产生了欧美的工业革命、商品经济和宪政体制等。[3]

然而,20世纪40年代的德国,希特勒的一个歪曲了的进化论观念——"次等民族"必须以灭绝为代价,让六百余万犹太人惨遭杀害,世界也为此付出沉重代价。有西方学者指出,在历史的关键时期,由几页纸阐述的某个观点便可把世界搞得天翻地覆。[4]

中国历史上,由外来观念引领的社会文化洗礼,主要有两次:一次是魏晋南北朝时期佛教观念的传入,使得中国原有文化发生了结构性的重组,形成了儒释道的基本文化格局;另一次则是鸦片战争之后的"西学东渐",形成了"中体西用"的策略,使得中国社会开始与现代国际社会接轨。[5]

突出的，如"科学"，该词在中国古已有之，指"分科之学"和八股取士，但完全不同于西方的 science，对该词的翻译自明末至晚清一直是"格致"。随着中西科学技术交流的加剧，"格致"逐渐被现代意义上的"科学"所取代，从而废科举、办新学成为势不可挡的潮流。进而，又引发了洋务运动、戊戌变法、新文化运动等。[6]

1898 年的戊戌变法，对于具有传统"统治"观念的慈禧太后是大逆不道的，势必遭到血腥镇压。但是十年之后，经过外国列强的欺凌、革命党人的起义、立宪派的驱动及五大臣的考察等，她逐渐接受了（哪怕是部分地）现代统治观念，于是由她批准的《钦定宪法大纲》，其新政内容包括政体、法制、经济、军事、教育等诸多领域，在广度与深度都远远超过了之前康梁的戊戌维新。只是历史没有给她留下付诸的时间，不久她便去世了。[7]

中国当代的"真理"观念，1978 年后，经过"实践是检验真理的唯一标准"的大讨论，上下有了重新认识，极大地解放了人们的思想，带来了随后"改革开放"的巨大成果。[8]

一切随着观念而改变。"人权"概念，在 1991 年 11 月 1 日之前的中国是不被接受的，因为那时以"阶级斗争"的理论框架来透视问题，即不承认有所谓抽象的人权。尔后，执政者摆脱了过时观念的束缚，从人性角度看问题，于是产生了中国有史以来的第一部人权白皮书，开宗明义："享有充分的人权，是长期以来人类追求的理想。"之后每年一部，直至如今。[9]

就人与自然的关系而言，自从人类找对了自己在宇宙中的客观位置，才有了真正的"学问"和"智慧"。同样，我们今天之所以关注气候变暖、生物多样性，也是因为我们看待地球的方式改变了——不再相信"人定胜天""唯我独尊"，而是将其看作一个相互影响和依存的动态系统。[10]

处在日益全球化的今天，我们不但要从中国看世界，更要从世界看中国，这样会有许多观念上的不同，从而采取许多明智之举。[11]

译文

It's All about Ideas

Although the most influential figures and inventions periodically appear in domestic and foreign media, the most powerful thing in changing the world is, so at least it seems to me, ideas. It has been the same in all ages. [1]

In the West, the word "idea" originated from the Greek ιδέα, meaning to observe or understand. From the 14th century, the term was used to denote "ideal type". Ideas, in a simple definition, are thus key words and essential elements to present a typified thought. The socialization of ideas will result in social action and social reform. [2]

Typical examples can be found in 15th century Europe where the famous Renaissance was caused by a renewed understanding of humans. The profound analysis and rational knowledge of enlightenment thinkers in the West, represented by Locke, Smith, Voltaire, Rousseau and Diderot, bred the Industrial Revolution, commodity economy and constitutionalism in Europe and America. [3]

However, in Germany of the 1940s, a distorted idea of Darwinism possessed Hitler's head – eliminating all the "inferior ethnicities" from the world at all cost – resulted in the massacre of 6 million Jewish people, while the world sacrificed a great deal as well. As some Western scholars point out, at certain crucial junctures in history, several pages of ideas are capable of turning the world upside down, or even destroying it. [4]

In China's history, two great events introducing foreign ideas to the country took place that transformed Chinese culture: One was the introduction of Buddhist ideas, reconstituting the cultural landscape as Confucianism, Buddhism and Daoism. Another emerged from the trend of "the eastward transmission of Western learning", which gave rise to the strategy of "basing on Chinese culture and employing Western techniques", initiating the process of connecting Chinese society with the modern international community. [5]

A classic example is the term *ke xue* 科学 (science), which was part of classical Chinese, referring to classified subjects and the eight-part essay examination, but had nothing to do with the idea of "science" in the West. In translating the Western concept, *ge zhi* 格致 had always been used from the late-Ming to late-Qing Dynasty before it was replaced by *ke xue* 科学 in its modern sense, as a result of the increasing exchange of science and technology between China and the West. Correspondingly, the abolition of imperial examinations, establishment of schools of Western learning, westernization movement, Hundred Days' Reform, and the New Cultural Movement followed. [6]

Concerning the Hundred Days' Reform in 1898, sticking to the traditional idea of ruling the country, empress dowager Cixi considered it extremely offensive and suppressed it bloodily. Ten years later, however, having gone through bullying and humiliation by foreign powers, revolutionary revolts, the constitutional movement as well as an investigation trip abroad by five ministers of the monarchy, the empress dowager gradually accepted the modern idea of government (even if only in part) by issuing the *Imperial Constitution Outline*, which was substantially more progressive than the proposals of Kang Youwei and Liang Qichao (two representative personages of the Hundred Days' Reform) in the areas of political and legal systems, the economy, the military, education and so on. Pitifully, history did not leave enough time for her to accomplish these reforms before her death. [7]

As for the idea of "truth" in modern China, the mass debate on "Practice is the sole criterion for testing truth" in 1978 was widely launched and emancipated people tremendously from their ideological confinement so as to bring about the enormous outcome of the "reform and opening up to the outside world". [8]

Ideas change everything. "Human rights", another example, was rejected by the Chinese government as an "abstract concept" before 1991, mainly due to the confines of the "theory of class struggle". Having freed itself from this obsolete idea and taking a more humane perspective, the Chinese government issued its first White Paper on Human Rights on November 1st of the same year, which has become a yearly event up to now and stated its purpose from the very beginning: "It has been a long-cherished ideal of mankind to enjoy human rights in the full sense of the term." [9]

As far as the relations between man and nature are concerned, human beings did not establish their knowledge and wisdom, so to speak, until their proper position had been located in the universe. By the same token, global warming and biological diversity capture our attention only after we have altered the way we approach nature from "man's fixed purpose is superior to heaven" and "supremacy over all" to a more balanced view of the universe, to treat it as an inter-dependent, mutually effective and dynamic system. [10]

In today's increasingly globalized world, we should not only view the world from China's perspective but view China from a global vision. In that way, many wiser decisions will be made using such transformed ideas. [11]

译 注

［1］"定期评选"，字面上似乎应为 periodically select…，但从读者角度，不妨换一种表达，用 appear…。

［2］"思想类型"，还有多种译法，如 thought pattern、typology of ideology 等，但参阅有关学术著作，ideal type 更为确切。

［3］"理性发挥"，似乎为 rational play、fully function 等，或二者的结合，如 study it rationally to exert its function fully 等，此处用了名词 knowledge 稍做变通。

［4］"几页纸阐述的某个观点"，其完整的表述似为 an idea expounded in several pages，此处则简略处理。"天翻地覆"一般还可译为 snafu、earth shaking/tremendous/radical changes 等。

［5］"文化格局"也可为 cultural pattern 等，而 cultural landscape 不应仅仅理解为"文化景观"，如：In China, a cultural landscape with so few signposts, this knowledge is harder to obtain—but even more essential.（在中国文化格局上标识性的东西不多，而这方面的知识又很难获得，故显得愈发必要。）"接轨"，还可有多种，如 integrate with、be in line with、be in agreement with 等，取决于具体语境，如"与世界经济接轨"（incorporate into the world）、"与国际接轨"（follow international practice）等。

［6］"突出的"一般理解为 prominently、outstandingly、in highlighted…等，但此处实则有"典型"之意。"随着"还可

以用 with、along with、following、in the wake of 等，此处 as a result of... 是一种倒置，突出的是前者。

[7]"大逆不道"一般为 outrageous、commit high treason、monstrous crime 等，此处用了 extremely offensive，更为通俗。"广度与深度"的字面意思是 extent and depth、width and depth，如："一些经济学家，包括我在内，认为这个项目太小，应该在广度与深度上大大扩展。"(A number of economists, myself included, think the project falls short and should be substantially increased.)

[8]"画等号"，这里没有用字面意思 equate，而是用 identify，有"认同"的意思，如："我对他的一些观点不能认同。"(I cannot identify with some of his points.)"上下"直白的译法为 top and bottom、high and low，这里以 widely 概述。

[9]"抽象的人权"不是 abstract human right，而指的是"概念"。

[10]"看待"一般为 treat、look upon、regard、look on、size up 等，但这里更多的是 to deal with 之义，故用了 approach；类似的如："就是教同一班的学生，也要因材施教。"(In teaching students even in a same class, you may have to approach them differently as individuals.)"人定胜天"还可有"Man's will conquers Heaven.""Man is the master of his own fate."等。"唯我独尊"，其他译法如 egoistic、everything but mine、assume air of self-importance、be puffed up with pride、exalt only one's own self、extremely conceited 等，在不同语境中似乎也可考虑。

[11]"观念上的不同"未用 different opinions 等，而用 transformed ideas，有在更深层次上改变观念之意。

碎片化与深思考

随着互联网技术的发展，信息的传播越发便利，使得人们的阅读出现了碎片化的趋势。随时随地，可见"低头族"们通过手机、平板电脑、电子书等进行着断断续续的刷屏。[1]

长篇大论，似乎不再受人青睐，而吸引眼球的是那些关键字眼和闪光警句。甚至源于纸媒的稿件，经过网络编辑的"集纳化"处理，也达到了 1+1>2 的效果，于是更加强化了大众传播中的碎片化写作风格和阅读习惯。[2]

例如，某大学的网站，为报道一研究生在宿舍卫生间用毛巾上吊自杀一事，提炼出了若干词语：带母上学、蜗居、毕业即失业、读书无用、知识难改命运、研究生自杀……构成了事件经过，而不求深度的读者也便就此满足。[3]

碎片化阅读为人们带来了"俯拾即是"的前所未有的便利，但也引起了专家、学者的忧虑，因为它改变了我们文化发展的节奏，破坏了印刷文化的深度性、连续性和统一性。[4]

然而，我以为，碎片化阅读在本质上是社会碎片化和多元化的体现，是传统社会向现代社会转型的过渡期的一种必然。回看人类的阅读史，人们曾在甲骨、竹简、羊皮等媒介上阅读数千年，知识传递和发明创造并未截断。关键在于阅读者本身，而不在信息的载体。[5]

其实，对于传统的书刊也可做碎片式阅读，而对于电子终端接收器上的信息亦可做连贯式处理，重要的是对内容的把握。阅读习惯是可以改变的，是为思维方式服务的。[6]

正如语言课中有精读和泛读，"读"与"思"完全可以在时空上相交融、相和谐。所以，不应把"碎片化"与"深思考"相对立，而应在社会转型中学着逐渐将二者有机地统一起来。[7]

译 文

Fragmentary Reading and Thoughtful Reflection

With the advance of Internet technology, information is more easily available than ever before, thus fragmentary reading has become a phenomenon as well. Smartphone addicts can be seen busily "refreshing" their mobile phone, iPad or e-book screens whenever and wherever possible. [1]

It seems that lengthy articles have gone out of favor with the general public, attention-grabbing phrases and glamorous aphorisms are instead catching people's eyes. Even contributions for printed media are culled by web-editors to achieve the results of 1+1>2, reinforcing both writing style and reading habits of this kind in mass communication. [2]

In reporting the event of a postgraduate who hanged himself

using towels in a campus dormitory, for example, a few key words are filtered on the university website, such as "bring Mom to university while studying", "humble abode", "unemployed following graduation", "undesirable learning", "fate has nothing to do with knowledge", "a postgraduate's suicide" ... And readers are quite satisfied with the superficial media coverage. [3]

Fragmentary reading, while providing unprecedented convenience for getting informative material, has also caused concern among experts and scholars, who believe that our cultural tempo as well as the profoundity, consistency and integrity of our print culture have all been jeopardized. [4]

In my view, however, fragmentary reading is in fact a natural reflection of the diversification and plurality of our society which is undergoing a transitional period. Looking back at the history of man's reading, for several thousand years people read from oracles, bamboo slips, sheepskins, which did not interrupt knowledge dispersal or the recording of inventions. Everything was and still is about the reader, not the medium. [5]

In fact, traditional print materials may also be read fragmentarily while materials on electronic terminals can be perused consistently as well, centering on their contents. Reading habits form and vary following thinking patterns and serve these patterns. [6]

Reading and thinking, whether they are fragmented or thoughtful, can actually be integrated harmoniously as a whole in our mind, in the same way that both intensive and extensive reading are combined in language learning lessons. Combinations of this kind, I think, have to be learned during the social transition. [7]

译 注

[1] 中的"碎片化"(fragmentation)源于 20 世纪 80 年代"后现代主义"的有关研究文献，原义是指将完整的东西打破成诸多零块，逐渐应用于政治学、经济学、社会学和传播学等多个不同领域。在大众传播领域，该词又常与"吸引眼球""浅层阅读"等相关联，如 eye-catching phrases、attention-grabbing phrases、shallow reading、scan the text 等。这里将其转译为 fragmentary reading（碎片化阅读）。

[2] 中的"集纳化"，一般是 collection、assortment 等，但这里更多的是筛选之意，故用了 cull，其原义为 look for and gather，如："All this, needless to say, had been culled second-hand from radio reports."（不用说，所有这些都是从电台报道中筛选来的二手材料。）

[4] "俯拾即是"一般译成 can be found everywhere、be extremely common 等，但这里强调的是获得信息的便利化（convenience）。

[5] "关键"一般常译成 key、crux、hinge、linchpin 等，这里变通为介词 about，类似的如："教育的关键其实并不在怎样教，而是怎样学。"（Education is after all not about teaching, but about learning.）

理论的胜利

令科学家们魂牵梦绕了一百年的引力波，终于在 2016 年 2 月 11 日被美国研究者发现了，这个重大的科学进步，实质上是一个理论的胜利。[1]

在科学中，理论固然来自实践——是对事实的发现和研究，但事实本身不是科学，正如房子是由砖砌成的，而砖的堆积不能称之为房子。[2]

科学还需要想象力和创造性思维，从而形成科学理论，用以解释过去、设计现在、预测未来。爱因斯坦便是这样优秀的科学家。[3]

早在 1916 年，爱因斯坦便突破了牛顿力学（在牛顿引力学中，假定物质互动传播是以无限速度进行的，因而引力波不可能存在），根据广义相对论，预言引力波会作为引力放射向外传送能量。所谓引力波，是物理学上从动力源作为波浪向外传播时在时空弯曲中的一种波动，即宇宙中的时空结构会因巨大物体而发生弯曲。当巨变发生时，如黑洞合并、行星爆炸，这些曲线便作为引力波扩散他处，正如有人在池塘里扔入了石头。[4]

然而，这些波纹传送到地球时，因体积极小（大约是原子的十亿分之一），很难发现，故耗费了科学家们近百年时间才得以发现，多亏 LIGO 实验室利用激光在两根 4 公里长的管道内来回探测，使得物理学家能够测量到时空中难以置信的微小变化。[5]

在科学史上，这类以科学理论来"预知"科学发现的实例很多。例如，俄国化学家门捷列夫在发现了化学元素周期表后，从该表中的几个空洞，预测了新元素的存在。果然，15年后，其他科学家发现了与预测相符的三种元素。理论物理学家狄拉克研究电子的性质，认为"真空"正如充满电子的海洋，那里其实没有电子的"泡泡"，却预测了正电子的存在，等等。[6]

在中国历史上，类似的"理论先于实践"的例子，其实也并不罕见。例如，两千多年前老子的关于"有"和"无"的论断，就不断被许多现代科学实验所证实。[7]

此次引力波的重大发现，证实了爱因斯坦广义相对论的最后一项重大预测，使我们不但可以去观察，而且可以去聆听宇宙，因而进入了宇宙研究的全新时代。[8]

译 文

A Victory for Theory

Gravitational waves, which scientists around the world have been fondly dreaming of for a hundred years, were finally found by United States researchers on 11th February 2016. This significant scientific progress actually marks a victory for theory.[1]

In science, theory is drawn from practice – the discovery and study of the facts. However, facts by themselves are not science, just as a house is built with bricks, but a pile of bricks can hardly be called a house. [2]

Science also involves imagination and creative thinking so as to establish scientific theories, explaining the past, designing the present and predicting the future. In this regard, Einstein is one of the most outstanding scientists. [3]

As early as in 1916, Einstein broke through the Newtonian theory of gravitation (gravitational waves cannot exist in the Newtonian theory of gravitation, which postulates that physical interactions propagate at infinite speed), and predicted that gravitational waves transport energy as gravitational radiation on the basis of his theory of general relativity. The so-called "gravitational waves" are ripples in the curvature of space-time which propagate as waves, travelling outward from the source; in other words, the fabric of space-time which can become curved by anything massive in the Universe. When cataclysmic events happen, such as black holes merging or stars exploding, these curves can ripple out elsewhere as gravitational waves, just as if someone has dropped a stone in a pond. [4]

However, by the time those ripples get to us on Earth, they have become very tiny (around a billionth of the diameter of an atom), which is why scientists have taken a hundred years to realize their dreams. Thanks to LIGO (the Laser Interferometer

Gravitational-wave Observatory) laboratory, scientists have finally been able to detect them by bouncing lasers back and forth in two 4-km-long pipes, permitting physicists to measure incredibly small changes in space-time. [5]

Reviewing scientific history, many predictions of this kind can be easily found. Taking chemistry as an example, the Russian chemist Mendeleyev discovered some gaps in the Periodic Table and predicted several new chemical elements, three of which were found by other chemists fifteen years later. Similarly, the theoretical physicist Dirac revealed that just like the ocean filled with electrons, there were no electronic "bubbles" in a vacuum during his research into the nature of electrons, and then predicted that something called a positron might exist, and so on. [6]

Similar cases of "theory guiding practice" are also not rare in Chinese history, such as the theory of "Being versus Nonbeing" hypothesized by Lao Zi about two thousand years ago, has constantly been proved by modern experiments. [7]

The significant discovery of gravitational waves was the last major prediction of Einstein's general theory of relativity, ushering us into a whole new era of research in which we are able not only to observe but also listen to the Universe. [8]

译 注

[1] 中"魂牵梦绕",常用的译法还有 dream、dream about、

haunt、obsess 等，如："I've had my 'China dream' for years and I'm here to realize this dream."（我多年来魂牵梦绕的中国之旅，就这样实现了）；"这就是我魂牵梦绕的那所房子啊！"（This is the house I've always dreamed about.）；"……这让他魂牵梦绕"（… which haunted and haunted him day and night）；"那些天她正对中国画魂牵梦绕。"（She is obsessed by Chinese painting those days.）

[4] 从定义角度，这里的"波动"不宜再用 waves，如同不能定义 "Computer is… computer"，而须定义为 "Computer is a machine whose function is to accept data and process them into information"。同时，ripple 与 wave 亦有细微区别：a small wave or series of gentle waves across a surface 和 an oscillation of small amplitude imposed on top of a steady value 等。

[5] "得以发现"，为呼应前面的 fondly dreaming，这里没有用 to discover 等。LIGO 全称 the Laser Interferometer Gravitational-wave Observatory，中译文为"激光干涉引力波天文台"。

[6] "空洞"不是一般意义上的 empty、cavity、hollow、void 等，而是指根据理论推测应存在的尚未发现的某种物质，即理论和实践之间的差距，故用了 gaps。

[7] "先于"不是简单意义上的 in advance of、antecedent to、anterior to，其实质是理论对实践的指导作用，故用了 guiding。

[8] 将"全新时代"提前，并将中文的定语"宇宙研究的"转化为译文的状语"in which we are able not only to"。

自由成就了他——饶宗颐

不久前,他的去世引起了广泛的报道,特别是在学术界,人们不禁叹道:最后一位百科全书式的人物走了,一个时代结束了。[1]

他是饶宗颐。蹊跷的是,作为著名的学者,人们有时又很难把他的学问归类于某一学科,因为他所涉及的学科和领域实在太广了。他曾对自己的学生说,你们要跟我学,到头来会很惨——弄到"无家可归",即没有了固定学科。可是,现在有了结论:他是跨学术领域的旷世通才。[2]

在我看来,饶公所以能够取得如此成就,全在"自由"二字。[3]

首先是心灵上的自由。1917年他生于广东潮州的首富之家,却没有任何纨绔子弟的习气,而是倾心阅读。刚入初中,发现老师教的他全都学过,毫无兴趣,于是毅然退了学,埋头自家巨大的藏书楼里。看似孤独,但他却在书中徜徉于古往今来,极大满足了他的求知欲。"万古不磨意,中流自在心。"日后,他说,自己后来所以能做成点事情,就在于没有继续上学,更因没有上大学。[4]

在学术上,他也毫无学科的禁忌——从上古到明清,从国学到西学,从研究到艺术……在书林学海中,他独来独往,任意驰骋。他去日本发掘罕见甲骨文，写出惊世著作；赴印度研究梵文、佛学，被特聘为学术研究员；到法国开拓跨文化的比较研究，获得"儒林汉学特赏"（相当于西方汉学诺贝尔奖）。[5]

若以现代学科而论，饶公的学术成就，似可主要纳入下述领域：史学、甲骨学、考古学、金石学、楚辞学、敦煌学、哲学、宗教、词学、目录学、书画、音乐等。但他自己并不这样认为，而是一向主张打通学科，左右逢源；以学问积淀艺术，用艺术滋补学问。著名的西泠印社，一向秉承艺术与学养并举的传统，于是推选饶公做社长，非他莫属。同时，他还通晓英语、法语、德语、日语、印地语、梵文、阿拉伯语文、巴比伦古楔形文字等。[6]

就性格而言，饶公身上充满了好奇心、孩童心和自在心。他在学问中寻找乐趣，在玩笑中讲究学问；他少年老成，作文如长者，老来又活泼风趣，酷似顽童；他因境而形，在天为云，在地为水，随心所欲不逾矩。他不计功名，却功成名就。[7]

当年，只有小学文凭的他，却受聘于各著名大学，这恐怕也是当今中国教育体制所不能允许的。在这个意义上，他的成功又不是可以简单复制的。[8]

回看中国现代文化史，上一位这样的学术通才，要追溯到九十多年前（1927年）去世的王国维先生。陈寅恪称赞他"自由之思想，独立之精神"。王、饶两位大师可谓心犀相通。饶公的百年寿命整是王公的两倍，学术成果自然更加丰厚；但在治学方面，饶公既有"古法"，又有"新意"，实乃接续了王公的潇洒风范，并且将其发挥到了极致，令后人难以企及。[9]

Rao Zongyi: Freedom Made the Man

Not long ago, his death attracted widespread coverage, especially in academia, where people could not help but sigh: the last encyclopedic figure has gone, together with his era. [1]

Strangely, Mr. Rao Zongyi, famous scholar as he is, may sometimes be hard to classify into what kind of scholar in certain disciplines since his academic career had extended so broadly. He told his students, "If you want to follow me, you may end up miserably – find yourselves 'out of scholarship'". The world, however, has now concluded: He was a generalist of remarkable talent in modern times. [2]

It seems to me that his accomplishments relied on nothing other than "freedom". [3]

Most free of all was his mind. Born into the richest family in Chao Zhou, Guangdong province of China in 1917, he was free of any naughty child's bad habits but enamored of reading. Entering junior high school, he found what the teachers taught was nothing newer than the books he had already read at home, which bored him to death. Determinedly, he dropped out of school and buried himself in his family's huge library. The now-lonely figure wandered through books from ancient to modern times, which greatly stimulated his thirst for knowledge. "My free mind remains as it is despite the abrasion of the ages", as he later put it, "and my absence of schooling (let alone at a university) has shaped me as a competent scholar". [4]

Academically, he was not bound by any boundaries – he roamed single handedly from the palaeolithic to the Ming and Qing Dynasties, from Chinese learning to Western culture, from research to artistic activities... In the vast ocean of knowledge, he travelled tens of thousands of miles alone and freely: in Japan he explored rare oracles in writing an outstanding book; in India he studied Sanskrit and Buddhism and was appointed as an invited researcher; in France he developed comparative cross-cultural studies and was rewarded the Special Sinology Price (known as the Nobel Prize in Sinology). [5]

According to modern disciplines, Mr. Rao's academic achievements may be classified into the following fields: history, oracle-bone inscriptions, archaeology, epigraphy, songs of the Chu (south), studies of the Dunhuang Caves, philosophy, religion, Ci-poetry, bibliography, painting and calligraphy, music and so on. However, he himself would disagree since he always promoted an inter-disciplinary approach to integrating resources in research, removing barriers between learning and art so as to mutually benefit each other. The well-known Xiling Seal-Engravers' Society, forever upholding the tradition of endorsing learning and art on an equal footing, selected Mr. Rao as its perfect president. Meanwhile, he was also proficient in English, French, German, Japanese, Hindi, Sanskrit, Arabic and ancient Babylon cuneiform. [6]

In terms of personality, Mr. Rao, filled with child-like curiosity, had always followed his own free will. He found fun in learning and cracked jokes with knowledge. He produced mature writings in his childhood, and became light, lively and funny when he got old. He was very open to changes in ambience and progress; in a sense, he never refused whatever his heart desired for the right cause. He couldn't have cared less about honor and fame, but has been widely recognized for his extraordinary achievements. [7]

In those years, with just a primary school certificate, he could be hired by several prestigious universities as a lecturer and professor. It would be extremely difficult for his success story to be simply replicated, as today China's educational system would hardly permit such a case to happen. [8]

In retrospect, the last such academic talent in modern China's cultural history can be traced back to 1927 (more than 90 years ago) when Mr. Wang Guowei, in his final year of life, was praised by Chen Yinque for his "freedom of thought and spirit of independence". The two masters' hearts beat in common. Surely, Mr. Rao's academic achievements are far more abundant than Mr. Wang's, given that his life-span was twice as long; in approaching learning, however, Mr. Rao had thoroughly inherited Mr. Wang's unconventional legacy – constantly refreshing ideas on classical scholarship – and used his talents to the utmost, which will be hard to match for generations to come.[9]

译 注

[1] 这里的"无家可归"显然是一种比喻，不宜简单地译成 be homeless and without a place of refuge、get the key of the street、without a roof 等，而实际指的是后面的"没有了固定学科"，故不妨译为 out of scholarship。

[4] "满足求知欲"，一般可译成 satisfy the thirst for knowledge、quench the thirst for knowledge 等，但这里不妨将其变通为 stimulated his thirst for knowledge，以更突出其对知识的兴趣。"做成点事情"，将此处的动宾结构短语变译为带有定语的名词短语 a competent scholar，以更切其意。"上学"，通常译成 go to school、attend school、be at school 等，但这里根据其句式，不妨用 schooling，同时将后面的"更因没有上大学"译为括号中的（let alone at a university），以做补充处理。

[5] "任意驰骋"字面意思 be free to gallop、any ride，若译成 roamed willfully / single handedly，又显重复，其实 roam 即可表明其意。

[6] "非他莫属"，似可译成 nobody else is worthy except him、he could be the next big thing 等，但这里可稍加变通，并更加点明为 as its perfect president。

[7] 这三"心"的核心是"自在心",故不宜并列译出,而是将其融于句子中。"因境而形"包含了后面"在天为云,在地为水"的内容,故不必译得太"实",如"he could become a cloud when in heaven and water on earth"等,可统而化之为"He was very open to changes in ambience and progress"。

[8] "……简单复制",此句译文的词序做了较大调整,即将其提前译出,而将上句的"当今中国教育体制所不能允许的"置后处理,以更加通顺、自然。

[9] "九十多年前",此处在译文中与原文中括弧里的"1927年"互换了位置,才更符合原意,更易表达,显出中英文的不同特点。"去世"通常意义上是 passed away、died、demised、departed、went aloft、went off 等,但这里似乎是"反其义"而译之为 in his final year of life,以更宜与"上一位这样的学术通才"相关联和比较。"既有'古法',又有'新意'",这里没有按通常意义上"既有……又有……"的句式译出,而是据其语境整合为 refreshing ideas on classical scholarship,并将词序调整,以更易表述。

当中医遇到西医

中医萌芽于周朝，以春秋战国时期的《黄帝内经》为标志，已有两千余年历史，治病救人，除疾养生，承担国医使命。但是近代以后，它却受到西医的冲击。[1]

西方的科学医学，自19世纪后飞跃发展，特别是在化学与微生物领域，确立了独立的科学体系。清末，随着"西学东渐"的潮流，中国迎来了"赛先生"，当然也包括其宠儿——西医。[2]

中西医结交的典型事例，是对于天花病的防治。天花，作为古老的烈性传染病，致死率高达90%。在中国，古人发现若一个人得过天花，便此生不会再得，于是根据"以毒攻毒"的原理，发明了人痘接种术，即通过接种人痘来预防"痘疮"。但由于技术不够成熟，风险很大。[3]

中国的"接种人痘"西传到欧洲，英国皇家学会研究并改进了中国接种天花的方法，由英国医生詹纳发明了接种牛痘预防天花的新方法，又传回了中国。所以，牛痘接种术的传入，真正显示了西方医疗技术在中国的实力，由此奠定了西医进入中国的基础。[4]

在19世纪下半叶之前，面对蓬勃而来的西医，应当说中医还是蛮有自信的。如著名中医王清任在1931年出版了《医林改错》，比照西医的解剖图式，纠正了中医里的许多错误。[5]

英国传教医生合信来华，于 1851 年出版了《全本新论》等详细论述医学的著作，有计划地把西医临床医学打入了中国知识界，从而使中医感受到了挑战。[6]

起初，中医试图"会通"西医。例如，唐宗海主张撷取西医的有用部分，掺入中医便可；朱沛文在对比研究中医的经络系统与西医循环系统之后，得出结论：医学中属于"形"的范围，应以西医为准（"从洋"），属于"理"的范围，应以中医为准（"从华"）。这显然受到洋务运动中"中学为体，西学为用"思想的指导。之后，又有恽铁樵、张锡纯等人的具体医学实践。[7]

中医面临真正的危机，是 1895 年甲午战败之后。严复发表《论世变之亟》，力言过去那种"增新不变旧"的洋务运动改革不能成功；郑观应出版《盛世危言》，批评传统学术，赞扬西方科技；梁启超成立知耻学会，发表《变法通议》。终于促使清政府在 1905 年取消了科举取士制度，象征着传统经学的全面崩溃，也使中医失去了固有国学支撑的优势。[8]

1914 年《中西医学报》发表了《中医救亡刍言》："自戊戌新政，新学渐露萌芽，迄至近世，民智勃起，科学昌明，而中西医学之优劣，判若天渊，昭然若揭。于是谋改良者有人，谋会通者有人，兴医报立医会者又有人，皇皇汲汲，不可终日。"颇为形象地概括了当时中医界的状态。[9]

之后，又有留日归国医生余岩掀起中西医论争，力促政府"废旧医，行新医"，认为"旧医一日不除，民众思想一日不变，新医事业一日不向上，卫生行政一日不能进展"，从而给了中医沉重一击。[10]

自20世纪20年代之后，西医在中国得到了迅速发展，其间得力于西方生理学、病理学、免疫学、遗传学、生物化学等学科的创建与突破。特别是自然科学研究与临床医学相结合，令科学医学发挥出显著疗效。至上世纪70年代，中国的西医人数终于超过了中医人数。[11]

译 文

When Traditional Chinese Medicine Meets Western Medicine

Traditional Chinese Medicine (TCM), originating in the Zhou Dynasty and symbolized by the *Inner Canon of the Yellow Emperor* in the Spring and Autumn Period (770-476 BC), has been saving lives and curing diseases as well as preserving people's health as the "national medicine" for the past two thousand years or so. However, it was challenged by Western Medicine (WM) when it entered modern times.[1]

Scientific medicine in the West has developed rapidly since the 19th century, especially in the field of chemistry and microbiology as individual disciplines. At the end of the Qing Dynasty (1644-

1912), with the trend of "Western culture emerging in the East", China received Mr. Sai (the initial syllable of "science" in translated Chinese) and its favorite son – WM. [2]

A typical case in merging TCM and WM was the prevention and treatment of smallpox, a virulent infectious disease with a mortality rate of up to 90%. In ancient China, people found that if a person had had smallpox, he or she wouldn't get it again. Based on the idea of "curing a poisoned patient with poison", a method of "human variolation" was invented to prevent the disease by vaccination. However, it was very risky due to the immature techniques. [3]

When the Chinese way of preventive variolation was introduced to the West, the Royal Society improved the method and the new vaccination invented by Dr. Jenner was reintroduced to China. In this way, vaccination proved an advantage of WM, laying the groundwork for it to expand in China. [4]

Before the second half of the 19th Century, in the face of vigorous WM, it should be said that TCM was quite confident. A well-known Chinese doctor, Wang Qingren, for example, published a book entitled *Corrections to TCM* in 1931, rectifying many traditional mistakes according to the anatomical schema of WM. [5]

The British missionary doctor Benjamin Hobson came to China and published his book *Treatise on Physiology* in 1851, among many others in later years, systematically planting the seed of Western clinical medicine into the soil of the Chinese intelligentsia, and posing a serious challenge to TCM. [6]

Initially, TCM tried to incorporate WM. For example, Tang Zonghai advocated infusing the useful part of WM into TCM; Zhu Peiwen, after comparing the meridian system of TCM and the circulatory system of WM, concluded that in treating external diseases one should rely on WM's techniques, while in dealing with internal illnesses, TCM's philosophy ought to prevail, which was clearly influenced by the idea of the Westernization Movement –"Applying Western technologies guided by Chinese philosophy". Consequently, Yun Tieqiao, Zhang Xichun and others practiced medicine in that way. [7]

The first real crisis TCM encountered was after the Sino-Japanese War of 1894-1895, when Yan Fu published an article entitled "An Urgent Transformation of our Time", pointing out that the failure of the reform simply "added something new to the old" under the name of the Westernization Movement. Zheng Guanying published his *Warnings in a Prosperous Time*, criticizing traditional Chinese learning and praising Western technologies. Liang Qichao also published his "On Reform", establishing a "Shame-Consciousness Society". Under various social pressures, the Qing government finally abolished the Imperial Examination System, symbolizing the collapse of traditional Confucian studies, which were the backbone of TCM. [8]

An article entitled "On Saving TCM" appeared in the *Academic Journal of TCM – WM* in 1914, vividly presenting the situation then: "Since the proposed reform in 1898, new learning from the West has sprouted and people have been enlightened in recent years. With the thriving of science, the advantages and disadvantages of the two medicines have been clearly revealed. People are in a constant state of anxiety now: some seek reform, some engage in social intercourse, some publish medical journals and set up medical associations..." [9]

This was followed by an overseas returnee, Dr. Yu Yan, stirring up the controversy between TCM and WM. He urged the government to abandon TCM and adopt WM, believing that if TCM was not deserted and people's old ways of thinking remained, the new medical era and health administration would not make any progress. It was a severe blow to TCM. [10]

Since the 1920s, WM has developed rapidly in China, benefiting from many emerging breakthroughs in disciplines in the West, such as physiology, pathology, immunology, genetics, biochemistry and so on. The combination of physical scientific research and clinical medicine, in particular, has produced remarkable curative effects. In the 1970s, the number of doctors in WM finally surpassed those practising TCM. [11]

译 注

[1] 中的"萌芽于周朝，以……《黄帝内经》为标志"在译文中可用动名词 originating 和过去分词短语 symbolized by 处理

成定语，以求简洁，便于表达。

［2］中的"确立了独立的科学体系"，原文是动宾结构，译文为表述方便，不妨作为介词短语 as individual disciplines；关于"西学东渐"，有多种译法，如 the eastward transmission of Western sciences、Western learning introduced into China、eastward spread of Western culture 等，这里做了些变通。

［3］中，"中西医结交"不是"中西医结合"，不宜译成 the combination of TCM and WM，而是两种医学第一次在中国相遇，共同治愈一种疾病，故可用"in merging ... prevention and treatment of…"句式。

［4］中的"中国的'接种人痘'"，因上文已明确，在译文里可简化为 preventive variolation；"实力"一般译成 strength、power、zenith 等，此处就其具体疗效，译为 an advantage。

［5］中的"蓬勃而来"，似可译为 prosperously、flourishingly、exuberantly developed 等，此处做了相应的变通。

［6］"使中医感受到了挑战"是被动语句，译文转换为主动句"posing a serious challenge to…"。

［7］中的"会通"，是文言文的用法，相当于现代汉语的"结合""融会"等，可用 combine、integrate、blend 等，此处用了 incorporate，其本义为 make into a whole or make part of a whole，以更恰当。同时，将"形"理解为 external diseases，将"理"释为 internal illnesses，不完全对等，是一种意译。"中学为体，西学为用"可有多种翻译，如"Chinese learning for the basic conduct of life and the Western knowledge for dealing with practical affairs""Chinese learning as the fundamentals and Western learning as techniques"等，这里做了较大的变通。

[8] 中的"洋务运动"还可译为 Self-Strengthening Movement、Westernization Drive 等。"使失去了……的优势"，一般以否定形式译成 making it lose its advantage，但此处顺其意，译为"which were the backbone of …"。

[9] 中，将"颇为形象地概括了当时中医界的状态"提前译出，以在表述上更为紧凑。

[10] 中，对于"旧医一日不除，民众思想一日不变，新医事业一日不向上，卫生行政一日不能进展"，首先，将直接引语改为间接引语；其次，并未逐句译出其意，而是将其涵义综合，如将四个"一日"概括在 was not、would not... 之中，将"新医事业……，……卫生行政"合并在一句中。

[11] 中，这里的"创建"未必总是 establish、set up、create 等，而是与"突破"相关联，合译为 emerging breakthroughs in...；此处的"中医人数"不是简单的 the number of TCM practitioners，而是指 the people who practice TCM，故用了 those practising TCM，以更切其意。

与细菌共生存

每当听到有人说要消灭我们身体中的细菌或战胜疾病时，便会感到不那么准确，因为事实并非如此。[1]

地球上有4000多万种细菌，它们先于人类很久来到这个世界。细菌繁衍了生物，进而是各种类型的生命，而任何生物都离不开细菌，包括人类。当人类在地球上消失之后，细菌还会生存很久。在这个意义上，是细菌把我们带来，又把我们送走。[2]

据科学发现，人体中的细菌大约是人体自身细胞的10倍，而人体本身所寄生的细菌、病毒等微生物的总量大约有1.5公斤到3公斤，主要分布在肠道，同时也大量存活于皮肤及其他器官。这些细菌在体内，由于免疫系统效应，大都对身体是有益的，它们通过输送溶解了的化合物向身体提供营养。换言之，人体正常生理功能的运转，完全依赖于这些细菌微生物的作用。[3]

当然，细菌也会引起疾病，如霍乱、梅毒、炭疽热、麻风病、黑死病等都是有名的细菌病。其根源是细菌变成了病菌。二者的区别在于，细菌是细胞间微生物，而病菌是细胞内微生物，它们对原细胞中基因物质的正常功能产生影响，引起病变。[4]

既然细菌于体内无时无刻不在，那么如何会在某一时刻发生病变？这主要由身体条件的变化所造成。在正常条件下，两个阵营和平共处，相安无事；而一旦身体免疫力下降，强的一方便会攻击过来，产生"异常"状态，这便是"得病"。所谓"治病"，就是将"入侵者"推回去，各就各位，回复原态。在西方，近来也形成了"与癌细胞共生存"的理念。[5]

根据中医理论，人类与微生物是共生共存、和谐平衡的关系。这些细菌组成了体内的微生态，是人体不可或缺的一部分。具体而言，就是人体中正气与邪气的关系，"正气不存，邪气入内"。"正气"是调节阴阳及虚实状态的物质，"邪气"是其对立面，在某种意义上是"毒"的概念。"邪之所凑，其气必衰。"因而中医理解的健康机制就是在体内不断"扶正祛邪"的过程。[6]

然而，"养正气，祛邪毒"并不是一味地要"消灭"什么，例如乱吃抗生素等药品，那样会打破人体固有的微生物平衡，使"风，寒，暑，湿，燥，火"（中医概念）乘虚而入，造成免疫力的进一步下降；而新的具有抗药性的细菌和病毒对人体健康会造成更大的危害。须知，"病"不是被战胜了，而是被平衡了。[7]

依据这种平衡理念，切忌乱投医，要少吃药，或不吃药，注重饮食养生、运动养生、心理养生，从而固本正源，才有真正的健康。[8]

可见，关于细菌、病症的理解，不只是个医学问题，更是个哲学问题、认识论问题；而中国传统文化的理念，在此与西方的科学发现又是不谋而合的。[9]

Living with Bacteria

Whenever people say that we should eliminate bacteria from our body and defeat diseases, it annoys me since it's not entirely correct. [1]

There are more than 40 million types of bacteria on earth, which came into being much earlier than human beings. Bacteria evolved as organisms which subsequently multiplied into varied types of life; no life, including human beings, can survive without bacteria. Even when humans disappear from the earth, bacteria will still be there. In this sense, we were brought in and will be sent off by bacteria. [2]

According to scientific discoveries, there are approximately ten times as many bacteria as there are cells in the human body, totaling 1.5 to 3 kg of various bacterial viral microorganisms, with the largest number of human flora being in the gut, and many others on the skin and in other organs. The vast majority of the bacteria in the body are rendered beneficially by the protective effects of the immune system, providing the nutrients needed to sustain life by converting dissolved compounds. In other words, the normal functions of the human body rely on converting dissolved compounds of bacteria. [3]

Certainly, some species of bacteria can generate infectious diseases, including some once epidemic diseases, such as cholera, syphilis, anthrax, leprosy, bubonic plague and influenza, caused by bacterial-viral conversion lesions. The main difference between bacteria and viruses lies in their structures: bacteria are intercellular organisms, whereas viruses are intracellular and are infectious to the host cell's genetically-normal function, resulting in pathological changes. [4]

Given the ubiquity of bacteria in our body, how do pathological changes take place all of sudden? Altered conditions in our body are to blame. Under normal conditions, the two equal partners peacefully coexist with each other. Once an immune system is impaired, the sturdier side will intrude and bring about an abnormal condition, manifesting as "illness". In the treatment, the "invader" is repelled and once the balance is restored the illness will be cured. In the West, an idea of "coexisting with cancer cells" recently emerged. [5]

According to traditional Chinese medicine (TCM), there are common bonds and harmonious relations between human beings and microorganisms which form an indispensable part of a micro-ecology within our body. In other words, there is a proper balance between vital *qi*, which is the substance regulating *Yin* and *Yang*, deficiency and excess, and evil *qi*, which is the opposite, symbolizing the idea of poison to a certain degree. Whenever the former is vulnerable, the latter starts its aggression. In this sense of TCM, recuperation is a process of strengthening body resistance and conquering malignant factors. [6]

However, engaging this rejuvenating process is not meant to extinguish everything unhealthy by indiscriminately trying the whole hog, such as by taking excessive antibiotics. Once the subtle equilibrium is lost, all the evil elements proscribed by TCM, such as wind, cold, heat, damp, dryness, fire, will break through at a weak point, further bringing down the immune system. And with antibiotic-resistant bacteria joining the attack, it will put our health at even greater peril. One should therefore note that sickness is not "defeated" as such, but ultimately "balanced out". [7]

Based on this idea of a balanced mechanism, people should avoid blindly seeking treatment and lavishly using medicines; instead, more attention should be paid to the root causes, which are a healthy diet, sufficient exercise and mental cultivation in terms of genuinely keeping fit. [8]

Apparently, things concerning bacteria and diseases are as much an issue of philosophy and epistemology as they are of medicine. On this point, however, traditional Chinese thought and modern Western science happen to hold the same view. [9]

译 注

[1] 这里的"准确"不妨与后面的"事实并非如此"结合起来翻译，并加上"感到"之意（annoys）。
[2] 将"繁衍"分为 evolved as 和 multiplied into 两个词组译出。
[3] 对于"细菌微生物的作用"没有按其字面意思译成 the micro-

organic function of bacteria，而是根据其性质译为 converting dissolved compounds of bacteria。

[5]"下降"未用通常的 decline、fall、drop、decrease 等，而是更准确的 impair，以说明其性质。"得病"一般译成 fall ill、be ill 等，但考虑到这里是因一方"入侵"导致失去平衡而出现的症状，故用了 manifesting as "illness"。

[6]"扶正祛邪"，关于"正"和"邪"的中医概念，这里用了多种词汇，如 vital / evil，resistance / malignant factors 等，下面还有 (healthy) / unhealthy 等。

[7]"一味地"一般多用 blindly、do far more than just…、obstinately 等，如："他终于意识到一味地追求虚荣是毫无意义的。"（He finally realized that blindly pursuing vanity was meaningless.）；"对于学生来讲，学习并不只是一味地上课。"（In terms of learning, students do far more than attend classes.）；"他只是一味地强调 GDP，而不顾环境保护。"（He obstinately emphasizes GDP at the cost of environmental protection.）这里用了 indiscriminately，语气稍重，但却是积极意义方面的，类似的如："我们不能一味照搬别人的经验。"（We should not copy indiscriminately the experience of others.）

[9]"更是"一般表达为 it is even more so、it is especially true 等，而这里用的句式是 … is/are as much… as it/they is/are…，强调的是前者。类似的如："这是给我的，也更是给他们的荣誉。"[This is as much an honor to them as (it is) to me./ This is honoring them as much as it is (honoring) me.]

城市的温度

每个城市都是有温度的,这指的当然不是自然气候,而是一种人文感觉。[1]

我到过世界上许多城市。初来乍到,新城市对我是陌生的,我对这地方也是陌生人。一来二往,慢慢熟悉起来,主要是通过人与人的交往。所以我觉得,最能体现一个城市人文温度的,是这城市里的人对于陌生人的态度。[2]

二十多年前,我初到澳大利亚的黄金海岸,在街上拿出地图,寻找地方,便有位长者主动过来,问我是否迷路了,需要帮助吗?那时,对于经过"文化大革命"、有着阶级意识的我,感到又惊又喜。后来,在那里住下了,类似的事情多了,也便习以为常,如路上散步,对面来人,无论认识与否,都问候一句。一天晚上,我在便道上骑车,一年轻女子喊了一声"带我一段",便蹿上了我自行车的后座。带着一身香水味,她告诉我刚参加完聚会,阴差阳错,没赶上车。我们一路还聊了会儿,又过了一段,她跳下了车,道了一句"谢谢,拜拜!"这时,我已经没了惊喜,有的倒是一种莫名的"被信任"感。[3]

还是在澳洲,我朋友的孩子与他的师傅要去悉尼参加跆拳道比赛,俩人为省路费,便试着在路边伸手搭车。一小伙子停下了,得知是同路,便让他们上来;由他俩轮流开车,自己躺在后座睡觉去了。八个多小时后,到了,车主醒了,于是互相道谢,各奔东西。[4]

十几年前,我到了台湾的高雄,上机场大巴,司机旁边的收费箱上写着"十八台币",我摸遍全身没有零钱,这时后面一男士将一大把硬币放了进去,说:"这是给你的。每个人在外都会遇到这种情况。"我和他素不相识啊!上车后,他告诉我:他是一家工厂老板,姓徐,在东莞有投资;听我是大陆口音,故有亲切感。我们后来一直保持联系,直到我手机丢了,找不到他的号码,甚是遗憾。[5]

原来以为,市场经济发达的地方,会人情冷漠,因为人们只是追求利益,匆匆忙忙,无暇顾及他人。后来发现错了,二者其实没有必然关系。在香港这样高度商业化的社会,人们也会很热情:有次问路,一位女士竟然陪我走过了桥之后,又转身回去赶路了。[6]

多年的经历,使我似乎悟出了一个规律:一个地方,在一定文明程度上,当人们的素质(不是种族)越相近(水平越相当),人们越少互相提防,越容易互相信任,因而对陌生人的态度也会越好。这里有两个条件,一是到达一定高度,一是高度的接近性。[7]

德国的美因茨,是个不大的城市,我在那里住的时间不长,但每天走同样的路,坐类似的车,有着各种形式的友好互动,与到访的地方和人们熟悉了起来,临走时竟然有了一种惜别旧友的感觉。[8]

当然,任何地方,个别的例外总是有的。譬如,在日本的京都，一次我请一位女士帮我照相，她明确表示拒绝，扭头走了（也许是有什么特殊原因），但我并不觉得那里是个冷漠的地方，因我同时得到了许多其他人的帮助。所以，就多数人而言，还是可以有一种总体的感觉。[9]

我想，一个地方，经济再发达，设施再先进，如果给人（特别是陌生人)的感觉是冷冷冰冰，甚至是防不胜防，恐怕也不能算是文明之地。[10]

其实，广义而言，每个人，即便生活在自己的家乡，也是生活在陌生人的世界：我们吃陌生人生产的粮食，住陌生人建造的房子，得到陌生人传播的信息，乘坐陌生人驾驶的公交车，接受陌生人的教育，受到陌生警察的保护，等等。所以，对待陌生人的态度，恰恰是一个地方人们整体素质的最自然的外在表现。[11]

译 文

The Warmth of a City

Every city, in fact, can be felt by its warmth – not in terms of its natural climate but its human touch. [1]

Personally, I have visited many cities in the world. On my first arrival, the new place and I are mutually alien to one another. We gradually become acquainted after getting down to business through social intercourse. In my view, the attitude towards strangers that the people have in the city thus mirrors its warmth. [2]

About two decades ago, I arrived in the Gold Coast, Australia. Searching for a place on a map in the street, I was approached by an elderly man who asked, "How are you? Are you lost? How can I help you?" which really impressed and warmed me, as a survivor of the "cultural revolution" where the consciousness of "class struggle" had overwhelmed common sense. I later became used to the courtesy and friendliness of the people after residing in the city, where people normally greet each other on the road during their strolls. One night, as I was pushing my bike on the sidewalk, a young lady shouted to me: "Carry me please!" and then jumped onto the back seat of my bicycle. With a gust of strong perfume, she told me that she had just joined a party and for some reason had been left out. While we had a little chat, she got where she wanted and hopped off my bike with "Thanks, Bye bye!" At that moment, I had a sense as much of pleasant surprise as of "being trusted". [3]

Still in Australia, son of a friend of mine who, with his master attempting to participate in a Taekwondo contest in Sydney, decided to hitch their way to there in order to save some money, so they went out onto the road to start thumbing. A young man stopped, luckily he was also going to Sydney, and so he let them in and even allowed them to drive while he went to sleep on the back seat. About eight hours later, they arrived and he woke up. Saying thanks to each other, they went their separate ways. [4]

A little over ten years ago, I visited Kaohsiung in Taiwan. When I entered the airport bus, I saw a ticket box marked "18 TW Yuan" beside the driver. Apart from big notes there was nowhere I could find the right fare from all my pockets then. Suddenly a handful of coins were put into the box by a man behind me, "All yours. Everyone may encounter such embarrassment in a new place", he said. But we were strangers! While we were seated, he told me that he was the boss of a factory, surnamed Xu, and he had also invested heavily in Dongguan in Chinese Mainland. My Beijing accent had appealed to him, and we kept in touch for quite some time until my cellphone was lost, unfortunately. [5]

It was thought that as a market economy develops people tend to be more apathetic since they all rush for profits which leaves little time for caring for others. The facts have proved that is incorrect, for the two are not necessarily related. Hong Kong, for example, is a highly commercialized city, where people can still be very considerate. One day, a lady accompanied me across a bridge to find a route I was looking for, and then went back along her own way. [6]

Having gone through these years, a regular pattern seems to strike me: wherever a place, when the quality of its citizens (whatever its races) has reached a certain level of civilization rather evenly (at an approximate level), people tend to take less precautions against but more easily trust one another, and a friendlier attitude towards strangers can be expected. For which two key points have to be met: a certain level and certain approximation of their overall quality. [7]

During my short stay in Mainz, a little city in Germany, I commuted roughly the same route and communed with similar people and places every day, we became acquainted through various friendly interactions. On my day of departure, I somehow felt like I was bidding farewell to an old friend. [8]

Certainly, there are always exceptions in any places. In Japan's Kyoto, for example, a lady bluntly declined my request to take a photo of me, she just simply ran away (perhaps due to some untold reason). However, it did not disappoint me at all since at the same time I was offered plenty of kind helps from all sorts of people in the city. In a way, you can always get the general feeling of a place by the people you meet on most occasions. [9]

In my opinion, no matter how developed and advanced its economy and infrastructure are, if in general a place presents itself with a cold and indifferent face to people, especially to strangers, even keeping them highly alert not to be cheated all the time, can perhaps hardly be classified as a land of civilization. [10]

Generally speaking, for all of us, including those living in their homeland, our wellbeing is in fact dependent on numerous strangers: the food we eat, the building we live in, the news we get, the public transport we use, the education we receive, the protection we acquire from the police and so on – are all provided by people unknown to us, living and dead. In this sense, people's attitude towards strangers in a place naturally reflects their overall quality. [11]

译 注

在［1］中，"温度"一般译成 temperature、hotness、heat 等，但这里主要是指人情冷暖，故亦用 warmth、warmness 等。

在［2］中，"一来二往"的字面意思为 one to two to the ground，如"一来二往地，他们相爱了"（One to two to the ground, they fell in love.），还有 in the course of contacts 的意思。这里主要讲的是人与人的交往，故用了 social intercourse。"又惊又喜"，通俗的译法还有"be surprised but glad""be both surprised and delighted""have mixed feelings of surprise and joy""half frightened, half pleased"等。

在［3］中，"骑车"通常译成 ride a bike、cycle、bicycling 等，但澳大利亚人的俗语是 push bike。

在［5］中，"亲切感"似乎是 intimacy、cordial feeling、affinity、affability 等，但此处更多的意思是引起了对方的注意和好感，故用了 had appealed to…。

在［7］中，"悟出"最直白的是 come to realize…、have learnt that…，此处用了 to strike me，语气强烈一些。

找北

最近读到央视洋主播埃德温·马厄在中国写的第二本书 *Caught on CCTV*，其中文书名译成《找得着北》。起初觉得有些不沾边，慢慢读下去，觉得颇有道理。[1]

埃德温是前澳大利亚电视台的主持人，我在澳洲生活了十几年，对他原本也是熟悉的。他在近退休之年，阴差阳错于2003年来到中国。初来乍到时，语言不通，人地两疏，闹出了许多尴尬、难堪及有趣的事，他把那段经历写了本书 *My China Daily*，中文名为《找不着北》，虽字义相差甚远，但其中内容还蛮贴切。第二本接续第一本，这样就顺理成章了。[2]

在字源上，古汉语的"北"字，象形为两个人背对背站立，其义为相背、违背，最初是指军队打了败仗，士兵四散而逃，所以称"败北"；后又引申为方位名词——北方；找到了北，也便找到了方向，入了门。[3]

作为一个外国人，在陌生的国度，埃德温的心理经历很正常。幸运的是，他来到的是有知识、懂外语的一群中国人里；他们都有素质，懂得并知道怎样帮他的忙。书中记载了许多这类的小故事，使他觉得中国人很有文化，中国社会很温暖。于是原先只想来华短期看一下的他，却意外地在这里工作和生活了下来，至今十多年过去了，还拿到了中国的绿卡。[4]

这也使我自然联想到二十多年前我初到澳大利亚时"找北"的感觉。我最初接触到的是那里的普通人，却都很热情。记得那时我在路上打开地图找地方，便有人过来主动问是否需要帮忙，实在让人感到惊喜。后来，在去过许多国家，有了各种各样的"找北"经历后，似乎发现了规律。一个地方对于外来陌生人的态度是否友好，与两点有关：一是人数多少，无论是城市还是具体部门，人员嘈杂，总会让人起烦；二是人口素质，无论是国家还是地区，人们受教育程度高、GDP高的地方，对人也会更和蔼、文明。[5]

让人没想到的是，若干年后回国，发现这里对陌生人防范警惕意识很高。家长、老师、公众媒体在不断地告诉人们不要轻易跟陌生人说话，更不能随便跟陌生人走。的确，不愉快或不幸的事情也会屡屡发生，对此我亦不乏切身体会。[6]

在中国文化里，固然有"由己推人""老吾老以及人之老""幼吾幼以及人之幼"等理念，但那并非是无条件的。在古代有"三纲五常"为框架，现代又有各种意识形态的困扰，再后来又遇到随商品经济而来的一些负面因素的冲击，使得我们的社会在公共领域助人"找北"方面，至今是个薄弱环节。似乎，中国人对于熟人是不乏热情的，但对陌生人却有"质"的不同。随着中国与世界日益接轨，日益显出我们的各种自信，我想，这方面的距离也应逐渐缩小。[7]

有意思的是，从中西比较文化角度讲，对于"北"的褒贬、好恶是相反的。在基督教里，北方是撒旦和一切恶魔居住的地方，是罪恶的渊源，如《圣经》所说"必有灾祸从北方发出，降临到这里的一切居民",而福音所以从祭坛的北端开始,正代表教会要做异教徒的转变工作。在中国,自殷周以来,由于政治中心大部分时期在北方,南方被统治,于是形成了"北上""南下"的观念,至今仍说"上北京""下南方";而北京人则更觉得北边是"上风""上水"。[8]

鉴于"找北"在中文里的吉利说法,所以中国人不妨把这种理念更多地转化到帮助陌生人的善举之中。[9]

译 文

Finding the North

I have recently read the second book written by Edwin Maher, an anchor in CCTV, concerning his experience in China, entitled *Caught on CCTV*. Initially, I was puzzled by its translated Chinese title *zhao de zhao bei*, or *I have Found the North*. Having read through the book, however, I find it's pretty relevant. [1]

As a former TV anchor in Australia, where I lived for more than a decade, Edwin is actually no stranger to me. Approaching his retirement, he came to China in 2003 due to all sorts of accidental mishaps. As a newcomer, he was in an unfamiliar environment with huge language barriers, and all sorts of anecdotes of embarrassments, difficulties and amusements were collected in his first book under the title of *My China Daily*, translated into Chinese as *zhao bu zhao bei* or *I Can't Find the North*. The two references to "the north" are equivalent not literally but as a linguistic metaphor. Following this rational line, the translation of the second book's title seems to be perfect. [2]

Etymologically, in the ancient Chinese writing system, as a pictogram the character *bei* (北) looks like two men standing back to back, hence it was originally meant "to be opposed to" one another, denoting that when an army suffered a defeat in a war or battle, all the soldiers ran for their lives with their backs toward each other, which was so-called *baibei*. Gradually, a sense of direction was further derived as "the north", expanding to mean having found a clue about how to do things in a new environment. [3]

The mental process Edwin has gone through as a foreigner in China is perfectly understandable. Fortunately, he was received by a bunch of Chinese who were knowledgeable, high quality, linguistically capable, happy to lend a helping hand. All the short stories recorded in the book contributed to his favorable feeling towards Chinese culture and society as he perceived them, and consequently led to his decision to remain rather than to stay temporarily. Over a decade has gone by and he is now a permanent resident of China. [4]

His story naturally reminds me of my experience in Australia as a newcomer in finding my way about. Initially the people I met in the street were all pretty friendly. What surprised me most was when I was searching for a place on a map quite often people nearby would come and offer to help. Having travelled to many places in the world, a regular pattern seems to have emerged in terms of how people seem friendly towards strangers, which has something to do with the density and quality of a population; a crowded place obviously causes irritation more easily and a place with high levels of education and GDP normally presents a more cordial and civil outlook. [5]

Unexpectedly, after all those years residing and travelling overseas, I came back to find that the highly alert place in terms of self-guarded consciousness is actually China, where parents, teachers and media repeatedly tell people not to talk to, much less go alone with strangers easily. Some unpleasant or unfortunate things do happen to people – unsurprisingly, and myself included. [6]

In Chinese culture, although there are considerate ideas, such as "proceed from the self to others", "take care of one' sown elders first and then extend the same care to others' elders", "love one's own children first and then extend the same love to the others' children", they are nevertheless conditioned by the feudal ethical codes and various ideologies in ancient and modern times, as well as being influenced by some negative factors of the commodity economy since China's "reform and opening up to the outside world". Rooted in this vulnerable area of their culture, the Chinese are people who instinctively treat acquaintances with passion, and strangers in a categorically different way. This practice is quite different from that of the West. As China is now increasingly confidently linked to the international community, the differences in dealing with "outsiders" should also be minimized. [7]

Interestingly, from a cross-cultural perspective, "the North" symbolizes both auspicious and inauspicious aspects in China and the West. In Christianity, the north is the abode of Satan and evil, the source of sins, as the Bible says "Out of the north an evil shall break forth upon all the inhabitants of the land", the gospel thus read from the north end of the altar represents the church's work to convert the heathen. In China, since the Shang and Zhou dynasties, the political center has for the most time been located in the north, with the south being ruled, therefore the traditional concepts for the Chinese have been the "Privileged North" and the "Disadvantaged South" even today. [8]

In the light of the propitious meaning of *zhao bei* in Chinese, the idea should be more favorably applied to people we meet in our life who are deemed to be "outsiders". [9]

译 注

在[1]中,"在中国写的第二本书"实际指的是作者在中国的经历,故不妨加入 concerning his experience in China;"不沾边"是觉得有疑惑,故用了 was puzzled by…;"有道理"不是一般的 with reason、hold water、have substance、it figures 等,而实则是对应前面,此处为"沾边",故用了 relevant。

在［2］中，"是熟悉的"可以是 familiar with…，此处反说为 no stranger to…，亦显自然。"中文名为《找不着北》，虽字义相差甚远，但其中内容还蛮贴切"，此句不宜按字面意思翻译，不妨分解为 literally 和 linguistic metaphor 两部分，即前者不等，后者相对。"顺理成章"原是形容写文章、做事情顺着条理，后比喻随着某种情况的发展而自然产生的结果。《朱子语类》说："文者，顺理而成章之谓也。"据此似应译成 logical、rational and clearly structured，但此处突出的是题目的涵义，故不必拘泥。

在［3］中，从该字的源头讲起，因汉字是象形的，故应在译文中有所体现（pictogram），而"找到北"引申为"入门"，又不宜简单地译成 introduction、induction 等，而更多的是 find a clue。类似的例子如："来了差不多半年之后，他总算对这套系统入了门。"（He at last found a clue to this system after almost half a year.）

在［4］中，（心理经历很）"正常"不是自身的 normal、regular、ordinary、common 等，而是从对方角度讲的容易"理解"，故可用 understandable、comprehensible 等；而"来到"（……一群中国人里），也同样可理解为是"被"（对方接纳的是……），故用了 " he was received by…"；"知道怎样帮他的忙"不妨稍做发挥："happy to lend a helping hand"。至于"拿绿卡"当然还可是 "had/got his green card"，或 "after gaining proof of his permanent residency of…" "he was granted legal permanent residency of…" 等。

在［5］中，"初到"是动词，可以是 when I first/initially arrived，但亦可为名词 a newcomer，以使句子更通顺。"让人感到惊喜"，可以按英语表达习惯置前处理。"发现了规律"，不是一般意义上的 have discovered/found the law，而是指 the repeated or regular way in which something happens or is done，故不妨用 a pattern... emerged，以显出其虽是人为的但却颇带规律性的现象。至于"一是""二是"也不必拘泥于中文的表达习惯，而可变通处理。

在［6］中，对于"家长、老师……跟陌生人走"这些事若分别列出，则显啰唆，故不妨整合成一个句子；而"我亦不乏切身体会"似可译成 and I myself have also had firsthand experience，但接续前文 do happen to people，此处可表达得更为简约。

在［7］中，是从文化根源上来找原因，如"由己推人"还可译为 put oneself in somebody else's position/shoes 等，"老吾老以及人之老"还可译为 extend the love to other elderly 等。"质"的不同，若译成一般的 qualitatively different、different in quality 等，显然不妥，故用了 in a categorically different way，以表示明显的区别对待。

在［8］中，这里的"褒贬"不是一般的 the positive or negative/commendatory or derogatory sense，而更多的是"吉利"与"不吉利"之义，故不妨用 auspicious and inauspicious aspects。"上"与"下"又可变通为 privileged、disadvantaged 等；对于"北京人则更觉得北边是'上风''上水'"，可接续前文，简约处理。

在［9］中，这里的"陌生人"更多指的是"局外人"，如刚来的人，文中特别指老外，故 outsider 比 stranger 更恰当。类似的例子如："这将有助于消除他们在异国他乡作为陌生人的感觉，而增强其语言技能。"（This helps to diminish their feeling of being an "outsider" in a foreign land and fosters them to develop their language skills.）

"道"与物理学

我在西方大学讲老子时,最难解释的是"道"。它看不见,摸不着,却又无处不在。然而,若与现代物理学研究的某些基本知识结合起来,似乎又不太难理解。[1]

老子说:"天下万物生于有,有生于无";"道生一,一生二,二生三,三生万物"。根据英国科学家霍金的研究,时间是从"宇宙大爆炸"开始的,在此之前是空白;现代量子宇宙学也断言,"观测宇宙始于真空"。所谓"真空",是系统的最低能量态(基态),特别是依照量子理论中的"测不准原理",真空中的能量并不等于零,而是形成某一常量。[2]

老子又说,"譬道之在天下,犹川谷之于江海",而百川归海便形成一种"道场"——在场里较高的能态都会自发地趋向基态(真空态),非常近似于现代量子场中的"真空场"。[3]

其实,真空不空,因真空中充满了无数倏忽产生又倏忽消失的"虚粒子对",故曰"虚空",如"虚电子对"就是一个虚的电子加上一个虚的正电子。所谓"虚",是指这些粒子生成的时间非常短暂,受到海森堡"测不准原理"的限制,因此原则上不可能用任何精密仪器直接探测其存在。[4]

量子力学的研究表明,在微观世界里,我们无法准确指出电子在某一时刻出现的地方,而只能确定电子在某一时刻出现在空间某一点的概率,即实物粒子在"恍恍惚惚",正是老子所言:"无物之象,是谓恍惚。迎之不见其首,随之不见其后。"[5]

老子的"有"又可视为物理学中的实物粒子,而"天下万物"均为实物粒子所组成。至于"道生一",无异于基本场,"二"或"三"则分别表示物质结构由低层次向高级层次的转化。由此看来,老子的自然宇宙观,居然与最新的科学发展(主要是与现代宇宙学和物理学所给出的宇宙本源、宇宙创生的基本图像)不谋而合。[6]

2003年2月1日,美国宇航局宣告,威尔金森宇宙微波各向异性探测卫星发现在宇宙中的绝大部分物质都是暗能量,亦即真空能量,从而更加证实了对于"道"和"无"的解释确为可信,其科学依据更为坚实。[7]

更有趣的是,量子物理学新近研究证明,如果高能光子的能量足够高,就有可能从真空中打出一对正负电子。即真空中的虚粒子对在一定外界条件下,如高能光子的打击或极强的电场和磁场的激发等,便可能"实化",变成可以观测的粒子对,于是产生了"无中生有"的物理效应,而这不正是老子的"有生于无"吗?[8]

早在1930年科学史专家萨顿就断言,新的启示可能会来自东方。物理学家卡普拉也曾感叹,远在2000多年前,老子就已经预见到了今天人类文明的状态。可见,中国古代哲学与西方现代科学之间,原本有着某种奇妙的契合。[9]

Dao and Physics

When I lectured Lao Zi at universities in the West, one of the most difficult things was to explain the concept of *Dao* to my students, given its ubiquitous and yet invisible nature. However, it may not be that difficult if we can relate it to some of the fundamentals in modern physics. [1]

Lao Zi hypothesized: "All things in the cosmos are generated from being and being arises from non-being"; "*Dao* produces one, one produces two, two produce three and three yield everything on earth". Stephen Hawking, the British scientist, has theorized that time began with the Big Bang, originating from nothing. According to the theory of modern quantum cosmology, the observable universe is in that empty space where energy is at its lowest (or "ground") state, formulated as a "constant quantity", but certainly not below zero in light of the "uncertainty principle" of quantum mechanics. [2]

Also, Lao Zi said, "All things under heaven are manipulated by *Dao*, in the same way as all streams and torrents flow to rivers and seas". By assembling in the sea, all rivers actually make a "field of *Dao*", where energy at high levels will naturally fill the void (ground state), which very much resembles a vacuum cavity in modern quantum field theory. [3]

Such a so-called vacuum is in fact full of fleeting virtual particle pairs, such as a "virtual electron pair" made up of a virtual electron with a positron, floating within a "vacant space". These particles, characterized by their transient nature, are hardly detectable even with the most sophisticated instruments, according to the "uncertainty principle" proposed by Heisenberg. [4]

Quantum-mechanical research reveals that in any microcosmos we cannot point out exactly where electrons will appear, except calculating their probability as "material particles" drifting in a certain space at a certain time, which is very much in line with Lao Zi's conceptualization: "Shapeless shapes are called vague resemblances – going towards them one can see no front; going after them one can see no rear." [5]

In this way, the "something" and "all things in the cosmos" described by Lao Zi can also be seen as equivalent to physical particles in modern physics. "*Dao* produces one" is in fact little more than ascending transformation, symbolized by "two" and "three" as materialized structures at more complex levels. In a way, Lao Zi's natural cosmology happens to hold the same view as the most recent scientific developments in terms of the fundamental profile of the origin and genesis of the cosmos portrayed by modern cosmology and physics. [6]

On 1st February 2003, NASA (the US National Aeronautics

and Space Administration) announced that the Wilkinson Microwave Anisotropy Probe (WMAP) had found that most materials detected had so far been "dark" or "vacuum" energy, which further consolidates the scientific foundation for convincing interpretations of the ideas of *Dao* and *Wu* in Daoist philosophy. [7]

More interestingly, recent research in quantum physics has proved that under enough pressure of high-energy photons, an electron-positron pair can be produced. In other words, imposed by an external force (such as when struck by high-energy photons or induced by an electric or magnetic field), virtual particles can materialize, becoming a pair of particles that are detectable – a physical effect of "creating something out of nothing". Doesn't that precisely coincide with Lao Zi's statement that "Being arises from non-being"? [8]

Sutton, an expert in the history of science, asserted in 1930 that a new enlightenment would probably originate from the East. Capra was also surprised that Lao Zi could foresee today's human civilization as early as 2000 years ago. Clearly, there are some marvelous conjunctions between ancient Chinese philosophy and modern Western science. [9]

译 注

[1] 根据英文表述习惯，翻译中不妨颠倒词序。

[2] "根据……研究" 一般都译成 "according to... research"，但

亦可根据不同语境做变通处理，如："据有关科学家的研究，暗物质一般不与大多数其他物质作用，而会直接穿过地球、房屋甚至是人的身体，并不会被原子所弹开。"（Dark matter, as some scientists have theorized, doesn't often interact with most other matter, but flies right through the Earth, your house, and your body without bouncing off atoms.）"测不准原理"又译为"不确定性原理"（uncertainty principle），是量子力学中的一个基本原理，由德国物理学家海森堡（Werner Heisenberg）于1927年提出。"而是形成某一常量"句式重组，将其提前、融汇。

［4］"故曰'虚空'"未译成 the so-called "vacant space"，而是作为状语 within a "vacant space"，融入整句之中。

［5］"而只能确定"似也可译成 but can only calculate。"恍惚"，这里不是主观上的 in a trance / absent-minded 等，而是指客观现象。

［6］"为实物粒子所组成"，将前面的"有"和此处的"天下万物"合并译出。"高级层次"若译成 more advanced / sophistic 等似都不够准确。"不谋而合"句中括号里的内容，在翻译中可不必拘泥形式，而将其扩展出来。

［7］"亦即真空能量"，与前面的"暗能量"一并译出（energy）。

［8］"实化"，数学里是 realification，物理学中多用 substantialization、materialization 等。

［9］"启示"，一般有 revelation、inspiration 等，这里特指对客观认识的启迪，故用了 enlightenment，其义为 to give someone more knowledge and greater understanding about something；而"契合",似可译为 agree with、tally with、correspond to、accord with 等,但这里讲的是某种同发性,即 the occurrence of them at the same time or place, 故用了 conjunctions。

科学与哲学

　　现代意义上的"科学"是个西方概念，是相对希腊理性科学而言的，指现代实验科学、应用科学、技术科学，至今不过一百五十余年的历史。[1]

　　实际上，早在中世纪末英语里就有了与拉丁文 scientia 相对应的 science，但即便是英国当时的大科学家，如哈维、牛顿、道尔顿等，没有谁认为自己是从事科学工作的，更没有自认为是科学家的，而被当世人称为"哲学家"或"自然哲学家"，从事的是哲学工作。牛顿的划时代著作标题为《自然哲学的数学原理》，道尔顿著作的标题是《化学哲学的新体系》。可见，在西方历史上，"哲学"是个比"科学"更高尚、更悠久的概念。[2]

　　的确，西方文明源自古希腊，更确切地说源于其理知传统，而其思想产物（episteme），我们称之为"知识"——那时只有一种，即哲学。后来随着人们对于客观事物认识的扩展和深化，科学逐渐从哲学中脱离出来，开启了"分科"化的进程。[3]

　　中文的"科学"来自日文，与"知识"概念相伴随传入中国，其实这两个词都源自同一个拉丁文 scientia，该词正是对希腊文 episteme 的翻译。之所以在中文里有了二者的区分，是因为英文里有了与之相对应的 science 和 knowledge 两个词，是英国

人在翻译 *scientia* 时对该词做了分解。[4]

可见，不同的概念，追根寻源，是对同一事物在不同历史时期、从不同侧面所做的不同理解而已。世界原本是统一的，人们的认识因为有限，所以分化了，才有了学科。[5]

就科学与哲学的关系而言，科学家与哲学家研究的原本是同一事物，不过看问题的角度和方法有所不同。科学家沿着传统思维，走入了事物的客观性，想通过实验证实世界是怎样一种存在；而哲学家沿着传统思维，深化了事物的主观性，试图通过推演，探究不同事物在人们头脑中是如何被接受的。换言之，前者要知道世界是如何发生的，后者要将这种发生理清头绪。[6]

科学通过实验将事实的信息连接起来，哲学则通过思辨的程序将人们对信息的认识加以整合与提升。对于同样事实的获取，前者要求系统，后者重在合理。同时，科学的每一步细化，都丰富了哲学的概念内涵。[7]

科学与哲学的分工产生了良性互动效应：哲学研究不断为科学提出课题，而科学的发展又需哲学的诠释来支撑。其中，最典型的莫过于相对论和量子论中物理学与哲学的高度结合。[8]

所以，世界顶级的科学家，一定具有哲学思维，才能站在相当的高度；而一流的哲学家，必然具有科学素养，方得可靠实力。科学与哲学在不同阶段、不同领域的结合，是回归本源，更是趋向未来。[9]

译 文

Science and Philosophy

"Science" in its modern sense is a Western concept, related to ancient Greek rational science, referring to modern experimental science, applied science and technological science during last hundred and fifty years or so. [1]

In fact, as early as the end of the Middle Ages, there was an English word "science" corresponding to Latin "*Scientia*". However, none of the scientists at that time, including the famous Britons Harvey (1578-1657), Newton (1643-1727) and Dalton (1766-1844), thought of themselves as scientists, so to speak, engaging in scientific jobs; instead, they were called "philosophers" or "natural philosophers", carrying out philosophical missions. Newton's epoch-making work was entitled *Mathematical Principles of Natural Philosophy* and Dalton's work *A New System of Chemical Philosophy*. Obviously, "philosophy" as a historical concept contained many more connotations than "science" in Western history. [2]

Indeed, Western civilization originated from ancient Greece, or more precisely from its rational tradition, and its ideological product – episteme, known as "philosophy" – was the only kind of knowledge at the time. As people's understanding of the world expands and deepens, science gradually broke away from philosophy, evolving different disciplines. [3]

The Chinese characters for "science" are 科学 (*kexue*) which were borrowed from Japanese, together with the characters for "knowledge" 知识 (*zhishi*). As a matter of fact, both were derived from the same Latin "*scientia*", which was translated from the Greek word "episteme". The dual versions of the translation actually resulted from "science" and "knowledge" when "*scientia*" was rendered into English. [4]

It can be seen that the seemingly different concepts were actually coined from different perceptions during different historical periods and from different perspectives. In other words, the integral world is divided by nothing other than the confines of people's comprehension. [5]

Regarding the relations between science and philosophy, the objects scientists and philosophers explore into are actually the same; it is the approaches they employ that differ. Following traditional thinking, scientists get into the objective nature of the world, willing to unravel the mystery of existence, while philosophers concentrate on subjectivity and delve down to the bottom of how things are perceived in the mind through reasoning. In short, the former is set to know how things have taken place, whereas the latter is determined to sort them out. [6]

In carrying out their studies, scientists systematically fit together information through experiments, while philosophers integrate and promote it by way of analysis. The former pays attention to systematicity, the latter to rationality. Meanwhile, with each step science moves on, while the connotations of philosophy are enriched. [7]

Science and philosophy, despite being different, nevertheless interact positively: philosophical research constantly puts forward new topics for science, which in turn provides substances allowing philosophy to become more substantive. Relativity and quantum theory are typical results of the high degree of interconnection between physics and philosophy. [8]

Therefore, the top scientists in the world are all equipped with philosophical minds, enabling them to have a grand vision. First-class philosophers, on the other hand, have to grasp certain scientific knowledge as part of their essential qualifications. This kind of combination in various fields at different stages is rooted in the past and points towards the future. [9]

译 注

[1] 所谓"希腊理性科学",实质指古代希腊的理性主义,即能超越自己感官欲望和利害关系并不计得失地探究各种抽象思辨的理智,故译为 ancient Greek rational science。

[3] "思想产物",主要是指 episteme,其本义为 the body of ideas that determines intellectually certain knowledge at any particular

time；因那时只有一种知识，即"哲学"，故二者可说是同义词。

［5］此处的"追根寻源"没有按其通常的意思译成 to trace it to its source、go to the heart of the matter、get to the bottom of its meaning 等，而是将其含义分解到 "coined from... during different historical periods... from different perspectives"之中。

［6］"通过推演，探究不同事物在人们头脑中是如何被接受的"，此句若按其字面意思和语序翻译，则不易表达，且会冗赘，故将其语义变通（如"探究"）、语序调整（如"通过推演"），译为 "delve down to the bottom of how things are perceived in the mind through reasoning"。

［8］"良性互动效应"，按字面翻译，似应为 benign interaction effect；此处据其语境，变通为 interact positively。"高度"一般译成 high degree、highness、altitude、height 等，但就全局和哲学角度而言，have a grand vision 更确切。

［9］"回归本源"一般译成 returning the origin、back to basics 等，但在此句式中，用被动语态 is rooted in the past，似更易表述。

哲学的用处

就专业来讲,"哲学"现在可能要算大学里的冷门了。不像电脑、金融、财会等,哲学似乎太抽象、遥远、不实用。[1]

其实,从根源上讲,哲学与科学的关系最紧密。"哲学"一词源于希腊文Φιλοσοφία,意为"热爱智慧",涵括了所有学问。那时的哲学家同时也是科学家,他们的智慧始于发问。在那由超自然的各种神灵主宰的世界里,泰勒斯敢于质疑其真实性,提出了万物由水而来的命题,阿那克西米尼认为空气是物质的主要元素,亚里士多德更是要检测空气与阳光等等,由此引发了最早的智慧——哲学。[2]

就人与世界的关系而论,主要有三大类,即人与自然、人与社会及人与自身的关系。第一类是人类认识、改造自然的知识,如物理学、化学、数学、生物学等;第二类是人们认识、改造社会的知识,即社会学、经济学、政治学、法学、伦理学等;第三类是你我认识自身思维的知识,包括脑科学、神经学、心理学、逻辑学等。但是,哲学不是这些具体学科,而是超越其上并对其加以抽象和概括的学问。[3]

典型的,如物理学中有作用与反作用,化学中有化合和分解,生物学中有同化和异化等等,哲学并不陷入这些细节,而是从整体上把握人与世界的关系,从具体学科的关联中抽象出最实质的内容和最普遍的规律，如"对立统一规律"。这种规律来自具体学科，又可反过来指导具体学科；因而，哲学看似无用，实则用大。[4]

首先，哲学可摆正自己与自然、社会、心灵的关系，正可谓"定位宇宙，安排人生"。苏格拉底认为，未经反省的生活是没有价值的生活；只有在大格局上把握事物发展规律的人，才不会被表面的现象所误导，被眼前的挫折所困扰。[5]

其次，哲学可使人的思维更加系统化，善于把零零碎碎的材料整合起来，提高逻辑分析能力，并与方法论相统一。哲学在性质上是一种关于"思考的思考"，不轻易相信任何未经各个角度深刻思考过的事情，特别注重缜密的反思，即对思维对象的再思、三思、多思，同时又反过来对思维过程本身进行思考，因而形成鞭辟入里的批判性思维。[6]

再次，哲学可锤炼人的品格。由于思考、推理、综合、分析本身是个艰难的过程，因而可在更深层次上使人坚毅。在根本上，哲学是关于"生"的学问，因而通过完善性格，使人懂得怎样活着才更有价值。[7]

在某种意义上讲，哲学是最实用的，哲学人才又是"通才"。不但许多自然科学、社会科学专家通晓哲学，哲学专业者从事相关领域，甚至转行成为名人的也大有人在，国内国外莫不如此。[8]

所以，哲学并不抽象，也不遥远，实有"大用"。[9]

译 文

Why Do We Study Philosophy?

As a "major" at university, philosophy may not be so popular nowadays, for it seems to be too abstract, remote and impractical, unlike such subjects as computing, finance, accounting and so on. [1]

Fundamentally speaking, the word "philosophy", derived from the Greek Φιλοσοφία, meaning "love of wisdom", originally embraced all kinds of knowledge. In that world dominated by supernatural deities, philosophers and scientists were identical, and their wisdom was initiated by asking questions: Thales queried the substance of the world by assuming the ubiquity of water; Anaximenes believed that everything in the world is composed of air; Aristotle attempted to scrutinize the air and sun – these quests developed their wisdom. [2]

The relations between man and the world may be divided into three categories, namely the relationships between man and nature, man and society and within the human self, which are studied respectively by the natural sciences (to understand and change nature), such as physics, chemistry, mathematics, biology etc.; social sciences (to understand and change society), sociology, economics, politics, law, ethics etc.; and sciences of thinking (to understand the nature and hyphology of the brain), such as brain science, neuroscience, brain psychology, logics, etc. Philosophy, however, is none of these branches of learning but their abstraction and generalization. [3]

Typically, various laws functioning in different fields of study – such as action and reaction in physics, combination and decomposition in chemistry, assimilation and alienation in biology – are not the focus of philosophical study. Philosophy, instead, contributes to abstracting the basic nature and general laws operating in these disciplines as a whole, such as "the law of the unity of opposites". These laws, once conceptualized, can in turn be applied to specific disciplines as devices, far more useful than they might at first sight seem to be. [4]

The benefits of studying philosophy may be realized as follows: First, it assists people to properly adjust the relations between nature, society and the self, becoming fully aware of where they stand both macrocosmically and microcosmically. As Socrates believed that no life is worth living without introspection, people cannot be misled and perplexed when they have grasped the general law of development in the world. [5]

Second, it makes people think more systematically, integrating various "segmented materials" into a coherent theoretical framework by enhancing logical analysis and combining methodologies. Essentially, philosophy is the study of thinking, penetrating into issues from different angles before anything can be taken in. Special attention is paid to rigorous reflection during every stage of thinking and this process itself is included as part of its study, so as to form a pattern of incisive critical thinking. [6]

Third, philosophy can also temper one's character. Arduous thinking, reasoning, synthesizing and analyzing results in people becoming firmer and more persistent in a deep sense. Since philosophy is ultimately about living, it leads to an appreciation of meaningful life through perfecting personality. [7]

In a sense, philosophy is in fact widely applicable and has been studied and acquired by experts of natural and social sciences and many philosophers, both at home and abroad, have become celebrities either in their specialist fields of study or in their switched professions as generalists. [8]

Therefore, philosophy is not abstract, nor remote, but of profound use. [9]

译 注

[1] "专业"在一般意义上是 specialty、profession、career、domain 等，但这里主要是指作为大学里的一门学科，故以 major 为宜。

[2] "万物由水而来"通常译成 everything in the world is made of water，但因后面用了类似的句子，故此处用了 the ubiquity of water，以有变化。

[3] 这"三大类"的分别表述，可不拘泥于原文，译成"第一类是" "第二类是"等，而应根据英文表达习惯，将句子加以整合。所谓"超越"不一定总是 surpass、transcend、surpass、

overreach 等，其义已包含在 abstraction and generalization 之中。

［4］这里的"陷入"没有用 be caught in、entrap 等，而是做了变通 "are not the focus of (philosophical study)"，以更切题。所谓"来自具体学科"，是指从各学科中总结、提炼出的概念与规律等，即 form some ideas of…，故可通融为 conceptualized，如："本专栏所讨论的数据模型来自计算机专家的推导。"（The data models discussed in this column are conceptualized by computer scientists.）

［5］"大格局"一般为 great setup、big structure、grand pattern 等，但这里的意思已尽含在 the general law of development，故可不必再刻意译出。

［6］"不轻易相信"，简单的译法如 not easily believe in/trust…。此处用了 "penetrating into…, before anything can be taken in"，以与哲学性相符。

［7］"更有价值"一般为 more rewarding、more valuable 等，如："许多人把他们的学识与他人分享，这些知识比时间或金钱更有价值。"（A lot of people share their knowledge which can be more valuable than money or time.）但就生活价值而言，又不妨用 meaningful life，如："如果我们经常思索这些问题，就会获得内心的平静，活得更有价值。"（If we can often reflect on these issues we will lead a more meaningful life of inner peace.）

［8］"通晓"一般可为 thoroughly understand、have a good knowledge、drench 等，这里变通为 "(philosophy) has been studied and acquired by…"，以适于句子表达。

无止境的认知

人类对于自然世界的认识经历了漫长的过程。希腊哲学家德谟克利特，在公元前450年认为，宇宙万物是由一种细微而不可分割的物质所构成。中国古代哲学家认为世界是由金、木、水、火、土五种元素组成。到了近现代，又发现了质子、中子、夸克。[1]

在20世纪30年代以前，经典物理学认为，物质是由分子和比分子小的原子构成，分子是物质中能够独立存在、相对稳定、保持其物质化学性质的最小单位。原子是化学反应的基本微粒，在化学反应中不可分割。[2]

1932年，苏联物理学家伊凡宁柯提出了"质子-中子说"。经科学家研究证实，原子由中心带电的原子核与核外高速运转且带负电的电子构成，原子核由质子和中子两种粒子构成。1964年，美国物理学家默里·盖尔曼提出新理论：质子和中子并非是最基本的颗粒，它们由更微小的物质——"夸克"构成。经过几十年的研究，虽然有的实验证实了夸克的存在，但单个的夸克至今还未找到。科学家们认为，夸克只能在束缚态内稳定存在，而不能单独存在，且瞬息即逝。[3]

就物理学的理论发展而言，以牛顿力学为基础的经典物理学，在17世纪提出了"物质不灭或实体不变"的理论，将物质视为实体,认为在任何机械运动及化学反应中,质量始终如一。然而,到了20世纪,爱因斯坦的"相对论"指出了物质实体观的谬误,认为质量与速度有关,同一物体相对于不同的参考系,其质量就有不同的值。例如,物体运动接近光速时,不断地对物体施加能量,物体速度的增加却越来越难,原因何在?其实能量并没有消失,而是转化成了质量。再如,原子弹的核裂变和链式反应,证明了质量可以变成巨大的能量释放出来。[4]

到了20世纪后期,物理学界又出现了"弦理论",认为自然界物质的基本单元不是电子、光子、中微子或夸克之类的粒子,而是无数微小弦的闭合圈;正是因为它们的不同振动和运动,产生了各种不同的基本粒子。换言之,无论宏观世界(星际银河)或微观世界(基本粒子),都是由"能量弦"组成的。[5]

所有这一切,还都是就"能见物质"而言的。然而,据科学家研究,人类对于世界的认知,目前为止也只有很小一部分。例如,人们所能看到的物质,只有百分之五,而对于构成宇宙的百分之九十五的暗物质,还几乎一无所知,因为它既不发射也不吸收任何光或电磁辐射,人们只有靠引力效应来推测它的存在。所以,我们对于自然世界的认知,其实还刚刚开始。[6]

译 文

Thinking Infinity

Human understanding of the physical world has gone through a lengthy development process. In 450 BC, the Greek philosopher Democritus believed that everything in the universe was made up of a tiny and indivisible substance. Philosophers in ancient China thought that the world was composed of five elements: gold, wood, water, fire, earth. In modern times, protons, neutrons and quarks have subsequently been found. [1]

By the 1930s, according to classical physics, matter is composed of molecules and atoms which are smaller than molecules. Molecules are the smallest units of matters in terms of existence, stability and chemical properties; atoms are the basic indivisible particles in chemical reactions. [2]

But in 1932, the Soviet physicist Ivanenko proposed his "proton-neutron theory" in which scientists proved that an atom consists of a positively charged nucleus (made up of protons and neutrons) and negatively charged electrons revolving around it at high-speed. In 1964, American physicist Murray Gell-Mann put forward a new theory, which held that protons and neutrons are not the smallest particles, since they are made up of quarks. After several decades of research, although the existence of quarks has been confirmed by experiments, no single quark has so far yet been isolated. Scientists thus believe that quarks are fleeting and exist only under certain stable and confining conditions. [3]

On the theoretical front, in the 17th century classical physics, based on Newtonian mechanics, put forward the theory of the "conservation of matter" or "entity invariance", regarding matter as an entity which remains constant under any mechanical movement and chemical reaction. However, in the 20th century, Einstein pointed out the fallacy of this theory in his Relativity, relating mass to speed since the quality of the same matter varies with different reference systems. For example, when an object moves close to the speed of light, it is increasingly hard to speed up despite more energy being infused. The energy, rather than disappearing, is instead transformed into mass. Also, it has been proved that mass can be transformed into immense energy through nuclear fission in the chain reaction of an atomic bomb. [4]

By the late 20th century, "string theory" had emerged in the field of physics, believing that the basic units in the physical world are not particles such as electrons, photons, neutrinos or quarks, but numerous tiny closed loop strings, whose vibrations and movements produce various basic particles. In other words, both the macroscopic world (e.g. the milky way galaxy) and microscopic world (e.g. fundamental particles) are made up of "energy strings". [5]

All this is about "visible matter". According to scientific research, however, the knowledge humanity has so far acquired covers only a tiny part of the universe. Visible matter detectable by humans, for example, accounts for just 5%, the rest (dark matter) making up 95% of the cosmos, which, neither emitting nor absorbing light or any other electromagnetic radiation at any significant level and inferred only from its gravitational effects on visible matter, still remains almost unknown to humans. Therefore, our journey to identify and understand the physical world has in fact only just begun. [6]

译 注

[1] 中的"自然世界",容易译成 natural world,如:"自然界中存在着一些守恒定律,其中有些是严格的,有些是近似的。"(In the physical world there exist a number of conservation laws, some exact and some approximate.) "微细"一般是 minuteness、minuscule particle 等,此处将其与"不可分割的物质"相结合,译为 tiny and indivisible substance。

[2] 中的"独立存在、相对稳定"未必译成 independent existent and relative stable, 而用 in terms of existence, stability…, 可更好地融入该句式。

[3] 将"就物理学的理论发展而言"译为 on the theoretical front, 据上下文而省去了 physical;"物质不灭",字面意思是 the

immortality of the material、indestructibility of matter 等，但更确切的译法应为 conservation of matter。

[6] 中一般意义上的"认知"，可译成 cognize、perceive、acknowledge 等，而 to identify and understand 是稍加诠释。

李约瑟的疑惑

李约瑟，研究中国科技史的著名英国学者，写出了六卷本的《中国科学技术史》，但有个问题一直困扰着他："中国古代科学技术很发达，为什么没有产生近代科学？"[1]

这是一个非常矛盾的问题。首先关乎对"科学"概念的理解。李约瑟经常将科学与技术（science and technology）两个词合在一起使用，似乎以"技术"充当了"科学"。应当说，中国古代的技术，并不是西方严格意义上的"科学"；如果他说中国古代有技术，而且远比西方发达，便易于理解，但他用的是"中国古代科学"，这便让人费解。[2]

而且，李约瑟用的是现代西方的科学分类概念来对中国古代的"科学"进行整理、归纳，于是不免使人误解，认为中国古代的"科学"就等于近代意义上的科学，例如：第三卷论数学、天文学、地理学，第四卷论物理学，第五卷论化学和化工，第六卷论生物学、农学和医学，等等。于是就有了矛盾：既然近代中国都没能产生近代科学，何以古代便出现了近代科学，而且还很"发达"？[3]

通观《中国科学技术史》，在李约瑟笔下，人类的科学似乎有一个统一的发展模式，即原始型—中古型—近代型，欧洲人走完了这一进程，而中国人却止步在了第二个形态。显然，这是把欧洲的科学发展模式当作世界通用模式，套用在了中国古代科技史上。[4]

其实,科学有广义和狭义之分。广义的科学是指有关主客观世界的系统知识,狭义的科学则"其推理重实验,其察物有条贯"。当今世界所通称的科学多指狭义的科学,即西方现代实验科学,而这不同于对中国古代科技的理解。[5]

从根本上讲,决定西方近代科学的基因是希腊理性科学,而中国传统文化中却没有出现这一理性科学基因。西方理性科学是自古希腊以来一直贯穿西方文明发展过程的主流知识形态:在古希腊和古罗马,其典型学科是哲学和数学;在中世纪,为神学;在近代,则是自然科学(数理实验科学)。有理性科学,不一定产生实验科学(如古希腊);但没有理性科学,一定不会产生实验科学。这正是中国近代何以没有产生西方人认为的"近代科学"的历史原因。[6]

若不顾中国古代基本没有数理实验科学传统的事实,勉强依照数理实验科学的框架去梳理中国古代的自然知识成就,便难免出现两个误区:一是前面提到的以技术代替科学,二是得出许多脱离中国古代语境的术语、观点和结论,进而产生矛盾和混乱。例如,在中国古代的自然知识中,由于数学没有优先性,其各种知识没有显著的数学化特征,所以中国的传统数学在本质上是计算"技术",没有独立的知识地位,是"有术无学",完全不能等同于西方意义上的"数理科学"。[7]

由此而言,在我看来,李约瑟疑惑的根本原因,在于他没有充分认识到中西方文明发展进程的本质差别,从而混淆了两套完全不同性质的"科学"(包括"技术")概念。[8]

译 文

Needham's Puzzle

Joseph Needham, a well-known British scholar, studied the history of science and technology of China, and wrote the six-volume *History of Science and Technologies in China*. One question, however, had always puzzled him: given the highly developed science and technology in ancient China, why had modern science not emerged in its modern history? [1]

This is a very controversial issue. Above all, it has to do with the definition of "science". It should be pointed out that ancient Chinese technology and "science" defined in the West are two different things. Since Needham often used "science and technology" indiscriminately as a phrase, and "technology" usually served as "science", it may confuse people with the question as to whether ancient China's science or its technologies were more advanced than those of the West? [2]

Moreover, Needham identified and typed "science" in ancient China based on modern Western scientific classification, which was bound to misdirect the reader to modern "science", such as mathematics, astronomy, geography in volume 3 of his *History*, physics in volume 4, chemistry, chemical engineering in volume 5 and biology, agronomy and medicine in volume 6. That being the case, a contradiction occurred: Now that modern China had failed to produce modern science, how come science had appeared in its ancient times and was even highly developed? [3]

Taking a comprehensive view of the *History* mentioned above, in his work there is a unified model in the development of human science, namely from primitive to medieval to modern. While the Europeans went through this process, the Chinese apparently halted at the second stage. Obviously, the European model has been used as a universal one ethnocentrically applied to ancient China's history of science and technology. [4]

In fact, the idea of "science" can be defined in both a broad and a narrow sense. Broadly speaking, it refers to systematic knowledge about the subjective and objective worlds. In its narrow sense, it can be understood as "reasoning on the basis of experiments while analyzing by logic". In today's world, so-called "science" is generally denoted in its narrow sense, namely modern experimental science, which is quite different from ancient China's "technology". [5]

Fundamentally, the core that determines modern science in the West is ancient Greek rational science, which was absent from traditional Chinese culture. Western rational science has long been the mainstream knowledge developed throughout Western civilization: in ancient Greece and Rome it was mainly in the forms of philosophy and mathematics, in the Middle Ages theology, and in modern times natural science (mathematical and experimental sciences). Experimental science may not necessarily follow rational science (such as in ancient Greece); however, without rational science, experimental science is out of the question. This was precisely the historical reason why "modern science" as defined by Westerners did not occur in China. [6]

Should we ignore the fact that there was no such thing as mathematical and experimental science in ancient China, the rigid classification imposed on the history of Chinese explorations in natural knowledge would inevitably cause misconceptions on two fronts: One, it is very easy to substitute the concept of technology for that of science, as previously mentioned; Two, many academic terms, viewpoints and judgments that have been taken completely out of their context would subsequently be produced, causing confusion and mess. For example, since "mathematics" did not prominently develop in ancient China, other kinds of knowledge were not expressed in mathematical terms, therefore its mathematics in essence remained as a technique of calculation and never gained the status of "mathematical science" as in the West; there was no equivalence between the two. [7]

From this perspective, the root cause of Needham's puzzle in my view lies in his lack of recognition of essential differences between the developments of civilizations in China and in the West, and consequent confusion of the two sets of concepts – "science" and "technology", which are completely different in their historical contexts. [8]

译 注

[1] "困扰"一般似可译成 bother、beset、perplex、persecute 等，但这里更多的是指被某一问题所疑惑，即 filled with bewilderment and unable to understand it，故用了 puzzled。

[2] "让人费解"还可译成 people hard to understand、be obscure/unintelligible for people、inexplicability 等，此处变通为"it may confuse people with the question as to…"。

[3] 此"误解"是使役句，不宜译成 misunderstand、misread、misconstrue、misapprehend、misconceive 等，而实则为"误导"，即 misdirect、misguide 等。

[4] "套用"通常译作 use indiscriminately、apply mechanically 等，但这里涉及以欧洲人的思维模式来理解中国历史，故用了有种族文化色彩的 ethnocentrically 一词。

[5] "条贯"为书面用语，即"条理、系统"，似可译成 order、procedures 等，但这里更体现为 logic、by logic。

[6] 所谓"希腊理性科学"，实质指古代希腊的理性主义，即能超越自己感官欲望和利害关系并不计得失地探究各种抽象思辨的理智。

[7] "有术无学"，这里不好直译，而"remained as a technique of calculation and never gained the status of 'mathematical science' as in the West"算是一种释译。

[8] 鉴于李约瑟文中的"科学"概念通常是 science 和 technology 并用，这里不妨将"'科学'（包括'技术'）"以同样的形式译出。

读史使人明智

我们生活在当下，筹划着未来，为什么要了解历史？培根说"读史使人明智"，是否有道理？[1]

如果把目光沿着人类走过来的道路向回望去，便会发现：我们其实都是历史的产物。不知道过去，就不懂得今天，何谈是个现代人！难怪在西方的一些国家，曾把是否具有历史知识，作为是否受过教育的标志。英国伊丽莎白女王在回忆录中说，她上学时最喜欢的就是历史课，而且成绩最好。历史代表了一种文明和风范。[2]

中国是一个具有五千年历史的文明古国，中国文化是世界上唯一没有历史中断的古老文化，因而"中国人"出现在世界任何地方，总伴随着悠久的历史文化背景。这也成为中国人的一种独特身份，因而应以熟知自己历史为荣，以不知为耻。[3]

在中国文化里，"六经皆史"。历史提供了知识与智慧的源泉。唐太宗说："以铜为鉴，可正衣冠；以古为鉴，可知兴替；以人为鉴，可明得失。"历史总有规律可循，正如事物的发展都有其内在的逻辑。这种历史感，在当今世界，自然也应是全球化的。[4]

唯其具有历史眼光，才能深刻理解当今社会现象，因为那不过是历史的延续。不知秦政，何以认识在中国延续两千余年并影响后世的专制制度？不知鸦片战争，怎能理解"西学东渐"，乃至香港问题？不知新文化运动，如何恰当区别文言文与现代文？面对西方，不知古希腊哲学，便无从理解其思想根源；不知文艺复兴、启蒙运动，便难以认知西方近代科学思想、市场经济、宪政制度、三权分立，乃至美国的总统大选。[5]

有历史感的人，看问题不会只聚一点，或只限于表面，而可通观脉络，深入实质。进而，形成立体性思维，以发展性眼光对待一切，因而也更容易明确自己的人生走向。[6]

学习历史还可不断锤炼人们的道德意识。历史上出现过形形色色的人，善恶美丑，不拘一格，但是历史的长河像一面巨大的筛子，将是非曲直理清，最终被后世称颂的是真善美，唾弃的是假恶丑。[7]

甚至，一件小事，也会铭刻在史，给人启示。例如，春秋时鲁襄公二十五年，齐国崔杼弑其君庄公，齐太史乃秉笔直书："崔杼弑其君。"崔杼怒而杀之，其弟接班，照写无误，又被杀……直杀到第四个兄弟，仍照写无误，崔杼才不得不放弃修改历史的企图。这四个兄弟，甚至在历史上没有留下姓名，但其风骨与情操，让人读后不禁掩卷长叹。[8]

的确，读史不仅仅使人明智。[9]

Histories Make Men Wise

We live in the present and plan for and worry about the future, so why are we bothered about knowing the things of the past? Is there any truth in Francis Bacon's saying "Histories make men wise"? [1]

Looking back along the road from which human beings have come, it is easy to find that we are all the products of history. Failing to know the past you will never fully comprehend the present as a modern human. It is thus no surprise to see the practice in the West where having a certain kind of historical knowledge has been seen as a sign distinguishing the educated from the uneducated. Queen Elizabeth II recalls in her memoirs that history was the subject she favored and scored best at during her school years. In a way, history symbolizes the quality and demeanor of a person. [2]

China is a country with an ancient civilization of five thousand years and Chinese culture is the only traditional culture in the world that hasn't been disrupted by history. "Chinese", whenever they go in the world, carry the badge of a long historical background whether they realize it or not. They should be proud of knowing their history and ashamed of ignorance. [3]

In Chinese culture, "all classics are history", which provides a source of knowledge and wisdom. As Emperor Taizong (599-649) of the Tang Dynasty said, "By looking in a mirror, you can dress up properly; by witnessing the rise and fall of dynasties in the past, you draw lessons from history; by learning from others, you realize both gains and losses". History has after all certain patterns emerging in its course, just as there is a logic underpinning the development of all things. A sense of history in today's world has certainly also to be globalized. [4]

Viewing things historically enables one to penetrate social phenomena which in one way or another are a continuation of their precedents. Lacking the knowledge of administration in the Qin Dynasty (221-206 BCE), for example, how can one understand the autocratic system of two thousand years that had far-reaching influence on China's succeeding politics? Being ignorant of the Opium War, how can one have a grip on the clue of "Western learning spreads to the East" or even the issue of Hong Kong? Having no idea of what the "New Culture Movement" is, how can one adequately differentiate between classical and modern Chinese? Likewise, in comprehending the West, one has to learn about ancient Greek philosophy, which is the root generating Western ideologies; to be familiar with the Renaissance and Enlightenment, which inspired its modern scientific ideas, market economy, constitutional system, separation of the three powers, and even presidential elections in the USA, and so on. [5]

With a sense of history, one will be equipped to judge issues more contextually and substantially, instead of being handicapped by bias and superficiality. Furthermore, with developed multi-dimensional thinking and a dynamic viewpoint, people can navigate their careers more wisely. [6]

Studying history can also temper one's moral conscience. Given that various characters, good and evil, beautiful and ugly, have appeared in history, which acts as a huge filter, by unraveling the rights and wrongs throughout history, one may conclude that virtue has its own reward and evil gets punished. [7]

Sometimes a little event is engraved in history, leaving much inspiration for generations to come. During the Spring and Autumn Period (770-221BC) in China's history, for instance, in 548 BC (the 25th year of the reign of Duke Xiang of the State of Lu), a grand historian in charge of its historiography in the State of Qi recorded the fact that "Cui Zhu assassinated his monarch." So angry was Cui Zhu that he had his historian executed. Then his younger brother took over the office of grand historian and recorded the event using the same words, and was likewise executed. Next came the second younger brother, who again recorded the identical statement, and so on. The killing didn't cease until the fourth brother was in charge, when Cui Zhu finally gave up the idea of "erasing" history. Having read this story, one can't help but sigh deeply about the character and sentiment of the four brothers who didn't even leave their names in that history. [8]

Indeed, histories contribute not only to wisdom... [9]

译 注

[1]"为什么要"似应译成"Why do we want to study history?",而 bother about 可体现出一种语气,如:"If you feel terrific now, you may not be bothered about learning things like refinance."(如果你认为现在很好,就不必去学选择投资那类的东西。)

[2]"何谈"似应用语气更为强烈的词语,如"how can…""what is…"等。例如:"如果中国不加入,又何谈世界贸易组织呢?"(How can you call it a world trade organization if China is not in it?)这里将其融合在一种更为平和的句式中。

[3]"总与",未必用 always,可用其他词语或表达方式,如:"不论发生什么事,上帝总与你同在。"(God will be with you no matter what happens.)"如果你总与过去的悲观打交道,那么很可能在面对错误的判断时,做出错误的决定。"(If you approach the past with pessimism, there is a possibility of making wrong decisions arriving at erroneous judgments.)此处用了 whenever…。

[4]说到"规律",用得最多的是 law、rule,但也可用 pattern,如:"所有列举的例子都遵循同一规律。"(All of the examples presented here follow the same pattern.)此处更有形象感。

[5]这里的"理解"没有用通常的 understand、comprehend、make out 等,而是用了更口语化的 have a grip on…。类似的

例子如："They have a good grip on the situation."（他们透彻了解并把握了局势。）"不知"没有延续前面的反问句式，而是改为陈述句，以示变化。

[6]"更容易明确"一般多用"It becomes more easier and clear…"等，但此处"navigate… more wisely"为更深层的释译。

[7]"理清"还可有 ravel out、clarify、clear… up、take… in shape 等。这里的"真善美"是一种泛指，不一定都具体翻译出来，如"the true, the good and the beautiful"等，而可概述为 virtue；与此相对应，"假恶丑"也不妨以 evil 代之。

[8]"仍照写无误"在表述和词序上都做了调整，将其译文放在了 the second younger brother 之后。

[9]为表述其还有更多的涵义，在译文里加上了删节号。

作者与读者

作者与读者是天然的一对。作者自然希望有读者，否则似乎没了写作意义，即便伤心欲绝的司马迁写完《史记》后"藏之名山"，也希望"俟后世圣人君子"来读。当然，也有不为他人而只为自己心灵写作的，那么读者便是自己——作者与读者合二而一了。[1]

特别是人文类的作品，作者根据自己的经验与理解写作，呈现给读者的无疑是经过加工的"现实"，当然又越"真"越好。其中，作者的诚实不应轻易受到怀疑，因为作者是在自己的四维时空里书写现实，自然含有其"合理想象"——甚至是无限的。唯其如此，才体现出作者的创意。[2]

一旦成书，作者便把这一时空交给了读者。二者的时空不可能完全吻合，原因是读者在第五维时空上发挥着想象力——调动起自己的经验与理解进行另一种创作。有作者对读者说，"我提供文字，你们制作画面"，形成了"共同创作"，但效果却是扩散性的。正如鲁迅所说，由于人们的经历、观念、学养及兴趣不同，在阅读《红楼梦》时，自然会从中读出不同的内容："经学家"看见《易》，道学家看见淫，才子看见缠绵，革命家看见排满，流言家看见宫闱秘事……"在西方也说，有一千个读者便有一千个哈姆雷特。[3]

同时，作者与读者的关系又不是直线、单向的，而是动态、多维的。读者不同于观众（特别是电视、电影等的观众），因为他们有更多的余地去想象、还原、扩展"真相"，因而更利于其知识和智力的滋养；而作者从读者的反馈中也会有新的发现，收到"结局大于期望"的效果，有助于原著的再版和新著的创作。[4]

阅读的魅力在于把人带入一个未曾经历或未曾深入理解的境况，好奇、挑战、获益，丰富和开阔了有限的生活时空，也相对延长了人生，因而真正尝到阅读甜头的人，是会上瘾且乐此不疲的。[5]

其实，阅读的最高境界，不是读到了别人的世界，而是读出了自己的内心世界——在更深、更广的领域，发现和丰富了"自我"，更加充实，更爱生活，更有创造力。[6]

作为"合作人"，作者应当首先是个好的读者——不会阅读何以写作？而好的读者不妨拿起笔来，体会遣词造句的经历，从而在阅读中获得更丰厚的感悟。[7]

译 文

The Author and the Reader

The author and the reader are a natural pair. It is only meaningful for an author to write if there are readers. Even Sima

Qian (145-90 BC), the well-known heart-broken historian of the *Records of the Grand Historian*, who decided to "conceal his writings in a sacred mountain", was still hopeful that a "certain kind of sage or gentleman" would appreciate them. There are certainly some writers who wish to express themselves only to themselves – in that case, the author and reader are united as one. [1]

Works in the humanities, in particular, are presented to the reader by the author based on "processed reality" (it ought to be as "real" as possible) according to his or her personal experiences and understanding. The author's sincerity should not be questioned lightly for what he or she writes is actually nothing more than their "reasonable" (sometimes infinite) stretching of the imagination – their creativity within their four-dimensional plane of space and time. [2]

Once the book is released, the author hands control to the readers, who start their own process of imagination – their creativity based on their own experiences and understanding, producing a "fifth dimension", which may not overlap totally with the author's. As one author says, "I make the words, you make the pictures": in a way, they are "co-creators", proliferating results. In reading *A Dream of Red Mansions*, as Lu Xun (1881-1936), the famous Chinese writer, pointed out, people naturally have different views and opinions due to their different experiences, ideas, learning and interest: "The Orthodox realize *change* in it; moralists see pornography; scholars sense romance; revolutionaries witness anti-Manchurian actions; gossips discover royal court secrets and scandals…" In the West, there is also a saying that "There are a thousand Hamlets in a thousand people's eyes". [3]

In fact, the relations between the author and reader are not uni-dimensional and one-way, but dynamic and multidimensional. Unlike, say, TV or film audiences, readers are left adequate leeway to fire their imaginations in terms of retracing (even expanding) the "truth", and consequently they obtain more knowledge and develop further intellectually. By receiving feedback from readers, on the other hand, authors discover more "unexpected effects", which in turn benefits the revision or new books of their creative writing. [4]

The charm of reading lies in venturing into uncharted or unknown waters, where wonders, challenges as well as benefits only bewitch the journey, enrich and enlarge the horizon of life and, in some way, prolong life, for those who have tasted the sweetness of reading will be addicted to and never bored with it. [5]

The zenith of reading, in fact, is to explore no world of others except your own – discovering more of the self in a more in-depth and substantial way, feeling fulfilled by more love and creativity in your daily life. [6]

As a "co-creator", then, the author should first be a good reader, for how can an author be a competent writer without reading skills? Likewise, a good reader should also pick up the pen to experience the pain and joy of writing, in order to enjoy reading more abundantly. [7]

译 注

[1] "只为自己心灵写作"未必是 to write only for their own soul，而 express themselves 则涵义很多，例如："The value of this exercise is that it challenges the students to express themselves freely."（这项练习的价值在于它能促使学生自由地表达自己的思想。）

[2] "四维时空"，在数学上有各种多维空间，但目前为止，人类认识的物理世界只是四维，即三维空间加一维时间；现代微观物理学提到的高维空间是另一层意思，只有数学意义。一般译成 four-dimensional space-time，此处稍做变通。

[3] 鉴于空间是一个集合，最基本的元素是点（零维空间），点的集合便是线面体（一维、二维、三维空间），即在一个从"无"到"有"的发展过程中，而时间是个矢量，是空间运动的顺序性和持续性，即空间也就是时间的片断。所谓"五维时空"是指在基本点上，又衍生出空间集合长宽高三值、时间矢量和速度矢量，这里借以比喻读者的想象力是在作者维度上向任意方向的延伸。"创作"一句的词序做了较大调整，若完全按原文，试比较：The two kinds of space-time may not be completely consistent, because readers fire their imagination in the fifth-dimension – mobilize their experience and understanding to engage in another kind of creation. "看见"，原文连用了五个"看"，在译文里则不妨根据英文特点加以变

换，如 realize、see、sense、witness、discover 等，以丰富其表现力。

[4] 前面的"想象"用了 stretching of the imagination，此处用了 fire their imaginations；此外还可用 use/fuel/ignite/stimulate/stir imaginations 等。"滋养"一般译成 nourish、cultivate、nurture 等，但这里结合"(智力的)滋养"，不妨译为 develop further intellectually，以更合原意。"结局大于期望"似可译成 the outcome is greater than the desired effect，但此处可更为简约。

[5] "相对"，可有多种对应词，如 relatively、comparatively 等，但亦可用其他方式，如 in a way，类似的如："In a way, the smallness of the room added to its luxury."（相对来讲，房间窄小反倒显得更加华丽。）

[6] "最高境界"，可有 tidemark、the highest kind、high ground、the best of optimism 等，这里用了 zenith，其义为 the most successful point in the development of something，或 something is the time when it is most successful or powerful，如："His career is now at its zenith."（他的事业现在正处于巅峰时期。）

[7] 这里的"会阅读"，一般可用 (someone) can read /be capable of reading... 等，reading skills 为名词词组，与前面的 competent writer 对应。

简单容易快乐

生活，在不知不觉中，会变得累起来。究其原因，在于欲望，有物质的，也有精神的。[1]

东西会越积越多，总觉得，即使现在不用，以后也总会有用的。其实，凡留下来的，就意味着你要保管它，就要分散精力；而积少成多之后，就会影响到你最应关注的事。[2]

人们常说，"人生如旅途"，又说"路远无轻物"，显然在旅途跋涉中，以轻装为佳。所以，就需要经常清理。[3]

所存放的、"说不定哪天用得到"的东西，到该用的（且不说是否真的用得上）那一天之前，其实都是一种时空上的消耗。[4]

就生活而言，"生"容易，"活"也不难，因为一个人物质上的消耗是有范围的；但是"生活"却不容易，因为生活是要有思想、有目标的。任何外在、物质上给人带来的快乐，都是短暂、有限的，而内在、精神上的愉悦则是更深刻、持久的。[5]

但是，目标若太大、太多，也会活得累起来。所以要像清理物品那样，经常"清理"目标，将其简化、再简化。须知，人生很短，一生真正做好一件事已经很不容易。[6]

随着现代科技的发展，人们每日得到的信息，不但充足，甚至"过量"。人们的正常生活，其实未必需要那么多信息，因为信息并不等于知识，过多了也会造成干扰，使人劳累，所以要学会随时过滤、清除信息。[7]

不妨写出一个清单，将自己的目标、所需罗列出来，而将其他所有可有可无的删去或拒绝。那样，生活不但不会受到影响，反而会更加轻松、快活，"腿脚敏捷"。[8]

人生旅途中只有负担少了，才能静下心来，慢慢体味生活，而不会让宝贵的时光在无味的纷扰中消耗掉。[9]

简单并不等于简陋，而是对于生活在更高层次上的理解和把握，是一种生活质量的升华。[10]

译 文

The Simple Life, Happy Life

Consciously or unconsciously, our life may become burdensome in one way or another. And the reason for that can after all be found in desires, either material or spiritual. [1]

Stuff, gradually accumulated for later use one day in the future, requires mindful care and energy, which may deviate one from the most important thing concerned. [2]

It is said "Life is a long journey" and "Every little thing may become a heavy burden in a trek". Packing light and constantly getting rid of the superfluous during a journey thus seem always to be desirable. [3]

Stuff being stored for future use (whether it can be useful in future remains uncertain) is actually a kind of consumption in terms of space and time. [4]

Concerning livelihood, it may be less difficult to exist than to live, which requires objective-orientated thought instead of mere physical consumption. Profound and everlasting happiness is in fact drawn not from external and material satisfaction, which can only infuse temporary elation, but from internal and spiritual contentment. [5]

Objectives one sets out to pursue, however, may overwhelm one's life should they be too remote or multiple. In the same way as cleaning a house, we should regularly check and narrow down our personal focus, bearing in mind that it will take a lifetime to accomplish a masterpiece. [6]

As technology advances, we daily receive quite sufficient, if not excessive, information which, we have to realize, is not the same thing as knowledge, and can be disruptive to us if it is oversupplied. One has therefore to be competent in filtering and eliminating information. [7]

It may be a good idea to write down an inventory, listing all your objectives and necessities, meanwhile deleting everything redundant, including unnecessary commitments. You may find that your life is in a better shape: instead of being inconvenienced, you will feel more lively and dynamic. [8]

Having eliminated all those burdens will leave room for tranquility to savor the taste of life, or else one's valuable time may just be wasted on complexity. [9]

Simple is not equivalent to rudimentary; rather, it reflects sublimation where the quality of life has been better understood and managed. [10]

译 注

[2] "积少成多",没有译成"Many a little make a mickle""Many small makes a great"等,而是结合在前面的"越积越多"里,一同译为 gradually accumulated。

[3] "清理",未译成通常的 clean up、put in order、clean、disentangle、check up 等,而是就"人生旅途"的具体涵义,用了 get rid of the superfluous。

[5] 这里将"生"(包括"活")和"生活"分别译为 exist 和 live,类似的如《21世纪大英汉词典》的例句:"She's not living, she's merely existing."(她不是在过活,只不过是在挨日子。)再如,迈克尔·杰克逊(Michael Jackson)在《拯救地球》(Heal the World)里的一句歌词"We stop existing/ And start living"(我们不再苟活,而开始生活);《圣经》里也有这样的句子:"If you haven't known the purpose of life, you aren't truly living; you're merely existing."(若没有生活目的,你就不是真正地生活,而只不过是活着而已。)"有思想、

有目标的"，未必分别译成 thought 和 objectives，而不妨整合为 objective-orientated thought 等。

[6]"'清理'目标"不是一般意义上的 clear up objectives，而是就个人所关注的事情（personal focus）而言的，故可译为 check and narrow down。

[7]"未必需要那么多信息"，未必正译，而不妨与后面的意思合并，反译为 it is oversupplied。

[8]"拒绝"，这里指的是推辞那些 unnecessary commitments。"腿脚敏捷"，是以"人生如旅途"为比喻而用的俗语，不必实译，可变通为 lively and dynamic 等。

[9]"纷扰"，不宜译成一般意义上的 confusion、turmoil、disturbance 等，而可对应 the simple life，不妨译为 complexity。

[10]"生活质量的升华"，未必译成 the sublimated quality of life，而是将全句意思融会贯通，综合译出。

生活中不能没有音乐

小的时候,记得每天要花很多时间练琴。那时真是迷上音乐,走了极端,甚至想,谁要是不喜欢音乐,我简直没办法和他沟通。[1]

后来"懂事"了,知道功课的重要了,对我爸爸说:"那时我真不懂事,浪费了许多学习时间!"他总是回答:"那怎么是'浪费'呢?以后你会知道,人需要多方面的素养,而音乐对你很有好处咧。"后来我慢慢明白了,音乐给人的影响是潜移默化而持久深远的,音乐对人的作用异常复杂而丰富。[2]

学生时代,去看世界著名指挥家小泽征尔的音乐会,他的一句话让我刻骨铭心:"如《二泉映月》这样的音乐,人们应当跪下来听!"我想,一个经过了怎样生活历练的音乐家才能说出这样深刻的话![3]

一个受了音乐启蒙的普通人,其感情也会从此被音乐所渗透,其喜怒哀乐和个人经历也会永远和音乐融合在一起。音乐的语言是那样地独特,那样地不能被其他任何一种艺术形式所替代,因而对音乐的感受也就那样地"自私"——其深浅和丰富的程度,完全取决于其阅历与修养。[4]

音乐在空中运行,是抽象的,正因如此,可以省略细节,使人们可以在不同的想象空间,演绎各自版本的贝多芬的悲壮,柴可夫斯基的优雅，柏辽兹的浪漫，舒曼的恬静悠然，莎拉·布莱曼的轻柔。音乐又是具体的，因为她会与生活中某些特定时间中的感受融合在一起，甚至会以特定的方式深化那种感受——一种除了音乐语言，其他任何语言都表达不出的感受。歌德认为，"音乐不仅是一种人类的主观语言，而且是体会更高境界的妙不可言的途径"。叔本华说："音乐是对生命奥秘的解答，是所有艺术中最富涵义的，表达出生活中最深刻的思想。"[5]

音乐的魅力，在于引起人们的共鸣，令人陶醉。孔子在齐国听到《韶》乐后，竟然三月不知肉味："不图为乐之至于斯也。"音乐还可沟通彼此的情怀。在《琵琶行》中，白居易听到嘈嘈切切的音调和跌宕起伏的旋律后，不禁叹道："同是天涯沦落人，相逢何必曾相识！"在影视作品中，凡感人之处（或喜或悲或怒或怨），大都以音乐做烘托，将效果推向极致。就个人而言，记得在"十年动乱"刚结束时，听惯了那种战斗式音乐，第一次听到邓丽君的《何日君再来》，真如一股柔风，吹酥了全身，坐在那里几乎站立不起来。那是一种人性的打动。[6]

在国外，在不同的音乐场合，我见过不同种族、肤色、操着不同语言的人们，在动情的音乐中相互沟通，传递感情，共同行动，产生了巨大的共鸣。音乐的语言可以冲破一切藩篱。[7]

当然，音乐给人更多的是陶冶。音乐家冼星海说："音乐，是人生最大的快乐；音乐，是生活中的一股清泉；音乐，是陶冶性情的熔炉。"悦耳的音调、旋律和节奏，通过感官，作用于人的大脑，使情绪沉淀下来，得以梳理，进入陶醉境界，激起心底的积淀，与世间美好的事物相联系，从而使整体境界得以提升。[8]

音乐是在空间中表现的，而空间离不开时间。根据爱因斯坦的相对论，时间和空间并不独立存在，而相互缠绕在一起；空间因必须至少有两个点才能存在，故不是一个纯粹的实体，需与相关因素来共同界定，而点与点之间的运动便构成了时间，同时也确立了空间。在这个意义上，音乐是构成人们心理历程必不可少的要素。[9]

然而，俗话说："外行看热闹，内行看门道。"对于音乐的领会和欣赏，我的体会是，如果学得一点乐理，抑或一两门乐器，效果会更理想。[10]

个人而言，我四岁学拉二胡，六岁学小提琴，后来又相继学会了大提琴、钢琴、手风琴和笛子。二胡和小提琴曾在不同场合独奏过，钢琴、手风琴曾为别人演唱伴奏，大提琴则是大学乐队的第二把。机缘巧合，我还曾与当今著名音乐家刘索拉同在一个乐队演奏过；当时我拉小提琴，她拉手风琴。[11]

尽管后来我没有从事音乐专业，但这些音乐经历，却使我获益良多。比如，对于交响乐，我会从弦乐组、木管组、铜管组和打击乐组来欣赏，而尤其关注弦乐部分，认为通过手指加工传递出的音色会更带感情。由于知道在每根弦上的音节和揉弦、运弓的力度，我便会情不自禁地随着他们而"使劲"，或轻拿，或用力，或顿挫，或松弛……真正使音乐融入细胞。[12]

练习乐器，据说还有益于提高智力。在演奏乐器时，要眼看乐谱，十指配合，双耳辨音，使整个身心协调起来，不断地刺激左右脑，从而促进智力发展。仅从这一角度，过去练琴的时间，好像并没白费。[13]

近来又有国外医学研究的最新成果，说健康长寿的最佳活动是唱歌，甚至超过游泳和跑步，因为唱歌最能改善心脏状况。这让我似乎又找到了放情于此的理由，时常会或约朋友或独自吼上几嗓子，以舒筋活血、开阔肺量。[14]

从根本上说，人是音乐的动物。远古时，人们便以音乐来沟通和组织活动，后又渗透到宗教、政治、学术及其他各种社会活动之中。在神话传说里，超自然的圣灵常把音乐作为馈赠人类的礼物，或抽象（属于感知或交流的一部分，如成为语言的一部分），或具体（如用人或动物身体的某一部位制成乐器，从而获得形而上的意义）。音乐从一开始就与人类自然地融为一体。[15]

现今而言，音乐其实业已渗透到人们生活的方方面面。不可想象，生活中若没有了音乐，会是怎样的。所以，作为一个现代人，无论每天多忙，都不妨有片刻时光静下心来，以各种形式从音乐中体会到某些生活的意义。[16]

译 文

Music: We Can't Live Without It

When I was little, as I remember, a lot of my time was occupied by practicing instruments. So fascinated was I with music,

I even went to the extreme of believing that anyone who is not a music lover would be hard to communicate with. [1]

Later, I realized the importance of acquiring knowledge and said to my Dad: "I was really ignorant then when I wasted a lot of time which could be used for study." He always responded: "How can you say it's a waste of time? You will understand better in your life that a person needs to possess all sorts of qualities, and learning music will definitely do you good." Afterwards I gradually appreciated the powerful function of music and its profound influence on people's lives in a subtle and incremental way. [2]

During my school days, I attended a concert conducted by the world famous conductor Seiji Ozawa whose words impressed me: "When you listen to a piece of music like *The Moon Over a Fountain*, you need to kneel down to really get into it." For me, it takes what tough experience for a musician to have such appreciation! [3]

Ordinary people, having been inspired by music, will forever be saturated with music in their emotions. The language of music, irreplaceable by any other form of art, is so unique and rich that one can only feel it "selfishly" depending on his or her personal experience and accomplishment. [4]

Traveling through air, music is abstract, which enables people to skip over the details to get into their own versions of different music – the solemn and stirring Beethoven, the elegant Tchaikovsky, the romantic Berlioz, the quiet and leisurely

Schumann and the gentle Sarah Brightman. Idiographically, music carries or even deepens personal feelings at a particular time in a unique form. Johann von Goethe saw "music not only as a subjective human 'language' but as an absolute transcendent means of peering into a higher realm". Arthur Schopenhauer said, "Music is the answer to the mystery of life. The most profound of all the arts, it expresses the deepest thoughts of life." [5]

The charm of music enables people to resonate with others and be intoxicated. In that way, after hearing the *Shao* music in the State of Qi, Confucius could not identify which kind of meat he was eating for several months and sighed, "I never expected I could be so lost in music!" Music can also link up feelings between individuals. When the well-known poet Bai Juyi in the Tang Dynasty (618-907) listened to a raucous and fluctuating melody played by a Pipa player from time to time, he could not help but groan: "Those who have the same misfortune can share their weal and woe through music even though they have not known each other before!" as he narrated in "The Song of a Pipa Player". In films and television programs, in every touching moment – be happy or sad, angry or resentful – music is always drawn on as a foil to maximize its effects. Personally, during the aftermath of the "ten years of turmoil" when we were bombarded by the music of "fighting style", my first encounter with the pop star Teresa Teng's song "Goodbye Again", intoxicated me thoroughly like a magic breeze, depriving me of my ability to stand up again. That was truly an effect on human nature. [6]

Overseas, on different musical occasions, I witnessed the power of the language of music which broke down the barriers of race, skin color and language among different peoples who communicated, passed on emotions through the moving music, acted in concert and produced huge echoes. [7]

Mostly, music nourishes and edifies people. The famous Chinese musician Xian Xinghai said, "As a pleasant spring and melting pot, music can mould a person's temperament, and bring huge pleasure to people." Euphonic tones, melodies and rhythms are carried through the senses to the brain, calming down and precipitating people's emotions and transmitting them into intoxication; meanwhile, music can also stir up something deposited in the bottom of people's hearts and link them up to the pleasure. In a way, it elevates overall personalities. [8]

While music is expressed in space, time is its prerequisite. According to Einstein's theory of Relativity, time and space cannot exist without one another. Space, determined by two points, is not a pure entity: it has to be identified by relevant elements. The movement between the two points verifies both time and space. In this sense, music constitutes an essential element of human psychology. [9]

However, as the saying goes, "While laymen are keen to watch the excitement, the connoisseurs appraise and appreciate the skills." In my understanding, to comprehend and appreciate music, acquiring some basics of music theory or certain skills of playing one or two musical instruments will make a big difference. [10]

For my part, I started to learn both the *erhu* and the violin at the age of four and six respectively. Subsequently, I mastered the cello, piano, accordion and *dizi*. On several occasions I played *erhu* and violin solos, provided piano accompaniment and accordion accompaniment for other singers during my youth, and was a second cello in my university orchestra. Luckily, I once played the violin in the same band with today's popular musician Liu Suola, who was an accordion player then. [11]

Although I didn't pursue my career as a professional musician, my experiences with music have benefited me substantially. To appreciate symphonies, for example, I can approach them from the perspectives of strings, woodwinds, brass and percussion, with particular attention paid to strings, since in my view timbers manipulated by fingers fuse better with emotions. Knowing the syllables on the strings and the tricks of vibrato and bowing, enables me to "perform" with them in ways of gentleness, strength, pause and transition in rhythm or relaxation… In that way, the music can truly be blended into my cells. [12]

It is said that playing musical instruments is good for the intellect, since during the process one has to look at the music score, coordinate the ten fingers, discriminate syllables binaurally at the same time, and the mind and body are thus harmonized. By constantly stimulating the left and right hemicerebrums, one's intelligence is improved. So from this point of view, my time spent in practicing instruments in the past seems not to have been in vain. [13]

Recent foreign medical research suggests that singing is the best activity for health and longevity, even better than swimming and running, since it can effectively improve heart conditions. This seems to have provided me with a good reason to indulge myself in the entertainment – either accompanying friends or simply alone to "roar a few voices", just for the fun of relaxing tendons, stimulating circulation and enlarging lung volumes. [14]

Fundamentally speaking, human beings are creatures of music. In ancient times, people communicated and organized activities with music, which then permeated into religions, politics, academia and other social activities. In myths, supernatural beings often conferred music upon humans as a gift, which could be abstract, a component of perception or communication, such as a part of language. It might also be concrete, for example, in forging musical instruments from physical objects (e.g. human or animal bodies), which thereby acquired metaphysical connotations. It is therefore fair to say that music and human beings are naturally integrated from the very beginning. [15]

Today, as music has penetrated into every aspect of our lives, it is unconceivable what life would be without it. As modern men, no matter how busy we are, it's better for us to have a moment each day to calm down and sense the meaning of life from music in one form or another. [16]

译 注

[2] 这里的"懂事"似不宜为 mature、maturity、thoughtful、sensible 等，而应与后面的"功课"相结合，是中国人说到学生时所指的"学习"，故以 acquiring knowledge 和 study 译出。

[3] "深刻的话"其字面意思为 deep words、penetrating insights、profound meaning 等，但作为一个音乐家对于音乐作品的评论，其涵义应为"欣赏"，即 appreciation。

[4] 这里的"渗透"与后面的"融合"所指相同，故可结合起来翻译，不必重复；相应的词还有 fuse、mix together、amalgamate 等。

[6] 对于孔子的"三月不知肉味"一般译成"for three months did not know the taste of meat" (Arthur Waley), "for several months he did not know the taste of meat" (Roger T. Ames), "for many months he did not notice the taste of meat (by being moved)"（谷学）等。鉴于其中不免有渲染的成分，这里不妨做一变通，译为"could not identify which kind of meat he was eating"，以更为贴切。"同是天涯沦落人"一般译成"those who have the same misfortune sympathize with each other"，这里根据音乐的语境，增添词语，译成"those who have the same misfortune can share their weal and woe through music"。"柔风"一般译为 gentle / soft breeze，但这里用了更重的词 magic breeze，以强调音乐的魅力。

[7] 此句不妨在词序上做一大调整，将"冲破一切藩篱"提前，

以"种族、肤色、语言"做定语；同时，将"音乐的语言"变通为 the power of the language of music。

[8] 在"音乐，是……"这一排比句中，不妨将"清泉"与"熔炉"并列译出，而将"人生最大的快乐"置后，以求英文词序的通顺。"境界"是一很有中国文化特色的概念，若译成 realm、state、extent、boundary、reached、plane attained、ambit 等，似乎都难与其原义对等，有的外国汉学家索性采用音译。例如，王国维的"词以境界为最上。有境界则自成高格"，被译成"The most important element in a consideration of tz'u is ching-chieh. If a tz'u has ching-chieh it will naturally achieve a lofty and naturally possess eminent lines."（Adele Austin Rickett），但英文读者理解起来仍有困难。这里，就音乐对人的熏陶而言，意译为 overall personalities。

[10] 对于"外行"一般用 layman、non-expert、nonprofessional、unprofessional、lay、laic 等，如"外行领导内行"，可译为"laymen lead experts""non-experts direct expert""non-professional guide professionals"等。对于"外行看热闹"的俗语，亦有多种表达，如"Dilettantes watch the scene of bustle, experts look at the way""Laymen watch the sight of bustle, adepts the contents""Laics watch the panorama of bustle, adepts guard the entrance"等，但就此处音乐语境而言，更多强调的是对艺术、技能的欣赏，故不妨用 connoisseur、appreciate、skills 等词语。这里的"更理想"是就效果而言的，不宜简单译成 the more ideal effect，而可译为 the desired

result 等，但这里讲的是一般人对音乐欣赏的不同，故可用 make a big difference。

[12]这里的"使劲"不是一般意义上的 exert all my strength、put in my energy等，而是因为学过这种乐器，故好像随之演奏一样，故用了 perform。

[14]"舒筋活血"是中医术语，一般直译为 to relax the muscles and enliven the blood，这里稍做变通。

[16]"现代人"可译为 modern、modernist、neoteric、homo sapiens 等；应注意，这里原文虽是"一个现代人"，实际可译成复数 modern men、modern people 等。

我的北京冬天

对于冬天，人们一般会用些冷酷、萧瑟的字眼来形容；但北京的冬天对于我，却有着别样深切、浓重、惜情的感觉。[1]

作为一个"老北京"，儿时的冬天是漫长的，但并不乏味，因为好像好吃、好玩的，特别是那种别具特色的北京味儿，一定是在冬天。[2]

到了青壮年时，阴差阳错，我移民到了澳大利亚的昆士兰省（"阳光省"），那里一年四季阳光普照，温暖如春。开始觉得很舒服，后来受不了了。那时每当想起北京，就会与这些事情联系在一起：鲁迅笔下清冷的四合院，那里"有两棵树，一棵是枣树，另一棵还是枣树"（后来明白了，那寓意着斗士孤傲、刚强的性格），老舍的骆驼祥子在呼呼的西北风中奔跑，林海音的"城南旧事"，李敖冬天中的法源寺……，还有就是那些遍布于北京各大公园、城根、河沟的正规、不正规的"冰场"。于是，在国外居住了十余年后，第一次回国，专门选了冬天，来重温我的北京梦。[3]

父母说，我有三样"童子功"，会受益终身：滑冰、外语和写字（当时还未上升到"书法"高度）。滑冰是我从小学开始学的，这也沾了北京传统文化的光。[4]

那时听老人讲，自打清末起，滑冰便是一项时尚的运动，称为"冰嬉"。因清朝贵族来自东北,而北京的冬季也是河湖结冰且冰期很长,冰嬉曾作为皇家冬季一项重要消遣活动,还被乾隆皇帝定为"国俗"。冰嬉的项目主要是冰上蹴鞠,酷似打冰球。再有是跑冰,即冰嬉者穿上一种带有铁齿的鞋,在冰上溜行,比赛争先者夺标取胜。还有是"打滑挞",冰嬉者从特制的冰山上往下滑,不倒者为胜。此外就是冰上杂戏了。故宫博物院藏有乾隆年间的《冰嬉图》,描绘的就是当时宫廷盛大的冰嬉场面。[5]

据说清代每年腊八前后,受过训练的八旗子弟都要举行一场正式的比赛与表演,即"冰嬉大典"。除了集体队列表演外,最引人眼球的是个人竞技部分,如金鸡独立、凤凰展翅、蜻蜓点水等高难度动作,绝不亚于今天的花样滑冰。[6]

由于官方的大力推动,冰上运动在北京民间遍地开花,小孩儿很早便在冰上混,最开始时是坐冰车,记得是用一把木椅子,下面钉上铁条或铁丝,由别人推着或用铁钎子在冰上扎着走,从而有了最初的在冰上滑动、速行的感觉。稍大之后,不满足了,要在冰上站起来独行,于是以能穿上冰鞋为荣。[7]

就冰鞋的历史而言,晚清时,京津一带曾流行一种自制的冰鞋,俗称"凌鞋",由两块木板组成,上面分别钉着细铁条。人们将木板紧扎在鞋上,便可在冰面上如履平地。每逢数九寒天,水面结冰,滑冰高手们便聚集到护城河冰面上,穿着凌鞋参加滑冰比赛,"如星驰电掣,争先夺标为胜"。据说,有人曾穿着这种自制的冰鞋,清早从朝阳门出发,顺着河道一路滑到通州,下午回来时手上端一碗通州的酱豆腐,以示自己跑了个来回。这在当时也成为老北京冬日的一景。[8]

到了民国初期，滑冰鞋的皮鞋可以由我国自行生产，再配上一副进口的冰刀，就成为中西合璧的滑冰鞋了。滑冰鞋价格的降低，以及北京天然滑冰场的开设，都为北京群众性冰上运动提供了必要条件，由此，北京的滑冰运动迅速普及起来。[9]

我的第一双冰鞋是上小学时从王府井著名的利生体育用品商场买的（好像全北京只有那里卖冰鞋），当时觉得是天价，要省吃俭用好久；买来它是一件大事，开始舍不得穿，睡觉时要放在床头。每次滑冰后，又要仔细擦干、包裹起来。可是，天有不测风云，一次滑冰时被冰缝子卡了一下，冰刀中间被弄掉了一大块，当时好不心疼，难受了好一段，几乎下定决心不再滑冰。直到后来听说什刹海冰场旁边有位老师傅可以补修，于是找到那里，还真行！他用高温把刀面熔化，又加上了一块生铁，居然把缺口补平了，真是大喜过望！师傅说，他在日本占领北京时，就学了那门手艺。北京真是藏龙卧虎，什么人才都不缺。[10]

说到北京的溜冰去处，首先想起的自然是什刹海冰场，如果北京的冰场也有老字号，那就非什刹海冰场莫属。什刹海本来就历史悠久，经过700多年的文化积淀，形成了其独特的魅力。这里原是古高梁河道，是一处天然水域，包括了前海、后海和积水潭。元建大都后，郭守敬奉旨修通惠河，引昌平白浮泉及以下诸泉入积水潭，形成了什刹海宽阔的水面，南来北往的粮船、商船停泊于此，以致"舳舻蔽水"；她的自然风光为燕京胜景之一，垂柳依依，远山如黛，中国书画的意境在这里表现得淋漓尽致。到了冬天，什刹海万顷水面又变身为琉璃似的光滑冰面，成为一处天然的大冰场,"引无数京人来嬉冬"。那里面,又镶嵌了我儿时对北京的多少记忆![11]

那时正值动荡年代,"罢课闹革命",而只有来到冰场才可逃逸那种压抑的政治气氛,一览开阔的冰面,呼吸清新的空气,形成鲜明的对比;也正是因为"罢课",才给了我们更多的时间。在那里,我们可以随便说,随便跑,随便闹(自然不是"闹革命"),当然也少不了随便摔跟头。回想起来,那才是真真切切的童趣![12]

当年的文学作品《血色浪漫》里,男主角的一句问话,成了流行语:"同学,你去什刹海溜过冰吗?"而电视剧《梦开始的地方》中在什刹海溜冰的场面,女主角所说的"五湖的、四海的水,不如什刹海的冰场美",更是为人所乐道。[13]

那会儿的时髦形象都在冰场上:小伙儿穿着压箱子底的将校呢军装,戴羊剪绒的帽子,而姑娘们会围着大红的拉毛围巾,脚上蹬一双大老远从上海托人买来的黑色或白色小高跟滑冰鞋,吵闹、拉扯、"拍婆子",尽情在冰场上释放着自己。[14]

不久前,在北京一室内真冰场滑冰,一小伙子过来对我说,一看您这范儿,肯定是当年什刹海冰场出来的吧?在电影《老炮儿》中,看到那最后茬架、冲刺的场面,也正是在冬天的什刹海拍摄的。电视里,有天习近平主席去那片居民区访问,说他年轻时也常到那里的冰面去玩儿。可见,有着什刹海冰场情结的人,实在不是少数。[15]

当然,那时适合滑冰的去处,绝不止什刹海一地。特别是在正规冰场开放之前,天又足够冷了,我们便背起冰鞋,"哪里有冰那里去"。譬如，护城河，那原是古人用来维护城内安全、抵御攻城者的，后形成了一道风景，特别是在冬天，结了冰，变成了雪白色，上面又出现了东倒西歪的滑冰者。其实，北京的护城河，不是一潭死水，玉泉、白浮泉、密云诸水，皆是它的上源，而护城河还与转河、金水河、坝河、通惠河及"六海"相通，在京城的外围，形成了一个巨大的水路交通网。印象深刻的，是在故宫的护城河上滑冰，忽然感到，一边是历史的凝重，一边是现代的欢愉，古今对话，自然和谐。[16]

此外，"寻冰"的地方还有北海公园、中山公园、紫竹院公园、玉渊潭、陶然亭等，如今随着北京—张家口冬奥会申办的成功，在这些地方相应都增加了一些冬季的游乐项目。[17]

与此同时，是在冰面上的"抽汉奸"。所谓"汉奸"其实就是个木制的陀螺（那时候买不起机器旋出来的陀螺，都是自己动手做的），即找一段圆形的木棍或树干用小刀慢慢地将一头削成锥形，然后把握好需要的长度从锥形的上方锯下来，再到修自行车的车铺捡一颗滚珠镶在圆锥的底部便可。重要的，是把握好"汉奸"的身高和腰围，太胖了转不起来、太瘦了又容易倒。做好了"汉奸"再找一根小木棍，拴上一条布条，就能"抽"转起来。老人们说，因为小日本侵占了北京城，不少汉奸助纣为虐，于是老百姓就把陀螺当成汉奸来抽，以解心头之恨，后来这竟成了孩子们的一项冬季运动。在北京冬天的冰面上，还常可看到孩子们一边滑冰一边抽着"汉奸"，像是打冰球时带球滑行。鞭子功夫好的，可以边滑行边用鞭子控制高速转动的陀螺紧随自己平移，甚至让陀螺腾空跃起，越过障碍后再"钉"在冰上继续旋转。[18]

在不少"老北京"的记忆里,一定忘不了当年火爆至极的冰球赛。1981年,男子冰球世锦赛C组在北京举行,能容纳1.8万人的首都体育馆几乎场场爆满。据说,比赛引发的热潮席卷了整个京城,火爆度足以和今天的CBA总决赛相媲美。[19]

可惜,后来因为种种原因,北京的冰上运动逐渐衰落了。明显的是,就个人来讲,现在的80后、90后中,比我滑冰好的实在不多,因为他们缺乏"童子功",尽忙着考试、补习、打游戏了。[20]

可喜的是,自2016年以来,为积极响应"三亿人参与冰雪"的号召,北京市各区县已经开始统筹冰雪运动优势资源,因地制宜,加大力度推动冰雪项目的发展。同时,北京市体育局和市教委联合还启动了"百万青少年上冰雪"活动,在未来将从六方面开展落实这一冰雪运动普及活动。[21]

回顾起来,其实我从小就受益于滑冰。研究表明,寒冷空气对于人体的刺激,本身就是一种良好的健身锻炼,因为空气和皮肤温度之间的差异,增加血液循环,有效改善机体功能,这使我从小有了一个好身体;在思维上,知道了在"沉闷"之外,还有一个"清冷"的开阔天地,从而不至于死钻牛角尖。同时,滑冰与外语、书法有着许多内在相通的素质,比如模仿、毅力、感觉、平衡、节奏、韵律、力度、品味等等,甚至有一种难以言状的内在美,有时我简直把它们混同起来了。[22]

现在,每当我冬天回到北京,都喜欢独自漫步在西北风中的小胡同,清冷寂静的公园,高耸的故宫城墙下,当然更少不了那结冰一片的湖畔。这时会深深意识到，所走的每一步，都是历史，都是经历，都是现实；它们似乎都已过去，但又永远那么真切。唯其寒冷，更能显出其厚重与包容。我甚至想，没有在冬天来过北京的，不能算是真正到过北京。[23]

这样的北京是我的，也是你的，是千千万万有过同样感受的人的。2022年的冬天，当全球的冬季奥运健儿们来到这里时，多么希望他们都能从各自的角度，来分享一份北京冬天里的情结！[24]

译 文

Beijing in Winter: It's So Dear to Me!

In describing winter, people prefer to use cold and bleak words. I have, however, formed a deep and strong attachment to Beijing's winters. [1]

As a native Beijinger, winters in Beijing during my childhood were lengthy but never boring since the delicious food and amusements characterizing Beijing were all related to winter. [2]

As a young adult, I accidentally immigrated to Australia's Queensland where the sun shines all year round: branded as a "sunshine state", the climate is mild and springlike even in winter. After the initial excitement, I started to miss Beijing, which has always been intricately intertwined with such things as the chilly courtyard where "There are two trees, one is jujube and the other is jujube as well" wrote Lu Xun, symbolizing a fighter's spirit and personality of solitude (as I later understood), the camel Xiangzi (a character in a Lao She's novel) running in the whirring of the northwest wind, Lin Haiyin's Memories of Beijing, and Temple of Origin of the Dharma Gate by Li Ao, and all the authorized and unauthorized ice rinks in parks and rivers and near ancient ramparts spreading over Beijing in winter. It was precisely for this reason that I chose a winter to come back Beijing to revive dreams from my past. [3]

My parents once told me that I had acquired three "skills gained from childhood" that would benefit me throughout my life, which are skating, foreign languages and hand writing (which didn't quite reach the level of calligraphy at the time). I learned how to skate when I was a mere primary school student, nurtured by the traditional culture of Beijing. [4]

According to the elderly, ever since the late Qing Dynasty, skating had been a fashionable sport, dubbed bing xi or "ice playing". Coming from the northeast, the aristocrats of the Qing Dynasty found the winter of Beijing quite agreeable, where the rivers and lakes were frozen for a pretty lengthy period. Once a royal pastime, Emperor Qianlong then further declared "ice-playing" a *guo su* or "national custom". The "ice-playing" was all about *cuju*, very much like ice hockey, together with "running on ice" (putting on a pair of shoes with iron teeth then drifting on ice to compete for the first prize). Another game called da hua ta or "the big descent" was to sliding down a manmade iceberg and the slider would win if he or she could manage not to fall over. In addition, there were various ice-acrobatics. A painting named "Ice-playing" in the Palace Museum collection depicts the grand scene of the sport. [5]

It was said that every year around laba (on the eighth day of the twelfth lunar month), the trained Banner Children would hold a formal game as an "ice-playing ceremony". Apart from the collective cohort performance, the most eye-catching part was their individual athletics, such as posing as a "pheasant standing on one foot", "phoenix spreading wings", "dragonfly skimming the ice surface" and so on, their difficult moves being nothing less than today's figure skating. [6]

Thanks to the official vigorous promotion, ice-sports became very popular among Beijing folks. Children started to play on the ice in their very early years, mostly with an "ice-chair" made by fixing iron bars or iron wires to the bottom of a wooden chair. They moved forward either by another's pushing or by using iron drills, to gain their initial feeling of movement and speed on the ice. Later on, as they grew up a bit, they normally desired more independent moves on the ice and took great pride in wearing skating boots. [7]

As for the history of making skates, in the late Qing Dynasty, homemade skates known as "ice-shoes" were made from two pieces of wood with iron bars on the bottom. By tying the wood tightly to the shoes, one could "walk" fast on the ice as easily as on firm earth. Once the rivers were all frozen, the skillful skaters gathered on the city's moats to compete being described as "moving as fast as flashing light to win the first prize". It was also said that, wearing such homemade skates, someone could skate from Chaoyang Gate in the morning along the river course all the way to Tong Zhou and return in the afternoon with a bowl of *tofu* in their hands to show they had made the return journey, which was a typical scenario of old Beijing. [8]

In the early of the Republic of China, skates could be produced by ourselves: a pair of ice-skate blades imported from the West and a pair of shoes made in China could combine to become perfect skates. The declining price of skates and the commercial operation of several natural ice rinks in Beijing provided the necessary conditions for ice-sports becoming popular among the locals in winters. [9]

I bought my first a pair of skates, as "a major event in life", in my early school days from the famous Lifetime sporting goods store located in Wang Fujing (it seemed to me that it was the only place where I could buy skates in Beijing at the time) at a sky-high price which cost me quite sometime of frugal living. Initially, I begrudged wearing them and put the skates beside my pillow at night. And carefully dried them out and wrapped them up every time after skating. Unexpectedly, one day one of my skates got stuck in an ice crack and excised quite a large piece in the middle of the blade. Oh my gosh! So depressed, I didn't want to carry on skating anymore until one day I heard there was a repairman near the ice rink in Shicha Lake and I went there. He melted the blade together with a piece of cast iron – and surprisingly, he fixed it! I was overjoyed. The artisan told me he had learned his skills during the period of occupation by the Japanese troops in the early 1940s. Really, Beijing is a place of "hidden dragons and crouching tigers", where you can discover just about every kind of talent. [10]

Concerning the places where people can skate, the first one that comes to mind has to be the ice rink in Shicha Lake: if there was such a thing as an old and famous skating enterprise, it would be nowhere but here. Shicha Lake, a place amassing a cultural history over 700 years, possesses a unique charm. Originally, it was an ancient sorghum-growing river, a natural water area comprising the former sea, backwater and billabong. After establishing the Yuan Dynasty (1271-1368), Guo Shoujing (1231-1316) was ordered by the emperor to repair the Tonghui river, channeling water from the White Spring and other small springs in Changping County to form the broad surface of the water in Shicha Lake, providing a port for victuallers and merchant ships of all routes to anchor, and the surface of the water was densely covered during busy times. Its natural beauty – weeping willows against the dim backdrop of distant hills – forms one of the eight sceneries of Yanjing and presents a perfect artistic conception depicted in traditional Chinese paintings. In the winter, the water surface becomes glassy ice, shaping a natural ice rink where "countless Beijingers are attracted to play". For me, it is the place encapsulating endless memories during my childhood and youth! [11]

During that turbulent age of "boycotting classes and fomenting revolution", only by coming to the ice rink could we escape the depressed political ambience and breathe in the nice cold fresh air as a distinct contrast. Strangely, the boycott actually provided us with more valuable time when we could freely talk, run, foment something (surely not "revolution") and tumble as well. In retrospect, that was nothing but real childhood. [12]

In those years, the hero's query in the literary work Romantic Life became a popular sentence: "Classmate, have you skated in Shicha Lake?" And in a teleplay named The Place to Dream the heroine's phrase had excited much interest among the public as well: "The water flowing to the east and west, when frozen in Shicha Lake is the best". [13]

Fashionable images of the time were to be found on the ice rink: Boys wore worsted coat uniforms (often family heirlooms) and put on sheep skin hats, while girls normally sported scarves of royal scarlet with black or white medium heel skates on their feet, which were probably bought by somebody in Shanghai a thousand kilometres away. They were noisy, dragging and pulling and courting with abandon. [14]

Not long ago, while skating in an indoor ice rink in Beijing, a young guy came to me after my skillful performance: "Looking at your stylish skating, you must have practiced in Shicha Lake?" In the movie *Mr. Six*, the last scene of fighting and sprint was also shot in Shicha Lake. Another day, on TV I saw that president Xi Jinping visiting the area and saying to the local people that he used to play on that ice rink as well. Clearly, people who have a special preference for Shicha Lake are not few. [15]

The places we searched out for skating were surely not confined to Shicha Lake. Especially before the authorized ice rinks started to operate and the weather was cold enough, we picked up our skates and determinedly looked for rivers and lakes wherever they were frozen. Most often, we went to the city moats, which were originally used by the ancients to maintain security and defend invaders, later forming a landscape, especially in winter when they were frozen and became white, and stumbling figures appeared on the ice. In fact, moats in Beijing are not stagnant pools but are sourced by the waters of the Yuquan, Baiquan, Miyun, as well as Zhuan, Jinshui, Ba and Tonghui rivers and the "Six Seas", constituting a huge waterway network on the outskirts of the capital. One thing engraved in my memory was that one day when skating on the Forbidden City moat, I suddenly realized the harmonious communication between the solemn ancient and the entertaining present. [16]

Additional places suitable for skating, so at least it seemed us, also included Beihai, Zhongshan, Zizhuyuan, Yuyuantan, Taoranting and other parks. Since the success of Beijing-Zhangjiakou's bid for the Winter Olympic Games, some facilities for winter sports have been installed in these parks. [17]

At the same time, another activity taking place on ice was "slashing traitors". The so-called "traitor" was actually a wooden gyro. Since people then could not afford to buy machine-made ones, they all used ones made by themselves from a round stick or trunk. By shaping it into a conical block with a knife, chopping off everything above the cone-shape, taking it to the bicycle shop to set an iron ball on the bottom and enabling it to spin, a perfect "traitor" was then made. The point was to balance the proportion between the height and waist to avoid being too "fat" to spin or too "slim" to be stable. Holding a small stick tied with a piece of cloth one could then slash it to spin. As related by the elderly, during the Japanese occupation, some Chinese traitors assisted the invaders to perpetrate, so people made "traitors" to be slashed to resolve the hatred in their hearts, which later became a winter sport for children. On the ice during the Beijing winter, you can often find children skating while slashing "traitors", very much like playing ice hockey. Some skillful ones can control the speedy gyros with the whip and make them roll in parallel, even levitate them to cross over hurdles and then descend to "nail" the ice, while still continuing to rotate. [18]

For many native Beijingers, an extremely popular ice hockey game may never be forgotten. In 1981, the men's ice hockey Group C world championship was held in the capital stadium, where every section was filled to its full capacity of 18,000 people. It is said that the game triggered the upsurge in interest sweeping the whole city, matched by today's CBA finals. [19]

It is a pity that for some reasons winter sports in Beijing have gradually declined. Personally, I notice that it's very hard to find skaters who are as skillful as I am, since they didn't have the "skills gained from childhood" and are all occupied with their exams, tutorials and computer games. [20]

To my delight, since 2016, in responding to the call to "involve 300 million people to participate in winter-sports", Beijing's counties have started to co-ordinate their advantageous resources in promoting the development of ice and snow events. Meanwhile, the Beijing Municipal Sports Bureau and the City Board of Education have also jointly launched a project to "encourage a million youngsters to partake in ice and snow", so as to popularize the winter sports from six aspects. [21]

Looking back, I have actually benefited greatly from skating. Studies suggest that the body's response to the stimulation of cold air is itself a good fitness exercise, and the stimuli of differences between the air and skin temperatures can increase blood circulation and strengthen body functioning, which resulted in my vigorousness from early childhood. Mentally, it inspired me to think of another cold and open world when I was stuck in an unpleasant circumstance, and to avoid being trapped in this dead end. In fact, there are a lot of things in common in practicing skating, foreign languages and calligraphy, such as imitation, perseverance, sense of feeling, balance, rhythm, rhyme, strength, taste and so on, even a kind of indescribable inner beauty. Sometimes, I simply mix them up altogether. [22]

Nowadays, whenever I return to Beijing in winters, I like to stroll against strong winds in small alleys, cold and quiet parks, under the towering ramparts of the Forbidden City, and of course, along the frozen lakeside. With these steps, I cannot help but gain a deep sense of history, experience and reality. Things may have passed but they still appear vivid. The coldness in fact may manifest more of its profoundity and inclusiveness. I even wonder whether those who have been to Beijing outside of the winter season, have really been to Beijing. [23]

This kind of Beijing belongs to me, you and everybody who has been touched by the capital. In the winter of 2022, when the winter Olympic athletes of the world come here to participate in the events, I sincerely hope that they will all enjoy their own unique experience in the winter of Beijing. [24]

译 注

[1] 这种"感觉"不是一般的 feeling、sense、perception、sensation、become aware of 等,而是与前面的"深切、浓重、惜情"相关联,故形成一短语"formed a deep and strong attachment"。

[2] 这里的"北京味"不宜用 Beijing taste、Beijing flavor 等,而

是 the character of Beijing，这里用了其动词 characterize。

［3］这里的"受不了"，不是一般的 cannot bear something、cannot stand/take it anymore，而是与下面留恋北京冬天的情感相融合，故变通为"I started to miss Beijing"。这里的"重温"不是一般意义上的 review、furbish、go over，而是相对北京旧梦的回顾，故用了 revive an old dream。

［4］"童子功"，一般的词典没有解释，只有根据其意思译为 skills gained from childhood，也未见得完全吻合。

［7］"遍地开花"的表面意思是 blossom everywhere、flourish everywhere、be blooming everywhere (throughout the country)、be a mass of flowers，但这只是比喻，实际表现 became very popular among Beijing folks。

［10］"什么人才都不缺"，反译为"there is no shortage of any talents"，正译则更为强调"you can discover just about every kind of talent"。

［11］"依依"，在古诗词里常用，如《诗经·采薇》的名句"昔我往矣，杨柳依依；今我来思，雨雪霏霏"，其中的"依依"，许渊冲注释为"杨柳柔弱随风摆动的样子"，但译为"When I left here / Willows shed tear / I come back now / Snow bends the bough"；此处又做了些变通："weeping willows in the dim backdrop of distant hills"，即与后面的"远山如黛"融合在一起。

［12］"闹革命"一般可译为 carry out revolution、make revolution、rise in revolution、incite revolution 等，此处用了 foment，其

本义为"try to stir up public opinion; If someone or something foments trouble or violent opposition, they cause it to develop",如:"They accused strike leaders of fomenting violence."(他们指责罢工领导人煽动暴力。)"They accused him of fomenting political unrest."(他们指控他煽动政治动乱。)

[13]"流行语"一般译为 catchword、catch phrase、buzzword、buzz words,但这里是一句话,故用了 a popular sentence。"为人所乐道"一般可译为 delight in talking about、take delight in talking about、indulge in elaborating on、dwell upon with great relish 等;这里稍加引申,为 excited much public interest。

[14]"箱子底"字面意思是 the bottom of the box,如:"I found the card at the very bottom of the box."(我正是在箱子底找到这张卡片的。)但此处实际指的是"传家宝",故可译为 family heirloom、hereditary treasure 等。"拍婆子"是20世纪六七十年代的流行语,意为 to chase girls、to hang around with girls,这里将其泛指为男女青年间的打情骂俏,故不妨用 banter、flirt、court 等。

[15]"范儿"字典上一般释为 style,其实不仅如此,还有 glamour、charisma、charm、personality 等,这里略加变通为 stylish。

[16]这里的"自然和谐"没有按字面意思译成 natural harmony,而是与前面的"古今对话"相结合,译为 the harmonious communication。

[21]"冰雪"实际指的是"冰雪运动",故宜译为 winter-sports。"上冰雪",作为口号中的简化说法,意思是让他们参加冰雪运

动,不妨也简译为 to take part in ice and snow。

[22]"好身体",不一定总是 good health、healthy body、fitness 等,根据具体语境,还不妨用 vitality、vigorousness 等。"钻牛角尖"还可译为 take unnecessary pains to study an insignificant or insoluble problem、split hairs、get into a blind alley 等。

[23] 这里的"每一步"不一定是 every step,而是"融入在了这些步子之中",故用了 with these steps。

[24] 这里的"感受"不是一般的 feeling、experience、receipt 等,而是一种感染,即 emotionally affected,故用了 touch。"分享"一般用 share、partake of 等,而 enjoy 的本义是 get pleasure from…,用在这里,有更积极之意。

富与贵

日常生活中，人们容易把"富"与"贵"相混淆，如把有钱人家统称为"富贵之家"。其实，二者是不同的：富者未必贵，贵者未必富。[1]

随着中国综合实力的提高，国内的富人逐渐多了起来。但他们中不乏这样的人：住豪宅，却大放噪音，干扰邻居；开豪车，却把垃圾从车窗扔到马路上；到国外旅游，如入无人之境，喧哗，吵闹，加塞儿；为自己，一掷千金；捐善款，一毛不拔……他们虽然富有，却没有半点儿贵族精神，有的只是暴发户的俗气。[2]

对于贵族精神，可有多种理解，但几个基本要素必不可少：诚信，担当，主见，教养。[3]

诚信的实质是守规则、重荣誉。在春秋时期的泓水之战中，宋襄公因恪守规矩，不乘机攻打立足未稳的楚兵，结果吃了败仗，被现代国人讥为"蠢猪式的仁义"，却不知其被古代史家所称颂。欧洲骑士间的战争，类似春秋时代的贵族战争，均摆好阵势，堂堂正正地对攻；搞突然袭击，对真正的骑士，是一种耻辱。而绅士间的决斗，更是规矩在前、动作在后；若投机取胜，则只会赢得性命而丢失荣誉，落个千古骂名，得不偿失。所以，境界不同，评价各异。[4]

担当的实质是社会责任、使命感,在中国讲的是"修身、齐家、治国、平天下"。春秋战国时,整个贵族阶级都以执戈披甲为荣,视冲锋陷阵为己任。秦国国君在选择后嗣时,首要条件是"择勇猛者立之";而楚康王即位五年无战事,自责为是莫大的失职。在欧洲,贵族享有特权的同时,意味着担当特殊的责任,包括关键时候挺身而出,为君主、国家献出生命,而历次民族战争,冲在前面、牺牲最多的是贵族。在西方航海业有一条不成文的规定,在船沉没时,船长必须最后一个逃生。英国的威廉和哈里王子,都被送往陆军军官学校受训,毕业后哈里还被派往阿富汗前线,当过机枪手,以为国家尽职为荣,体现的都是典型的贵族精神。[5]

主见的实质是独立思考、高贵人格。他们不会是"千人之诺诺"中的一员,却宁可为"一人之谔谔"而终。如陈寅恪评价王国维:"来世不可知者也,先生之著述,或有时而不章。先生之学说,或有时而可商。惟此独立之精神,自由之思想,历千万祀,与天壤而同久,共三光而永光。"马寅初认定自己"人口论"的正确性,在巨大的政治迫害下,仍不"悔罪"。在西方,哥白尼、布鲁诺、伽利略不畏教会的监禁、摧残甚至火刑,誓死捍卫"日心说":"你们可以杀死我,但地球仍在转动。"[6]

教养的实质是文化素质、雅致得体。这些多体现在日常的细节之中,如孔子的弟子子路,在战争中受了重伤,临死前不忘系好被对手砍断的帽缨,"正冠而殁"。康有为的女儿康同璧,在上世纪狠批资产阶级的六十年代,赴好友的家庭宴会,手提包里另藏雅装(当时不容在街上穿着),进入四合院后,临时换装,也要体面出席。二战时，英国国王爱德华到伦敦的贫民窟视察，站在一个东倒西歪的房子门口，对里面一贫如洗的老太太问道："我可以进来吗？"体现的是一种贵族式的对人的尊重。法国大革命中，在巴黎的协和广场上，路易十六的玛丽王后不小心踩了刽子手的脚，马上下意识地说了句"对不起，先生"；而临刑前的国王则坦言："我清白死去。我原谅我的敌人，但愿我的血能平息上帝的怒火。"几分钟后，路易十六及王后便身首异处。两个世纪后，时任法国总统的密特朗在法国大革命200周年纪念活动上真诚宣布："路易十六是个好人，把他处死是件悲剧……"[7]

有贵族精神的人不一定都富有，有的甚至还很贫穷。陈独秀晚年贫困交加，但拒绝接受别人哪怕一文钱的馈赠；俄国著名作家托尔斯泰最后把所有的家产分给了穷人，像流浪汉一样死在一个荒芜的小车站。[8]

在精神层面上，贵而不富者，留下来的是文明、人道和慷慨；而富而不贵者，可以用大把的金钱换取有限时光的享受，却买不来半点别人发自心底的尊重。[9]

译 文

Wealth and Nobility

In daily life, people often relate wealth to nobility, such as *fu gui zhi jia* in Chinese or "a family of wealth and nobility". In fact, the two are not always necessarily associated; in some cases they are two quite different things. [1]

With the growth of overall national strength, more Chinese have become wealthy. Among them, however, are those who make a tremendous noise to annoy neighbors from their luxury homes, or throw out rubbish from the windows of their classy cars, or talk and laugh uproariously and jump queues as if entering an unpeopled land when traveling overseas. While throwing away money like dirt, they donate none like an iron cock... Wealthy they are, what they actually display is nothing more than the air of nouveaux riches, which is totally unrelated to the spirit of nobility. [2]

Speaking of noble spirit, although people may define it differently, there are certain components which are deemed to be essential, such as credibility, commitment, thoughtfulness and upbringing. [3]

To have credibility is to abide by the rules and behave honorably. During China's Spring and Autumn Period (770-476 BC), for example, in the battle of Hongshui, Duke Xiang of Song was defeated by the troops of Chu due to his rigidity in following the "gentlemen's agreement" which promised not to attack opponents when they were not ready. The Duke's act, praised by ancient historians, is nevertheless satirized by some people nowadays as asinine ethics. Likewise, wars between European knights were also launched in a dignified and imposing manner, openly confronting one another. Launching a surprise attack would be seen as a disgrace to a genuine knight. In a duel between gentlemen, action had to follow rules, otherwise any win (to save one's life) could only result in indignity, earning eternal infamy, which was utterly not worthwhile. Clearly, things are judged differently by different standards. [4]

By "willingness" is meant to be infused with a sense of mission and social responsibility. Guided by the creed of "cultivating the self, supporting the family, governing the state and ruling the world", from the Spring and Autumn Period, the Chinese noble class have been proud of charging forward wearing coats of armor, as exemplified in the king of Qin's imperial order to choose his heirs based primarily on their bold and powerful character. It may also be evidenced in King Kang's deep self-accusation over his five-year warless reign (so he had no chance to go into battle to defend his country) of the Chu State. In Europe, the privileged aristocracy were also those who threw themselves into the breach at crucial moments and history has witnessed sacrifices mostly by nobles when their sovereign or country required them. In Western seafaring, there is an unwritten rule that the captain has to be the last to escape when the ship sinks. Princes William and Harry were both sent to military academies for training, and Harry was then dispatched to Afghanistan as a gunner. In this sense, honoring one's national duty typifies a noble spirit. [5]

Thoughtfulness comes with independent thinking by those of noble character. "The blind obedience of thousands is not worth the straightforward advice of one person" is what a noble believes and practices. In commenting on the well-known scholar Wang Guowei (1877-1927), professor Chen Yinque (1890-1969) said, "Wang's works and theories may remain controversial for quite sometime in the future, but his noble spirit of independence and freedom of thought will mingle with heaven and earth, providing a light for thousands of generations, which will never fade away." Examples can also be found in these noble characters: Ma Yinchu, a prominent Chinese scholar, never confessed to his "Chinese Malthusianism" even under extreme political pressure. In defending their heliocentric theory, Western scholars Copernicus, Bruno and Galileo were not afraid of being imprisoned or even burned at the stake by the church: "You can certainly kill me, but the earth is still rotating." [6]

Upbringing, which embodies cultural quality and decency, is reflected in daily subtleties: Zilu, a disciple of Confucius (551-479 BC), while mortally wounded and on his deathbed, still managed to fasten his toories to have a "decent death". Kang Tongbi, the daughter of famous reformer Kang Youwei (1858 - 1927), attended a family banquet in the 1960s when the "bourgeois life-style" was severely criticized, and hid all her elegant dresses in her bag (since they were not allowed to be worn on the street); after entering the courtyard she found a "change room" in a corner to make up and appear gorgeous at the party. In Europe, during World War II, the British King Edward visited a shabby slum in London. "May I come in please?" he asked the owner, a poor lady, revealing noble respect for ordinary people. During the French Revolution, in the Place de la Concorde in Paris, a few minutes before their execution, when Queen Marie Antoinette (the wife of Louis XVI) accidentally stepped on the foot of the executioner, she instinctively said "Sorry, Sir" and Emperor Louis XVI then said to the crowd: "I will die as an innocent but I forgive my enemy. May I wish my blood calm the wrath of God." Two centuries later, President Mitterrand sincerely announced in the General Assembly on the 200th Commemoration of the French Revolution: "Louis XVI was a good man. It was so tragic to kill him..." [7]

A man of noble character does not have to be rich; some of them are in fact very poor. Chen Duxiu (1879-1942), a well-known figure in modern Chinese history, was impoverished in his later days, but he refused to receive a penny from others. Tolstoy, the famous Russian writer, shared out all his possessions to the poor before he died miserably like a beggar in a small deserted railway station. [8]

Evidently, as far as spirituality is concerned, those who are noble but not wealthy are enlightened, humane and generous for generations to come, while those who are wealthy but lack nobility, although enjoying a good (but limited) time of living like a king, can never buy any respect from the bottom of others' hearts. [9]

译 注

[1]"相混淆",多用 to confound... with...、mix、mingle、blur 等,这里用了 relate to... 更多有 deal with、get、involved in 的意思。

[2]"中国综合实力"还可译成 the integrated power of China、China's overall national strength、the comprehensive strength of China 等。"没有",最通常的是 no、none、without 等,这里变通为 is unrelated...,如:"这没有什么正式不正式的。"(This is not unrelated to the official.)

[3]"理解"一般为 understand、comprehend、digest 等,因这里特指"贵族精神"概念,故用 define,如:"这就取决于你如何理解了。"(It all depends on how you define it.)"担当"一般多用 commitment,该词义为 a promise to do something or to behave in a particular way、willingness to undertake,故也可用 willingness to oblige,如:"Her willingness to oblige has deeply moved everyone present there."(她敢于承担的精神感动了在场的每个人。)

[4]"重荣誉"似可译成 honor one's name、defend/maintain/preserve/protect/secure/uphold reputation 等,这里的 behave honorably 更为直白,也使句式更易表达。"蠢猪",一句骂人的口语,如同愚蠢、蠢驴、傻瓜、笨蛋等,可译成 idiot、stupid swine、ass 等,但又不可拘泥文字,因中西比喻所用形象不同,如文中的"一掷千金/挥金如土"(spend money

like water/dirt)，另"骨瘦如柴"(as thin as a lath、skin and bones、a mere skeleton)、"大海捞针"(look for a needle in the hay stack)等，都采用了不同的喻体（metaphorical objects），这里又稍做变通。

[5]"修身、齐家、治国、平天下"，根据语境中的句式，可有多种表达，如"self cultivation, family harmony, country management and world peace" "rectifying the mind, regulate the family, country and the world" "cultivate themselves, put family in order, administer a country and make the world peace"等。"失职"不是一般意义上的 neglect one's duty、dereliction of duty、negligence of duty、negligent in the performance of duties 等，而具体指的是无仗可打、无以报国的自责，故用了 self-accusation，并在括号中具体说明。

[6]"三光"，文学用语，古人称自然界发光的三种物体为三光，即日、月、星。史上有对联：三光日月星，四诗风雅颂（苏轼）。又，在古代神怪小说中，六道中修道者现真身时，往往要避日光、月光、星光。此处可不必拘泥，如"他不到黄河不死心"，不必译成"He wouldn't stop until he reached the Yellow River."，而是译成"He wouldn't give up until his hope has gone."即可。"人口论"一般指英国人口学家马尔萨斯（Thomas Robert Malthus）于1798年发表的《人口论》（工业革命时期政治经济学经典之作）中提出的人口理论，故作 Malthusism，此处借用为 China's Malthusism，特指马寅初的"人口论"。

[7]"得体"一般为 appropriate、behave properly (in the proper way)、befitting one's position、suited to the occasion 等,这里的 decent 更有形容性。"雅装"与 fashionable dress 不同,在此语境更宜用 elegant,如:"作为主持人,她今晚身着雅装,体态优美。"(As a hostess, tonight she is wearing an elegant dress and walking in a very elegant way.)"几分钟后",此处作为状语,可在译文词序上有所变动。

[8]"富有",rich 与 poor 相对应,故未用前面的 wealthy。

[9]"留下",若用 left (civilization, humanity…) 则不大确切,故不如译为形容词 "are enlightened, … for…" 更直白。"用大把的金钱",与前面的"一掷千金"类似,但换种表达;类似的还有 fling one's money about、scatter one's gold around as though it were dust 等。

老炮儿的讲究

颇受欢迎的国产电影《老炮儿》,开头有这样一幕:一民工模样的小偷,在拿走战利品中的现金之后,把钱包扔进了垃圾桶,这时老炮儿逼着他把证件给人寄回去,末了冒出一句:"讲究!"[1]

这个"讲究"很有学问。分析起来,主要有两方面的涵义,一是"规矩",一是"面子"。[2]

凭着这"规矩",老炮儿几乎成了胡同里的道德警察,他拉群架,挡城管,劝和气,有效地维系着胡同中的民间秩序。[3]

内在的,老炮儿心里也有那么一股高贵劲儿,支撑着他的"面子"。虽然身上没俩钱儿,但穷也讲礼数,如遛个八哥,且见面一定打招呼,嘴头上永远没有不得体的时候。[4]

但是,老炮儿的这些讲究,从性质上说,是江湖的。[5]

对于"江湖",我们的教科书似乎始终没有一个到位的定义,例如"泛指流落四方各地"等。[6]

其实,据我理解,江湖的本质是与官方相对立,另有一套,类似潜规则之类的,故不妨译为 street practice in sub-communities。[7]

这便有了两条致命的弱点:一、拿不上桌面;二、跟不上现代社会的趟。于是就很拧巴。[8]

例如，他跟已经发迹了的哥们借钱，人家二话不说把钱掏了出来，但他又嫌人家说"钱"了，不给面子；奇怪得很，来借钱又不能提钱的事儿，这不是虚伪吗？但是，当他病倒后被送入了ICU，哥们给他出了钱，他又不言声了。[9]

又如，当他儿子把人家的豪车弄坏后，赔不起了，他又要用"我们的方式"把事儿铲了，提议打群架，以输赢决胜负。结果架没茬成，儿子被对方姑娘救出，还顺走了10万块钱。实际上是没守规矩。[10]

老炮信守着"不报警"，但实在没招了，最后还是给中纪委寄去了举报信，扳倒了官二代的小混混。于是，江湖了一辈子，临了老炮儿还是和官方合作了一把。[11]

电影落幕时，老炮儿身着皇军大衣，手提日本战刀，向着一群"不讲规矩"的家伙冲将上去，不料却倒在了犯病之中——形成了一幅堂吉诃德式的北京老炮儿恶战当今腐败势力的黑色幽默图，令人产生无尽的时空倒错与无可奈何的感觉。[12]

译 文

Mr. Six's Way

At the start of the plot of the popular Chinese movie entitled *Mr. Six*, when a migrant-laborer-looking burglar throws out a wallet after empting all its cash, Mr. Six insists on him sending back all the cards to their owner, shouting "That's our way of doing things." [1]

"Our way of doing things" is meaningful on two fronts: following the rules and maintaining face. [2]

By applying his rules he has virtually become the moral policeman of the *hutong* (alleys), refereeing fights, reasoning with city inspectors and mediating among neighbors, so as to effectively maintain the folk order of the community. [3]

Inwardly, he has an air of nobility which well preserves his face. With little money in his pocket, Mr. Six manages to keep his decency by a gracious way of living (such as playing myna) and immaculate courtesy. [4]

However, his way of doing things is actually the way of *jianghu*. [5]

It seems that we haven't yet found the proper term to define *jianghu*: those in use, such as "all corners of the country", "a vagabond life" etc. in our dictionary, are far from satisfactory. [6]

In my understanding, the nature of *jianghu* is contrary to any official practice, since it is based on unofficial rules of practice recognized in sub-communities. So I am suggesting "street practice in sub-communities". [7]

Inevitably, this kind of practice is somewhat odd since it has to be under the table, and is deemed outdated by current society. [8]

For instance, when his *nouveau riche* friend offered to lend him a huge amount of money at his own request without any hesitation, he felt somehow hurt and refused, which is typical hypocrisy –

wanting the money but not wanting the money to be mentioned. However, when on another occasion he was fatally ill and sent to the ICU, and the bill was paid by his friend, he just quietly accepted it without apology. [9]

On another occasion, when his son damaged someone's luxury car and was unable to repair or pay for it, he proposed "his way of settling things"– a free fight, which is supposed to be a fair fight. However, his son was surprisingly rescued by a girl who also stole a prepayment of ten thousand *yuan* from the victim. This behavior that had broken the rules was nevertheless endorsed by Mr. Six. [10]

"Never go to the police" is the one tenet that Mr. Six vowed always to stick to. However, when he realized that he really was at a disadvantage, he reported to the Commission for Discipline Inspection of the Central Committee of the CPC about the crime his rival "officiallings" had committed. As a kingpin of *jianghu* throughout his life, he finally broke his own "way of doing things" by cooperating with the official. [11]

The final scene: wearing an overcoat of the Japanese imperial army and holding a Japanese sabre, Mr. Six singlehandedly rushes a crowd who are "lawless people" by his standard, but suffers an unexpected attack of his old illness, falls over himself and loses consciousness. What a Beijing-style Quixotic anticorruption crusader he portrays in a picture of black humor! In such manner he leaves his audience endlessly sighing over the chaotic jumble of time and space and desperation. [12]

译 注

[1] 这里的"讲究"京味十足，不是一般意义上的 stress、strive for、be particular about、pay great attention to、devote particular care to、daintily 等，而是一种特殊的做事方式，故成此译文。

[2] 是句京腔，不是平时讲的 have knowledge、learning、learned、literacy 等，即有特殊涵义。

[4] "嘴头上永远没有不得体的时候"，这句话颇有北京人的幽默，不宜照字面意思翻译，故不妨以 immaculate courtesy 来概括。

[8] "拧巴"，也是北京人的一句现代用语，有 awkward、uncomfortable、troublesome、difficult to deal with、hard to get along with 等意思，这里用了 somewhat odd，以表别扭。

[9] "这不是虚伪吗？"，此句不一定要译成疑问句，而可译为陈述句并做相应的句式调整。这里的"不言声了"不仅仅是不说话了，而是有着更多的涵义，即与他的讲究相抵触，故译为 quietly accepted it without apology，以做扩充处理。

[10] "铲了"，即北京话，把事摆平了，这里用了 settle things；"茬架"，似无准确的英文对应语，姑且用 free fight。"实际上是没守规矩"，此句没有单独译出，而是融入整句，以更通顺，特别是加入 the rules was nevertheless endorsed by Mr. Six，以揭示老炮儿信念的矛盾性。

[11] "江湖了一辈子"，此句中的"江湖"用作动词，即"一生行江湖之道"，是位"老炮儿"，故用了 kingpin，其义为 the most important person in a group or undertaking，这里当然是指 in sub-communities。

从法制到法治

"法制"与"法治",虽一字之差,却有本质不同。[1]

"法制"主要是个名词,意为法律、制度或国家机关及其公民活动的合法原则。我们说"法制建设""健全法制""加强法制"等主要是指这种意思。[2]

"法治"则为动词,是依法治国、依法执政,与"人治"相对立。前者以代表全体人民意志的法律为准绳,后者以个别当权者的意志为决策,即分别代表民主与独裁。[3]

关于这二者的争论,古今中外,从未停止。儒家主张人治(或曰德治、礼治),认为"道之以政,齐之以刑,民免而无耻;道之以德,齐之以礼,有耻且格"。法家则主张法治,认为"圣人之治国,不恃人之为吾善也,而用其不得为非也",故"不务德而务法"。[4]

在西方,柏拉图力主"贤人政治",认为除非哲学家成为国王,人类将永无宁日,而不应将许多法律条文强加于"优秀的人",只是在他的"贤人政治"的理想国方案失败之后,才称法律为"第二位最好的"。亚里士多德主张"法治应优于一人之治","法律恰恰正是免除一切情欲影响的神祇和理智的体现"。[5]

法治和人治的根本区别在于:当法律权威与个人权威发生

冲突时，是法律权威高于个人权威，还是个人权威凌驾于法律权威；换言之，是"人依法"还是"法依人"，二者必居其一。所以，法治和人治绝不可能结合起来。[6]

实践证明，人治社会有许多难以克服的弊病，如决策的随意性、非民主性、矛盾性，没有一套体现民意、有权威性、稳定性的规章制度，使人们的行为无章可循，整个社会的治理效率低下，腐败丛生。如邓小平所说，"制度好可以使坏人无法任意横行，制度不好可以使好人无法充分做好事，甚至会走向反面"。[7]

因而，"改革开放"以来我国全面地启动了法制的进程，至今在各个领域基本建立起了比较完备的法律体系。然而，"建立法制"并不等于"实行法治"，其间还有相当的路程要走，即如何解决有法不依的问题。[8]

其实，"法治"是一个政治概念，而不只是一个法律概念，因其实质并非是一种传统意义上的统治，而是现代意义上的社会管理，即依据通过民主程序制定的法律，使社会公众参与其中；人人既是治者，也是被治者，良性互动，从而形成"善治"，有效地解决社会问题，推动社会向前发展。[9]

令人欣喜的是，党的十八大之后，我们不但进一步完善了法制，而且加快了法治的步伐，有利于早日建成有中国特色的社会主义法治国家。[10]

译 文

From "Rule of Law" to "Rule by Law"

The essential meanings of "rule of law" and "rule by law" are quite different even there is only one character separating the two terms in Chinese. [1]

As a substantive term, "rule of law" means the laws themselves, the legal system of state organs as well as the legal principles that regulate the behavior of citizens. Phrases like "legal construction", "improving the legal system", "strengthening the legal system" that we normally refer to are mainly in line with this connotation. [2]

Contrary to "rule by man", "rule by law" as verb phrases means ruling the country in accordance with the law and managing state affairs according to law. In other words, the former presents a dictatorship where everything is determined by the will of the authorities, and the latter signifies a democracy in which the people's will prevails based on law as the criterion. [3]

How to rule a state has been a constant debate since ancient times. The Confucianists advocated the "rule of man", believing that "If the people are governed by law and kept in order by punishment, they will evade the laws with no sense of shame; if they are governed by virtue and kept in order through observing ritual propriety, they will develop a sense of shame, moreover, they will impose order on themselves." The Legalists, on the other hand, asserted that "In ruling a country, the wise man will not rely on self-consciousness, but on an environment and conditions where the people dare not to commit crimes. Therefore laws instead of virtues are adored." [4]

In the West, Plato advocated "sage politics", assuming that unless philosophers become kings, mankind will never be able to live in peace, and it is not right to impose so many legal provisions on "good men". Law he deemed to be the second best option only after the failure of his idea of Utopia. Aristotle, however, advocated that "rule by law" definitely excels "rule by man" since law is the way to manifest rationality and eliminate any gods affected by emotion. [5]

The fundamental difference between the rule by law and rule by man lies in decision making – according to law or men when conflicts occur involving different authorities. Legal authority and individual authority are the two entities between which the choice must be one or the other and they can never be compromised. [6]

Practice has proved that there are many insurmountable drawbacks in a society ruled by man, such as free-rein decision making, a non-democratic and contradictory process through which an unauthorized and unstable regulatory framework is produced, not reflecting public opinion. As a result, it is hard to persuade people to follow any valid rules, for social management to be efficient, and corruption becomes rampant. As Deng Xiaoping pointed out, "With a good system bad guys are unable to run amok, while a bad system is in place good people are hindered in doing the good things they intend to do, and even have to do some undesirable things." [7]

The "Reform and Opening Up" saw a comprehensive process of legal system building commenced, and a rather complete legal system has since been established. However, "establishing law" is not the same as "practicing law", which requires a considerable effort to solve the problem of individuals showing contempt for laws. [8]

In fact, "rule by law" is not merely a legal concept but a political one as well, since it no longer means to rule a country in a traditional sense, but to manage a society in the modern era. Namely, based on a democratic legal system, a "benign governance" is formed to involve everyone who is both a ruler and the ruled, in solving social problems and promoting social development. [9]

It is delightful to witness that since the CPC's eighteenth Congress, we have not only further perfected our legal system but also accelerated the pace of "ruling the state by law" in establishing a legal state with Chinese characteristics. [10]

译 注

在［1］中，很长一段时间里，人们对于"法制"与"法治"的区别是不敏感的，经常混用。其实在英文里，二者有本质区别，如："Democracy is predicated upon the rule of law."（民主是以法制为基础的。）"This is a basic requirement for modern civilization and nations subject to the rule of law."（这也是一个现代文明和法治国家的基本要求。）"这为中国走向法治准备了非常重要的前提条件。"（This has prepared very important prerequisite condition for that China moves towards rule by law.）"领导干部要实现从'人治'到'法治'的观念转变。"（The leading cadres' mentality has to be transformed from "rule by man" to "rule by law".）

在［2］中的所谓"名词"不是 noun，这里是名词的词组，故用了 substantive term；而且所列的"原则"和几个关于"法制"的短语都属这种性质。顺便而言，中文里以"法"为词头的词组，其英译文有着很大变化，如"法系"（family of law）、"法统"（legally constituted authority）、"法案"（act）、"法典"（code）、"法院"（court）、"法庭"（courtroom）、"法学"（jurisprudence）、"法则"（rule）、"法条"（provision, article）、"法医学"（forensic medicine）、"法理学"（jurisprudence）、"法律关系"（jural relation）、"法律行为"（juristic act）等。

在［3］中，可将"与'人治'相对立"调整到前面，以便行文顺畅。"依法治国、依法执政"其中有重复的部分，但可在译文中有所区别，如 in accordance with the law、according to law 等。"分别代表"似可译成 each separately represent，但还应力求对二者有所区别，如 presents 和 signifies 等。"以法律为准绳"一般译作 take law as the criterion，但亦可根据语境有所变通，如 "based on law as the criterion"，以及"现在，我告诉他们要以事实为依据，以法律为准绳"（Now, we tell them to emphasize the law and the facts.）等。

在［4］中，孔子的这段话出自《论语·为政》，历来有着不同的英译文，如："Govern the people by regulations, keep order among them by chastisements, and they will flee from you, and lose all self-respect. Govern them by moral force, keep order among them by ritual and they will keep their self-respect and come to you of their own accord."（Arthur Waley）；"Regulated by the edicts and punishments, the people will know only how to stay out of trouble but will not have a sense of shame. Guided by virtues and the rites, they will not only have a sense of shame but also know how to correct their mistakes of their own accord."（赖波、夏玉和）；"Lead the people with administrative injunctions (zheng 政) and keep them orderly with penal law (xing 刑), and they will avoid punishments but will be without a sense of shame. Lead them with excellence (de 德) and keep them orderly through observing ritual propriety (li 礼) and they will develop a sense of shame, and moreover, will order themselves."（Roger T. Ames）；"If you lead people by law and keep them in order by punishment, they will evade the laws with no sense of shame. If you lead the people by virtue and keep them in order by the rituals, they will have a sense of shame and reform themselves."（谷学）。

笔者认为其中不乏过时与不到位的地方，故于此做些变通。所引法家言论，则是《韩非子》中的一段话。

在［5］中，"贤人政治"容易译成 philosopher politics，但 sage politics 更确切，特别是考虑到后面一句"除非哲学家成为国王"。这里的"优秀的人"没有用 excellent men，而是 good men，是因 good 与 evil 相对应。"优于"，常用的还有 better than、overmatch、precede、excelled、outbalance 等。这里的"神"不是通常讲的 God（上帝），而是众神，如："Men have ascribed their own characteristics to their gods."（人们认为他们的特性属于诸神。）"In Greek mythology, Zeus was the ruler of gods and men."（在希腊神话中，宙斯是众神和人类的统治者。）

在［6］中，"二者必居其一"，常用的表达还有"The door must be either shut or open."等；"不能结合"，字面意思似乎是 cannot be combined / mixed / married / united 等，但此处的实质是不能含混、融合，故做此变通。

在［7］中，原文直至"腐败丛生"为一句，翻译中可将其截短，如在"稳定性的规章制度"处断开，以"As a result"另起一句，易于英文表述。而"走向反面"，可以是 go over to the opposite side、turn into its opposite 等，但此处的主要意思是因为碍于制度，无法做应当做的事，而做出一些很"无奈的事"。

在［8］中，"并不等于"一般译成 unequal to、not equal to 等，但更具说理性的宜用 is not the same as，如："Being poor and white is not the same as being poor and black."（白人致贫的原因和黑人致贫的原因也不一样。）"Establishing which chemical compound is active in a traditional medicine is not the same as knowing that the medicine is effective."（确定哪种化学物质在一种传统药物中具有活性与了解药物能起作用是不同的。）"有法不依"，更直白的翻译可为"there are laws but little observation of them""do not abide by the law"等。

在［9］中，"善治"一般译成 good governance、good governing、government of good、good domination，如："Good governance is one of the two cornerstones for the construction of a harmonious society."（善治是构建和谐社会的两大基石之一。）"为达到公民个人利益和公共环境利益的高度协调，善治是推进城市公共环境管理的理想路径。"（In order to coordinate highly the benefit between citizen and public environment, good-governance is the best ideal path to advance city public environment administration.）这里用了 benign governance 是有引申之义。

在［10］中，"令人欣喜"，还可译为 pleasurable、happily、joyously 等。就整段结构而言，译文相较原文做了某种程度的整合。

自由需要素质

"自由",在我的学生时代,不是个好词,因为它与个人主义、自私自利、自由散漫等联系在一起。特别是课文里还有一篇《反对自由主义》,历数了自由主义的种种危害性和反动性,于是觉得那简直是个有些令人生畏的词了。[1]

后来,"文革"结束,改革开放,自由之风一度吹遍了祖国大地——从思想界、文化界、教育界到各行各业,人们被压抑多年之后,终于舒了一口气,到处显出新气象。具体而言,有书看了,以前被严令禁止的"反动书刊",可以大量出版了。那时,第一次感受到了有自由与没有自由的区别。[2]

再后来,看了些书,知道了中国传统社会不是一个法治社会,人们因为没有"权利"的概念,也就没有"自由"的概念,所以在中国人的意识里对"自由"形成了错误的理解:要么不存在,要么是个坏东西。于是,想体验更加自由的西方世界了。[3]

初到国外时,看到了媒体上的言论自由,有各种政党、团体、个人的评论与批评,但那时忙于上课、打工、延续签证等,竟无暇顾及那些以前渴望看到的东西;人毕竟要为生存而自由,不能为自由而自由。不错,在总理办公的大厦门前,似乎每个人都有权把他拦下、理论,甚至骂上几句,但我那时突然觉得毫无必要了。于是,体会到了自由可以是有意义或没意义的。[4]

在那里生活下来之后，发现西方的"自由"与我原来想象的有所不同。逐渐明白了，一个更进步、更文明的社会，其条文和规矩不是更少了，而是更多了；一个更自由、文明的人，一定是个更加守法、更有道德的人。无论是在交通规则、交税退税、办理公务、诉讼裁决、公司程序，还是入学就业等方面，其严格细致的规定，都让人有动辄得咎的感觉，但一般正常人都会自觉遵守，不会以身试法。有些没有明文规定的，则要靠人们的道德和素质来约束。比如排队，人们不但会自觉地依次排列，而且会在人与人之间或走道之间留出相当的距离，没有人"忍心"去破坏的；若偶有莽撞者（多半不是本地人）破坏了，周围的那种气氛，也会构成无形的压力，令其有所醒悟。于是，又认识到任何自由其实都是受限的自由，因世界上原本没有不受限制的自由；而且，唯其受限，才更加自由。[5]

如果说，解决了生活问题便获得了"低级自由"，那么步入大学、科研领域，可谓享受到了"高级自由"。在那里，我获得了对于信息与学术探求的空前自由，极大地满足了我的求知欲望。正如古希腊人所认为的，知识本身就是最高的目标，获得知识就是获得自由。[6]

《现代汉语词典》对于"自由"的定义，有一条是"哲学上把人认识了事物发展的规律性，自觉地运用到实践中去，叫作自由"，即通过认识事物而获得的一种自觉。这吻合了斯宾诺莎的观点，"自由是对必然的认识"，而波普尔也说"通过知识获得解放"。根据古希腊哲学，最高的知识是科学；而科学既非生产力，也非智商，而是通往自由人性的基本教化方式，因而没有对科学的追求之心,就不具备做自由人的资质。在这个意义上,自由又有了质的高低之分。[7]

可见,自由具有不同种类和层次,不同的需求对应不同的自由;而享有真正的自由,一定离不开相应的素质。[8]

译 文

True Freedom Has to Be Based on Its Quality

"Freedom" wasn't a good word at all during my school-days, since it was associated with individualism, selfishness and laxity in discipline. It even became a daunting concept when we read an article entitled "Opposing Liberalism" in our textbook, enumerating all the dangers and reactionism. [1]

Later, as the "Cultural Revolution" ended and the wind of freedom blew in every corner of the country, people in all walks of life, including in the fields of ideology, culture and education, breathed a sigh of relief, ushering in a new atmosphere everywhere. Practically, we got books to read that had previously been prohibited from publishing. With abundant publications, it then seemed to be the first time that we had really tasted what freedom was. [2]

After acquiring some knowledge of history, I realized that traditional Chinese society was not ruled by law, where the legal concept of "right" was absent, and consequently its concomitant "freedom". Most Chinese had the wrong idea about freedom – that it either didn't exist or was highly undesirable. Intending to experience "real freedom" in another world, I therefore went to the West. [3]

Arriving in a Western country, dazzled by freedom of speech in the media, various comments and criticisms in public, I had the initial taste of the freedom I longed for. Ironically, I didn't have the time to appreciate it then since I was overwhelmed by all sorts of things, such as attending classes, working part-time and renewing my visa. A man has to survive before enjoying anything else; freedom can never be simply for its own sake. Sure, legally speaking, in front of the building housing the Prime Minister's office, everyone has the right to stop him, to argue or quarrel with him, but I suddenly realized that it was completely unnecessary for me now. Freedom after all can be meaningful or meaningless. [4]

Having lived there for some time, I started to differentiate between realistic freedom and the imagined freedom of the West. Gradually, the truth dawned: as a society progresses, its civilization requires more rules and provisions, not less; as its people grow to be more civilized and liberalized they become more law-abiding and virtuous citizens. There are strict and meticulous rules to regulate almost every aspect of people's lives and their boundaries are easily crossed, resulting in fines, such as for traffic offences, tax returns, business dealings, litigation, schooling and employment. Law-abiding people, however, just get along provided they don't defy the law. In circumstances where nothing is proclaimed in writing, morality and conventions will take care of, for example queuing. Not only will people consciously line up but also keep a specific distance between people or walkways, which no one "dares" to break. If, occasionally, a rule is broken by some reckless persons (possibly not locals), the offenders will sense the pressure of the atmosphere, and are very likely to back down. There is no such thing as unlimited freedom in this world; but their restriction actually grants people more freedom. [5]

Having got over the hassles of survival, which could be seen as "low quality freedom", moving to enjoy "high quality freedom" seemed to be the next logical step – enrolling in a university and engaging in research. The unprecedented academic freedom greatly enhanced my thirst for learning, as the ancient Greeks believed that acquiring knowledge is freedom since knowledge is itself the highest goal. [6]

According to the *Dictionary of Modern Chinese*, such freedom is applying laws that have been philosophically understood in a conscious manner, which is completely consistent with the viewpoints of Spinoza ("Freedom is the recognition of inevitability") and Popper ("Liberation is gained from knowledge"). In ancient Greek philosophy, since knowledge is science, which is neither a productive power, nor intellectual, but basic enlightenment guiding human nature, without the pursuit of science, one can hardly qualify as human. In this sense, freedom is differentiated by its qualities. [7]

Therefore, freedoms of different kinds at various levels are in fact correlated with different requirements, and true freedom has to be based on its quality. [8]

译 注

[1]"令人生畏",一般译成 formidable,如 formidable competitor（强大的竞争对手）等；这里指的是词语,故用 a daunting concept。

[2]这里的"区别",不宜简单地译成 the differences、distinction、discrimination 等,而是就真正自由而言的,故可变通为 really tasted what freedom was。

[3]"法治社会"一般可译为 society with rule of law,此处"不是一个法治社会"可译为 society was not ruled by law。"坏东西"似可译成 a bad/terrible thing 等,但 highly undesirable 更雅。

[4]"为自由而自由",似可直译为 freedom for freedom sake,而 "freedom can never be simply for its own sake" 则稍做扩展。此处"理论"不是名词,而是动词,即"辩论是非"之意,故译为 to argue。

[5]这里的"明白了"没有用通俗意义上的 I understood/got it/gotcha 等,而是更为书面的 the truth dawned,以表探明事理。

[7]"通往自由人性的基本教化方式",若按其字面意思则很难翻译,如 by a basic way of teaching towards freedom of human nature,且未必确切,此处变通为 basic enlightenment guiding human nature,以融入其语境。

解析篇

启蒙的真谛

"启蒙"的本义是开启蒙昧,识字读书,明白事理。在中国古代,人们从小要接受"蒙学",才能成为有教养的人,否则就是"教化未开"。据说,早年被启蒙到了什么程度,决定其日后可达到的智力高度。[1]

同样,人类社会从传统向现代转型的过程,也是与启蒙相伴随的;没有启蒙就没有现代化。[2]

然而,作为现代话语的"启蒙",却源自于近代西方。在人类历史上,近代启蒙思想和启蒙运动首发于17世纪后期的英国,后传播到法国、德国等欧洲国家,波及北美,19世纪后期又影响到日本、中国等亚洲国家。[3]

正是由于西方有了洛克、斯密、伏尔泰、卢梭、狄德罗等启蒙思想家,才有了之后欧美的工业革命、商品经济和宪政体制。在中国,自晚清时期出现近代启蒙思想后,中国知识分子在"救亡图存"的背景下,借助西方近代思想,改造中国传统文化,塑造新型国民,引发了洋务运动、戊戌变法、新文化运动等。特别是在当代,1978年关于"实践是检验真理的唯一标准"的大讨论,极大地解放了人们的思想,带来了之后"改革开放"的巨大成果。由此,思想的力量可见一斑。[4]

长期以来,人们对于启蒙运动有一种误解,认为那是先知先觉的知识分子和哲人启发、教育、训导被启蒙者，因而"启蒙"成了及物动词，其宾语是未开化的芸芸众生。其实，根据现代启蒙思想家康德的解释，启蒙的本质不是"他启"而是"自觉"，即人们从自我原因的不成熟状态（在缺乏指导下无力运用自我理性的状态）中觉醒，其根源并非是人们缺乏理性，而是缺乏对理性的运用。[5]

这种真知灼见至今闪烁着理性的光芒。[6]

在西方，启蒙思想的支撑源于人们对客观规律的认知，如哥白尼的"日心说"、牛顿的万有引力定律、伽利略的宇宙论等，认为整个宇宙中的一切物体都遵守同一定律，进而冲破千年的宗教束缚，将这一理性思考引入了人类社会，从而开创了一个不断进取的新时代。在中国，几千年的封建农业社会，使得科学科技落后、法制传统缺乏，直到受到近代西方启蒙思想的影响（包括马克思主义），才引入了科学、民主、法治的概念，开始与世界文明接轨。[7]

在这一历史大潮中，中国现在比历史上任何时期都更接近中华民族的伟大复兴。正如"一带一路"被越来越多的国家认识到不是中国的独角戏，而是沿线民族的大合唱，每个中国人对于客观与主观世界的深刻、自觉的理性开发，最终将汇集于前所未有的中国梦的实现。[8]

The True Meaning of Enlightenment

Originally, "enlightenment" so-called was to enlighten people by teaching them how to read and reason. In ancient China, from their childhood, people had to receive *meng xue* or private rudimentary education before they could become well-educated and avoid being labeled as "uncivilized". It is said that how far a person can go intellectually in his or her later life depends largely on how well they have been enlightened in their early days. [1]

Likewise, the transformation of a society from its traditional phase into a modern one is also impelled by enlightenment. In other words, without enlightenment there will be no modernization. [2]

As a modern term, however, "enlightenment" originated in the modernizing West. In human history, enlightenment ideas and movements started in England, and then spread to France, Germany and other European countries as well as North America in the late 17th century. By the late 19th century such Asian countries as Japan and China had also been influenced. [3]

It was due to the mobilization of some enlightenment thinkers in the West, represented by Locke, Smith, Voltaire, Rousseau and Diderot, that bred the Industrial Revolution, commodity economy and constitutionalism in Europe and America. In China, influenced by the West, enlightenment ideas occurred as early as in the late Qing Dynasty, Chinese intellectuals carried out the mission of transforming traditional Chinese culture, re-moulding its people, as well as initiating a westernization drive, the Reform Movement of 1898, the New Cultural Movement and so on. As far as current affairs were concerned, the mass debate in 1978 on "Practice is the sole criterion for testing truth" tremendously emancipated people from their ideological confinement so as to bring about the enormous outcome of the "reform and opening up to the outside world". In this way, the power of ideas was therefore clearly evident. [4]

Enlightenment has for quite some time been mistaken for a movement where privileged intellectuals inspire, illuminate and guide the populace (obviously, "enlighten" has been used as a transitive verb which takes the populace as its object of mobilization). According to Kant, enlightenment does not in fact mean people have to be awakened by others but need to be able to wake up by themselves – emerging from their self-induced immaturity which is the state where they are unable to use their own understanding without the guidance of another. And the cause does not lie in any lack of rationality but in inability to reason. [5]

This view still penetrates rationality even today. [6]

In the West, enlightenment was underpinned by the scientific truths they had plumbed, typified by Copernicus' Heliocentric

Theory, Newton's Law of Universal Gravitation and Galileo's Cosmology, believing that everything in the cosmos is ruled by a common universal law. Having breached a thousand years of religious bounds, they introduced rational thought into human society and ushered in a constantly progressive era. However Chinese society, dominated by feudalist agriculture for thousands of years, experienced sluggish development of science and technology and a barren legal tradition. It was not until modern times that China, under the influence of Western enlightenment ideas including Marxism, started to receive modern ideas about science and technology, democracy and the rule of law, and to proceed in line with international standards. [7]

Following the historical trend, China is now closer to its rejuvenation than at any other time in history. Just as more and more countries along the "One Belt and One Road" route have realized that this Program initiated by China is not a "monodrama" but a "cantata": the unprecedented Chinese Dream, involving every Chinese who is willing to carry out serious intellectual searching in both the objective and subjective worlds, will also eventually come true as a collective consummation. [8]

> 深度解析

确切　融通　整合
——《启蒙的真谛》汉译英点评

此文是本人为本届翻译大赛所写的一篇时文，就启蒙的基本涵义、历史演变、与文化及政治的关系和现实意义等做了简述和分析，言简意赅。看似平实，但翻译起来仍须精雕细琢、全方位考量。

1. 术语的确切

任何翻译赛的基本层面是词语、术语的准确性与确切性，即求其"信"。本文的中心议题是"启蒙"，有的用了 initiation，该词本义为 "the act of starting something for the first time; introducing something new"，似乎有"开启"之意，但通览全文，就知识、思维、理性而言，该词不够分量，还应用 enlightenment，其本义为 "education that results in understanding and the spread of knowledge" "wisdom as evidenced by the possession of knowledge" 等，特别是在题目中。而一般参赛者译成了 The Essence/Truth/Essential/Philosophy of Enlightenment，但更确切的应为 The True Meaning of Enlightenment，类似的用法如："The true meaning of the modern law society is judiciary independence."

（现代法治社会的真谛是"司法独立"。）需要指出的是，有的参赛译文漏掉了题目的翻译，形成最明显的"硬伤"。

[1] 中的"'启蒙'的本义是开启蒙昧，识字读书，明白事理"，典型的译文，如："The original meaning of enlightenment is to <u>open ignorance</u>[①], to read, to read, to understand." "The literal meaning of 'enlightenment' is to <u>discard ignorance</u>, receive education and become mature." "The original meaning of 'enlightenment' is to <u>smash ignorance</u>, to read and to understand." "The word 'enlighten' originally means <u>to explore ignorance</u>." "'Enlightenment' literally means to <u>remove one's ignorance</u> with literacy and good sense."等。这些译文都试图以字面意思表明"开启""启迪"之意，如"开"（open）、"除"（discard）、"碎"（smash）、"探"（explore）、"移"（remove）、"愚昧"（ignorance），但其表述的语义并不确切。其实，最确切的词义是其本身，即 enlightenment 的动词形式 enlighten，其原义为 to give someone more knowledge and greater understanding about something (Cobuild, 2002)。

从词源学上讲，"启蒙"在英文里是 enlighten/enlightenment，德文里是 aufklaerung，均有光或光明、启发智慧之义。在西方思想史上，德国哲学家最早对"启蒙"概念进行了深入探讨。1783年 12 月，德国神学家策尔纳（Zerna）在《柏林月刊》发表文章，希望学者对"启蒙"概念进行界定，具体回答"什么是启

---

① 下划线是笔者为方便讲解所加，后文均如此。

蒙"的问题。1784年,德国的一些著名哲学家纷纷给出了自己的理解与答复。如门德尔松（Mendelssohn）认为,教育其实由文化和启蒙两部分组成,但二者的含义与作用不同:文化似乎更多地把兴趣引向实际问题,而"启蒙似乎与理论问题的关系更加密切:按照它们对人的命运的重要性和影响,启蒙关系到（客观的）理性知识,关系到对人类生活进行理性反思的（主观的）能力"①。莱因霍尔德（Reinhold）指出:"启蒙一般来说意味着从能够具有合理性的人当中制造出理性的人,导致这个伟大目的的一切机构（Anstalten）和手段,全部加起来,就给予'启蒙'这个词最广泛的意义。"② 因而启蒙就是把有理性能力的人培养成有清晰概念的理性的人；一个启蒙了的个体比一般人明显地具有理性和思维判断能力；一个启蒙了的民族是一个有理性能力和理性文化的有教养的民族；只有人的理性才能将人从黑暗中解放出来。

当然,对于"启蒙"最为著名的论断,是康德（Kant）在《什么是启蒙》（An Answer to the Question: "What is Enlightenment?"）中所做的: Enlightenment is man's emergence from his self-incurred immaturity. Immaturity is the inability to use one's own understanding without the guidance of another. This immaturity is selfincurred if its cause is not lack of understanding, but lack of resolution and courage to use it without the guidance of another. The

---

① 见施密特（编）,《启蒙运动与现代性——18世纪与20世纪的对话》,徐向东、卢华萍译,上海：上海人民出版社,2005年,第57页。

② 同上书,第68页。

motto of enlightenment is therefore: *Sapere aude*! (Dare to be wise!) Have courage to use your own understanding!① （启蒙即是人们从自我导致的不成熟状态中的觉醒。这种"不成熟"是指在缺乏指导下，无力运用自我理性的状态；其原因，并非人们缺乏理性，而是在无人指导下缺乏决心和勇气来运用理性。因此，启蒙的口号是"勇于智慧！"，即有勇气运用自己的理性！）②

对此，法国哲学家米歇尔·福柯（Michel Foucault）有过精辟的解读：启蒙是一种过程，是从"不成熟"状态走向"成熟"状态的过程；在不成熟状态时人们接受他人的权威，人们只有充分地、自愿地运用理性才能摆脱这种状态。但同时，他又怀疑启蒙的终极意义："我不知道我们有朝一日是否会变得'成年'。""然而，我认为可以赋予康德在思考'启蒙'时对现时、对我们自身所提出的批评性质询以某种意义。……我们自身的批判的本体论，绝不应视为一种理论、一种学说，也不应视为积累中的知识的永久载体。它应被看作是态度、'气质'、哲学生活。"③ 显然，福柯把启蒙由个人转向了社会的发展进程，认为社会的转型和现代化过程也是一种启蒙过程，而这一理念与当代西方学者对启蒙的理解，包括中国近代启蒙思想和社会现代化理念不谋而合。故此，该句不妨译为："Originally, the so-called

---

① 康德，《对什么是"启蒙"的回答》（英汉双语），肖树乔译，北京：中译出版社，2015年，第97页。

② 如无特别说明，书中引文均为笔者所译。

③ 南京大学中国现代文学研究中心（编），《启蒙文献选编》（外国卷），上海：上海人民出版社，2010年，第497页。

"enlightenment" was to enlighten people by teaching them how to read and reason."

在［2］中，"人类社会从传统向现代转型的过程，也是与启蒙相伴随的"，其中的"转型"，许多人并没有效地译出来，而只是译为"the modernization of human society from a traditional one""the process of human beings started from a traditional into a modern one"等，其实可用 transformation、transition，甚至 evolution；而"伴随"一般被译成了 is accompanied、in line with、hand in hand、come with、go together with 等，固然都不错，但在全面理解该文"启蒙推动社会进步"这一主旨基础上，可不妨加重其动词的分量，即用 impel（推动），这看似变形，实则确切，故该句可译为"the transformation of a society from its traditional phase into a modern one is also impelled by enlightenment"。

在［4］中，许多参赛者将"思想"译成 thought、thinking、will 等，但此处更为确切的应该是 ideas。例如，世界著名的企鹅出版社出了一套《伟大的思想》学术丛书，名为 Penguin's Great Ideas Series；又如"What Europe represents is much raw power as the power of an idea – a European dream."（欧洲所代表的，与其说是硬实力，不如说是"欧洲梦"这一思想的力量。）

在［5］中，"先知先觉的知识分子和哲人"，参赛译文一般为 the foresighted intellectuals and philosophers、prescient intellectuals and philosophers、intellectuals and philosophers of foresight 等。"先知先觉"很容易让人联想到 foresight，这是语

言层面的，但在社会层面，在17、18世纪的欧洲，成为知识分子，要有许多社会、教育、经济等方面的优越条件，是某种意义上的少数思想特权者，故不妨采用当时的流行术语 a privileged few，如 "During that time, higher education was available to only a privileged few but to all."（那时的高等教育只是为少数精英，而非面向全民。），变通为 privileged intellectuals。"哲人"也未必总是 philosopher，还可以是 wise man、sage、thinker、intellectual 等，而这又与前词相重合，故可归一。

对于"启发、教育、训导被启发者"，一般容易遵循其文字，译成 "to inspire, educate, and discipline the unenlightened" 等，似乎不错。但经辨析即发现：这里的"教育"不是一般的 educate（本义：to teach people better ways of doing something or a better way of living），而是一种 illuminate（本义：to make things clearer by explaining them carefully and intellectually）；"训导"亦非一般的 discipline（本义：the practice of making people obey rules or standards of behavior, and punishing them when they do not），而是 guide（本义：to provide people with enough information to help them understand or do things better），显然更具积极意义；此处的"被启发者"也不尽是 the unenlightened (the ignorant)，而是那一时期社会的普罗大众（the masses、people、populace、public、commonage 等）。故此，该句不妨译为 "privileged intellectuals inspire, illuminate and guide the populace"。

同样在［5］中，对于"自我原因的不成熟状态（在缺乏指导下无力运用自我理性的状态）"，参赛者做了多方面的翻译尝试，如 "That is, people awake from the state of immaturity aroused by themselves (be incapable of using the state of self-reason in the absence of guidance)" "Namely the original cause of people's awakening from the immaturity of self reason (the state of being unable to use self reason in the absence of guidance)" "This is to say that the primary reason why people can wake up in an immature condition attributed to their own reasons, which means in a condition where people unskillfully apply to their own rationality without appropriate instruction" 等，似乎都有一定道理，但又都不十分到位。这里须做点学术探究（academic search），即从上文康德的名著中找到他所创造的那个"自我原因的不成熟状态"（self-incurred/self-induced immaturity），而后面括号中的内容不妨展开来，形成从句："self-induced immaturity which is the state where they are unable to use their own understanding without the guidance of another"。

在 [6] 中，对于"这种真知灼见至今闪烁着理性的光芒"，有的直译比喻，如 "Such insightful vision has hitherto shone the light of reason." "This insight has so far shone with reason." "The insight of Kant still blazes with rationality." "Amazingly, Kant's insight has lent its rational radiance to this date."；有的偏重意译，如 "This remarkable view/idea has been guiding mankind with its rationality until today."；有的做了些变通，如 "Until now, this truth is still shinning with the light of reason."，但主语似乎有些错

位（应为 view、vision、insight 等）。笔者倾向对此采取意译："This view still penetrates rationality even today."

在［8］中，"一带一路"，有的用了 the strategy of "one belt and one road"，其实不妥，因为 strategy 的意思是 "an elaborate and systematic plan of action; a plan that is intended to achieve a particular purpose"，可见其主观性、计划性、预谋性太强，容易引起外国人的反感（有外国媒体称此为 Chinese Marshall Plan，即"中国的马歇尔计划"），故不如用 initiative，其本义为 readiness to embark on bold new ventures，由首倡者提出，具有主动性和号召力，更确切的应为 the initiative of "land and maritime silk road programs"。当然在表述时，又可做些变通处理，但 initiative 应加强调，如 this program initiated by China 等。

对于同段中的"中国梦"，有的译成 China Dream、China's Dream、Dream of the Chinese nation 等，但这难免给人一种感觉，即类似于美国梦，号召全世界的人来中国冒险、创业、发财，而这完全有悖其涵义，故应为 Chinese Dream，即中国人在这片土地上实现自己的远大理想。

此外，就人称而言，在［1］中"据说，早年被启蒙到了什么程度，决定其日后可达到的智力高度"，似乎并无所指，这显出中文模糊与含蓄的特点，但在英文里必不可少，以 he or she 或 they 加以指代。参考译文为："It is said that how far a person can go intellectually in his or her life depends largely on how well they have been enlightened in their early days." 有人认为其中的人称前后不一致，有语法错误；其实并非如此，因为这里不是简单的语法规则问题，而是英文实际使用中的约定俗成。

2. 语义的融通

在词语、术语层面确切翻译的基础上，应进而求其语义的融通，即要注重词语间的衔接与相关语境背景的内在关系。换言之，在"信"之上，进而求"顺"。

如前所述，就本文的中心词"启蒙"的语义而言，尽管已被广泛使用，但在学术界却并没有达成共识；由于立场和时空的差异，对其概念、内涵、原则等有着各种解释。中国古代，早在东汉应劭的《风俗通》中就有"每辄挫衄，亦足以祛弊启蒙矣"的记载，此后又有东晋顾恺之的《启蒙记》、南宋大学者朱熹的《易学启蒙》等。在中国传统文化里，此词是指掌握一定知识的人向初学者传授基础知识或传播某种思想、以去除蒙昧的教育活动；它虽具传授知识和思想的功能，但还主要是一种儿童教育，与近代意义上的传播科学、民主思想、塑造独立人格的启蒙是两回事。

以此为背景，在［3］中有"作为现代话语的'启蒙'，却源自于近代西方"。对此，典型的参赛译文有："As a modern discourse, 'enlighten' roots in modern West." "Nevertheless, as a contemporary word, 'enlightenment' originates in the modern west." "However, the 'enlightenment' in modern words originated from the west" 等。其中，"话语"未见得是 discourse，该词的主要涵义为 extended verbal expression in speech or writing，而 word 又

显宽泛，脱离了语境，不够专业；所以，可理解为词语或术语，即 term；"源自"似乎是 root，但应用其过去式，而更恰当的应为 originated in/from；enlighten 是动词，此处应为名词 enlightenment；modern 固然是个形容词，但 modernizing 更能体现一个过程，故全句不妨译为："As a modern term, however, 'enlightenment' originated in the modernizing West."。

之后，同样在［3］中，原文以简洁的笔触概述了"启蒙"的发展过程："在人类历史上，近代启蒙思想和启蒙运动首发于17世纪后期的英国，后传播到法国、德国等欧洲国家，波及北美，19世纪后期又影响到日本、中国等亚洲国家。"这当中是有几个层次的，须予表述："首发于""后传播到""波及"。一般参赛译文对此有所忽略，译得过于"平铺"，缺少层次变化与有机衔接，如："In human beings history, the thought and movement of modern enlightenment began in Britain in the late 17th Century, it expanded to France, Germany and other European countries as well as North America. It affected Japan and China and other Asian countries in the late 19th Century."。其实，不妨用此句式：In human history, ... started in... spread to... been influenced... 等，故不妨译为："In human history, enlightenment ideas and movements started in England, and then spread to France, Germany and other European countries as well as North America in the late 17th century. By the late 19th century such Asian countries as Japan and China had also been influenced."

对启蒙的定义和评价，应当说，与对其语境背景的理解紧密相关。就［4］中的历史背景而言，18—19世纪是西方资本主义的发展和上升阶段，与之相伴的启蒙与现代性所追求的是人性和社会的进步与发展。参赛者对于"<u>正是由于</u>西方有了洛克、斯密、伏尔泰、卢梭、狄德罗等启蒙思想家，才有了之后欧美的工业革命、商品经济和宪政体制"的翻译，一般都能做到意思基本正确，但缺乏对于前后因果关联的强调，如"There were the enlightenment thinkers including Locke, Smith, Voltaire, Rousseau, Diderot and so on to promote the industrial revolution, market economy and constitutional system in Europe and America."等，<u>显然缺失了</u>诸如"It was precisely because (the emergence of enlightenment thinkers…)""It was due to…""Thanks to the contributions made by…"等的介词短语引领，未形成有效句式。例如，"<u>It was due to</u> the <u>mobilization</u> of some enlightenment thinkers in the West represented by Locke, Smith, Voltaire, Rousseau and Diderot, <u>that</u> bred the Industrial Revolution, commodity economy and constitutionalism in Europe and America."其中，It was due to… that… 形成因果关系，而 mobilization 属增译（因原文并无此词），以此翻译出其实质内涵。

就中国的启蒙背景而言，历经了辛亥革命、新文化运动、五四运动等，但当时的知识分子并没有使用"启蒙"这一术语，也没有提出明确的启蒙概念；如今学者对于中国近代前期启蒙思想的表述是以"启蒙话语"建构的方式进行的。20世纪30年中后期，一些进步知识分子在总结五四运动经验的基础上，提出了"新启蒙"的概念，并发起了一场"新启蒙运动"。1937年

5月,张申府在《实报》"星期偶感"栏目发表《什么是新启蒙运动》一文,指出:"启蒙就是打破欺蒙,扫除蒙蔽,廓清蒙昧。因此,在字典上,所谓启蒙就是脱离迷信,破除成见等等的意思。凡是启蒙运动必有三个特性。一是理性的主宰;二是思想的解放;三是新知识新思想的普及。"① 这里的"理性"是指做事要有根据,重事实和逻辑。到了20世纪80年代,随着改革开放的进程,中国学界再次掀起了新启蒙运动的高潮,其主流是翻译、引进西方近代以个人主义为核心的自由主义思想。进入21世纪以来,中国学者们对于启蒙涵义的探讨并没有停止。刘擎认为,中国学界对于启蒙的理解和态度发生了变化;启蒙就是从蒙昧状态走向光明的过程,目的是建立理性的现代社会。② 这些都为我们理解此处原文提供了不可或缺的背景知识。因而,对于[4]中"在中国,自晚清时期出现近代启蒙思想后……"的翻译理解应该也是历史性的,即以历史为背景下的解释性翻译(explanatory translation)。例如,对于"借助"(西方近代思想),许多人用了 borrowed、with the help of、drew support from、in virtue of、in line with 等,虽字面对等,但似乎都不如 influenced by the West 更符合历史事实,即形成句式"In China, influenced by the West, enlightenment ideas occurred…, which resulted in…",以贴近其真实发生、发展过程。

---

① 见丁守和(主编),《中国近代启蒙思潮》(下卷),北京:社会科学文献出版社,1999年,第168页。
② 见许纪霖(主编),《启蒙的遗产与反思》,南京:江苏人民出版社,2010年,第11页。

在［7］中，"在中国，几千年的封建农业社会，使得科学科技落后、法治传统缺乏"，是一种并列叙述，如何使其衔接顺畅又错落有致，须费思量。参赛译文如："However, in China, thousands of years of feudal agricultural society makes the technology backward and lacks traditional rule of law"，似略显平铺，且语法值得商榷；"As to China, impeded by feudal agricultural society in thousands of years, China was lagged behind the world in its technology development and lack of the tradition of rule by law"，试图做些变化，但不免捉襟见肘，出现纰漏；"China saw its backwardness in science and technology as well as the lack of legal traditions caused by thousands years of feudal agricultural society" "Through thousands years of feudalism, Chinese people valued agriculture than science, technologies and laws"等，变通似乎是有效的，但表现力又显不足，特别是对于"法治传统缺乏"，很容易与前文唐突。故此，不妨译为："However Chinese society, dominated by feudalist agriculture for thousands of years, experienced sluggish development of science and technology and a barren legal tradition."当然，也许这并非是最佳版本。

即便是些简单句子，若不注意，也会有"脱节"之感。如［2］的"没有启蒙就没有现代化"，许多人译成"no enlightenment, no modernization" "no modernization without enlightenment"等，彼此孤立无缘，显然不如"In that way, modernization could not be achieved without enlightenment."或"In other words, without enlightenment there would be no modernization."

这种语义间的融通,与其说是一种语言技巧,不如说是一种语言思维的意识以及对相关背景知识的理解与运用。

3. 语篇的整合

在语义融通的基础上,需进一步注重语篇的整合,即信与顺在更高层次上的统一。

对于什么是"语篇",目前学术界有着不同的定义,这里不妨采用胡壮麟的观点,即语篇是"不完全受句子语法约束的在一定语境下表示完整语义的自然语言"。广义上,包括"话语"(discourse)和"篇章"(text),可以是一个词、一个短语或词组,甚至一个小句[1];狭义上,则可将其看作是大于句子的单位[2],即所谓的"超句结构"(super-sentence structure)。这里实际涉及狭义、广义两个方面。

在[1]中,对于"'启蒙'的本义是开启蒙昧,识字读书,明白事理",许多参赛译文采用这种句式:The literal meaning of enlightenment is to eliminate ignorance, to learn to write, and to read and to acquire common sense…。姑且不论用词的准确性,单在形式上就给人一种珠子洒落一地的感觉,需要用线穿起

---

[1] 胡壮麟,《语篇的衔接与连贯》,上海:上海外语教育出版社,1994年,第1页。

[2] 哈特曼、斯托克,《语言与语言学词典》,黄长著等译,上海:上海辞书出版社,1981年,第104页。

来，如上文所列，以 be 动词、不定式、介词、动名词、连词等形成相互连接的结构，如 … was to… by-v-ing… how to… and…等。同时，"……人们从小要接受'蒙学'，才能成为……，否则就是……"，其中也不乏层次与转合，如不妨采用此句式：… from their childhood, … had to… in order to/before they could... and avoid… or otherwise being… 等。

对于"早年被启蒙到了什么程度，决定其日后可达到的智力高度"，较多的译文使用了这种叙述："It is said that the education in one's childhood will determine his or her intelligence in the future" "It is said that the early enlightenment is to the extent related to his or her late intelligence" "It is said that the enlightenment of early stage is to what extent could decide a person's intelligence in the future"等，其中看不出"什么程度"与"（什么）智力高度"之间的内在的有机联系，故不如使用 … how far/high… (largely depends on/greatly relies on) … how well/much… 等，使其相互呼应，凝聚在一起。

同时，标点符号的运用在语篇的整合中也起到重要作用。例如［5］中，"长期以来，人们对于启蒙运动有一种误解……因而'启蒙'成了及物动词，其宾语是未开化的芸芸众生"，其中，前面讲的是文化，后是语言，或者说是从语言的角度来阐释文化，是一种转换了视角的补充与递进的说明，故不妨放入括号之中，如："Enlightenment has for quite some time been mistaken for a movement... (obviously, "enlighten" has been used as a transitive verb which takes the populace as its object of mobilization)." 其中的 object，既做 transitive verb 的宾语，又做 mobilization 的对象，形成了一种双关语。同时，将括号中的内容（在缺乏指导下无力运用自我理性的状态）提出，如上所述，形成从句。

同样，［7］中的"只是受到近代西方启蒙思想的影响（包括马克思主义）"，参赛译文大都按照原文的形式，译成"included Marxism"，其实完全可以展开，形成一种整体感："It was not until modern times that China, under the influence of Western enlightenment ideas including Marxism, …"

在［8］中，"在这一历史大潮中，中国现在比历史上任何时期都更接近中华民族的伟大复兴"，可以正说，如："Following the historical trend, China is now closer to its rejuvenation than at any other time in history."亦可反说，如："In such a long history, China was never closer than now to the Chinese nation's great rejuvenation ." "正如'一带一路'被越来越多的国家认识到不是中国的独角戏，而是沿路民族的大合唱，每个中国人对于客观与主观世界的深刻、自觉的理性开发，最终将汇集于前所未有的中国梦的实现"，许多人忽视了介词"正如……（那样）"，其潜台词是，"所以中国梦是每个中国人汇聚一起的合力"，而许多参赛者译成："<u>An increasing number of countries have realized that Belt and Road Initiative is not monodrama of China, but the chorus of all the countries alongside. If every Chinese could rationally dig the subjective world and objective world deeply and automatically, we will realize the Chinese Dream</u>

that has never ever seen before."这就使得前后两部分相脱节,从而也就失去了以"一带一路"中"大合唱"做比喻的意义。所以,应当使用 just as…、in the same way 等介词或短语等连接方式,将其段落整合在一起。

此外,关于段落符号,参赛规则虽然没有规定要注明,但大部分写上了就一目了然,而没有写的就不够清楚,有的还将整个段落漏译。经验值得记取。

综上所述,对本篇"启蒙"概念、涵义及相关历史作用的翻译,首先应在各种辨析之中求得术语的确切,进而在语义层面得到融通(包括对背景知识的理解与运用);在此基础上,还应着眼语篇意义的衔接与完整性,从而使译文既信且顺,浑然一体。

隐私：现代社会的文明概念

中国的传统文化对于"隐私"性质的概念是排斥和贬低的，并很容易将其混同于"阴私""阴暗""丑陋""侮辱""亵渎""不正当性行为"及其他有伤风化的事。古代君子标榜"慎独""君子坦荡荡""吾一生无不可语人者"，追求的是"内圣外王"的光明文化人格，因而在很大程度上压抑了个人隐私发展的正当性和可能性。查了一下著名的《辞海》（1989年版），竟然没有"隐私"和"隐私权"的条目。[1]

改革开放前，我们的社会受极左思想影响很深，那时任何与"私"沾边的事情都与"公"相对立，是落后、不光彩，甚至反动的。[2]

在语义上，该词由英语 privacy 翻译而来，指一种个人隐匿、隐遁，免于公开和受外来干扰的状态。在西方，到了20世纪中叶这种隐私观念形成了"隐私权"的法律意识和法律条文。因而，隐私、隐私观念、隐私权的漫长演变过程，实际记录了人类在物质文明与精神文明方面的发展历程。[3]

就人的本性而言，"羞耻之心"是人区别于动物的一种智慧。据《圣经》记载，在亚当和夏娃偷吃了分辨善恶的果子之后，第一件事便是用无花果的叶子为自己的赤身裸体编做裙子，而这种"护外阴"的心态便是人类认识隐私的开端。[4]

实际上，每个人都有与公共利益无关、不愿让人知道的个人信息，不便告人的个人私事以及不宜让人涉入的私人领域。换言之，一个人，无论其职业、地位、身份如何，在每天的生活中，不可能时时刻刻都以同一种面目出现。若真可能，要么此人不知变换自己的角色与责任，要么是个伪君子。[5]

二十多年前，我初到西方国家，感受最深的一点，是对于他人私人空间的尊重。体现在小事上，如排队时在人与人之间留够了距离，不像在中国"贴"得那么紧。又如，对于他人的私人信息绝不打听，而中国人则视打听私人信息为对他人"体贴入微"的关心。[6]

在某种意义上讲，隐私是一种特殊的独立，而隐私权是对于自己何时、何地、以怎样的方式进入社会关系的一种选择权和控制权。因而，没有了隐私，也就没有了个性。[7]

其实，界定了"隐私"概念和具体涵义，对于社会中人与人之间的关系便建立起了一种无形的安全网，否则"你的也是我的，我的也是你的"，实在不利于维持有效的社会秩序和对于独立人格的尊重。人格权，是每个人"生则带来，死则带走"的最基本的权利。[8]

我国是《世界人权宣言》的缔约国，也是《公民权利和政治权利国际公约》的加入国，这两部国际法是目前我国进行隐私保护可参照的最高层次的国际法律体系。[9]

事实表明，无隐私便无自由；一个隐私得不到保护的社会，不会是安定的社会。一个社会的物质和精神生活水平越高，对于人格权和隐私权就越重视，这也是其制度自信、理论自信和文化自信的一个方面。[10]

译 文

Privacy: A Civilized Concept in Modern Society

In traditional Chinese culture, any ideas regarding the nature of privacy are easily related to things offending public decency, such as "shameful secret", "dark side", "ugliness", "indignity", "blasphemy", "extramarital affairs", and have therefore to be repudiated or belittled. Conventionally, what admired by men of noble character in ancient China were confession, broad-mindedness and openness in a way that nothing should ever be concealed. In pursuing the "open-hearted personality" (characterized as "sageness within and kingliness without"), people's legitimate privacy was largely oppressed in almost every possible way. Surprisingly, there are no entries of "privacy" or "right of privacy" in the widely authorized *Unabridged Dictionary* (1989 edition) in China. [1]

Before the "Reform and Opening Up", China was under the severe influence of ultra-left thought, where everything related to "self" was deemed to be in contradiction to public interest, backward, shameful, even reactionary. [2]

Etymologically, the word *yinsi* (隐私) in Chinese is translated from English "privacy", denoting a state where individual hidden and eluded matters are immune from publicity. In the West, the concept of privacy started to take shape as the right of privacy was defined in legal terms in mid-20th century, resulting in legal consciousness and legal provision. In that way, the gradual evolution of privacy as a value and as a right witnesses a development in both the physical and spiritual well-being of human civilization. [3]

It is the human sense of shyness that differentiates man, as an intelligent being, from other creatures. As it is recorded in the Bible, having eaten the fruits of the tree of knowledge, the first thing Adam and Eva did was to weave fig leaves to cover their naked bodies; the awareness of concealing vulvae was perhaps the starting point of human privacy. [4]

Everyone has some information, matters or areas, irrelevant to public interest, that are inconvenient or inappropriate to be noticed, revealed or intruded upon. In other words, it is impossible for anyone, regardless of profession, status or identity, to appear the same 24 hours a day unless a hypocrisy or a failure to switch roles between different social responsibilities are to take place. [5]

When I first visited a country in the West about twenty years ago, what impressed me most was a respect for personal space, reflected even in trivial things. For instance, when people are queuing up they keep a set distance from one another, unlike the Chinese who always "intimately attach" to one another. As for others' personal information, Westerners normally and consciously take their hands off, while Chinese will traditionally have a hand on as a gesture of caring or concern for others. [6]

In a sense, as privacy symbolizes independence, the right of privacy entails the right for a person to choose and control when, how and in what ways to engage in social intercourse. Without privacy one would lose personhood. [7]

Defining the concept and connotations of "privacy" actually completes a safety net to maintain social order and a respect for personality that is the basic right a person is endowed with from the day he or she is born. Alternatively, a state of "all mine are thine, and all thine are mine" can only confuse boundaries and cause social chaos. [8]

China is the contracting state of the *Universal Declaration of Human Rights* and the acceding state of *International Covenant on Civil and Political Rights*, the two international laws are now highly referencable when dealing with privacy infringements in China. [9]

All facts show that it's hard to achieve stability in a society where no privacy is protected and consequently freedom is out of the question. As people's material and spiritual living standards improve in a society, the right of privacy and the right of personality will be much accounted of as part of its strength in the system, belief and culture. [10]

> 深度解析

比较法视阈下的"隐私"概念翻译

世界上各个国家、地区的法律千差万别,但又互相影响,于是有了比较法学、比较法律文化的研究,对于某些法律概念的分析与翻译别有意义。中国法律意义上的"隐私"概念,便是一例。

比较法的基础是对于法律文明的分类,通常划分的范畴,如:法律体系(legal system)、法系(legal family, legal genealogy)、法律文化(legal culture)、法律传统(legal tradition)、法律类型(legal type)、法律模式(pattern of law)、法律集团(legal group)、法圈(Rechtskreis)等。其中最为广泛接受和应用的是法系和法律传统,此为分析、翻译法律概念的前提。

就法系而言,该词由"法"(law)和"系"(family, genealogy)构成,在词根上源自生物遗传学。按其观点,生物体的生理构造、机能、特征可由上一代传给下一代;同样,"法系"指具有共同起源,从而具有亲缘关系的众多国家或地区的法所构成的族系。而对于法系的分类,比较权威的是达维德(Davide)的"四分法",即罗马-日耳曼法系、普通法系、社会主义法系、其他法系[①]。然而,就中国来讲,此种分类法又不

[①] 达维德,《当代主要法律体系》,漆竹生译,上海:上海译文出版社,1984年,第24页。

十分确切,因为中国法律体系基本属于大陆法系(即第一种),但又没有其通常在《宪法》及一般法律工具书中界定的"隐私权"([9][1])。同时,经过三十余年的改革开放,中国的法律范畴又超过了正统的社会主义法系;除了参与了《世界人权宣言》和《公民权利和政治权利国际公约》([9])外,还有其自身文化上的许多特性,如"慎独"等([1])因素,对此又须从法律传统上去分析。

在比较法学家看来,法律传统是指在过去的社会实践中积累而成,经过世代传承、演化、流传至今的法律知识、经验、制度和行为方式,及一系列根深蒂固并受制于历史的法律观念,包括有关法律的性质、法律在社会和国家中的地位、法律体系如何组织和运作等理念与方式①。究其根源,[1]中的那些中国特色词语,主要源于中国德治主义的法律传统。自古,中国的德与礼、德治与礼治便相提并论,重德与礼而轻法与制。如《荀子》说:"闻修身,未尝闻为国也。君者仪也,民者景也,仪正而景正。君者盘也,民者水也,盘圆而水圆"(《荀子·君道》);孔子更是强调"其身正,不令而行,其身不正,虽令不从"(《论语·子路》)等,重视的是道德修养和光明磊落的品格。"君子坦荡荡,小人长戚戚"(《论语·述而》),自然不但没有什么可以隐瞒的,而且还会加以鄙视。而要恰当地译出这些颇富文化涵义的概念,须在语义和句式上做些适当的梳理与变通。例如,"慎独"一般似可译成 inner concentration,但又须融入"君子"

---

① John H. Merryman. *The Civil Law Tradition* (2nd ed). Stanford, CA: Stanford University Press, 1985, p. 2.

之德而"坦荡荡",若译成"expansive, like a plastic bag",又无 open 之意;有的词典将"君子坦荡荡"译成"A gentleman is calm and poised",似乎完美,但在此语境中却失去了"耻于隐瞒"的重点,而"吾一生无不可语人者"又与此相重叠,故不妨将二者合译。"内圣外王"似有多种译法,如 a learning both sound in theory and practice、inner cultivation and exterior action、Saint and Emperor、being saintly inside and kingly outside、a saint in his heart and lording outside 等,但要与"光明文化人格"搭配自然,不宜唐突。显然,最佳方式是将其内涵整合在一起:"Conventionally, what admired by men of noble characters in ancient China were confession, broadmindedness and openness in a way that nothing should ever be concealed." 同时,又与"压抑了个人隐私发展的正当性和可能性"形成对比:"In pursuing the 'open-hearted personality' (characterized as 'sageness within and kingliness without'), people's legitimate privacy had largely been oppressed in almost every possible way." 当然,这不是唯一的组合方式。

[2] 中的"私",似乎可用 private、personal、secret、selfish 等,但这里指个体与公共利益的关系,private 主要是私有性,其涵义更丰富(详见 [3]);personal 为个人的,secret 主要为隐藏之意,selfish 为自私等,都不够确切。而 self,本义为"the type of person you are, your character, your typical behavior; one's own private interests, wishes, hopes, etc.",指的是客观的"自我",如 by one's self(独自,单独)、have no thought of

self（绝无个人打算）、one's better/worse self（本性中善良/邪恶的一面）等。同时，又要注意与下文［7］中的"个性"、［8］中的"人格权"的区别。

［3］中主要探讨了由英文 private/privacy 引发或引申的隐私、隐私观念、隐私权、隐匿、隐遁等概念。就原义来讲，privacy 指个人隐匿、隐遁，免于公开、受外来干扰的状态，与公共生活相对立，是私人生活领域。在汉语里，由于法律传统和法律文化的差异，竟然没有与 privacy 相对等的词语；然而，语言与语言所指现象的关系是专断的，其边界也是臆断的，在人们的长期生活中有所演化。于是，倚仗汉语的强大造词功能，将"隐"和"私"相结合，造出一个与 privacy 相对应的新词（"隐私"），表明中国人对这一概念的独特理解。

就"隐"字而言，大致有这样一些涵义：隐蔽（《说文》："隐，蔽也"）、隐瞒（《论语·子路》："父为子隐，子为父隐"）、隐测（《晋书·庾冰传》："又隐实户口，料出无名万余人，以充军实"）、怜悯（《孟子·梁惠王》："隐其无罪"）、隐逸不出（《论语·微子》："隐者也"）、隐没（《国语·齐语》："隐武事，行文道"）等。而"私"字的涵义，包括：本义从禾，（《说文》段玉裁注："盖禾有名私者也"）、男女阴部（《赵飞燕外传》："早有私病，不近妇人"）、日常衣服（《诗·周南·葛覃》："薄污我私"）、私田（《诗·小雅·大田》："雨我公田，遂及我私"）、诸侯国君的嬖臣妾媵（《国语》："君多私"）等。

概括来讲，"隐"主要有两层意思：一是隐匿，秘而不宣；

一是隐遁，生活态度。正所谓"有道则仕，无道则隐"，"大隐隐于朝，中隐隐于市，小隐隐于野"。"私"则限于个人享有的具体事物，如庄稼、私田、衣服、家臣、妾媵等。在拥有个人财产为"私"这个意义上，中西文化又是相通的。

然而，正如[1]中所述，在中国语境里，"隐私"曾常常与"阴私"等相混同，这主要是由于在我国压抑个人权利和泛道德化的传统背景下，男女不可告人之事成为对隐私的当然解释，因为"在人类社会形成的初期，……人们尚无更多的身外之物可供支配。因此，人类的隐私意识仅能及于自己的身体；在文明尚未达到现代程度时，人们只认识到阴私需要保护，而未意识到隐私的其他部分也应得到法律保护"[①]。于是有了"难言之隐""难于启齿""不可告人"等词语来形容"隐私"，甚至凡"私"必揭，把不择手段获取来的别人的私人材料作为"证据"，从而达到政治正确的目的。在这种隐私观念下，"隐私"自然被扭曲、贬低和排斥，更难成为一项具有正当性的法律权利。

只有当一个社会的法律文明进步到一定程度时，才会对[3]中涉及的有关隐私的概念及表述做出较为理性、恰当的解释和翻译。一般认为，"隐私"是 privacy 的翻版，但其本义其实更注重的是自我意识和感受。如其经典论述："Privacy: In traditional dualism, one assumes that whatever is mental, such as experiences, sense-data, representations or ideas, is private. This can be meant in two senses. In the first sense, my mental phenomena are

---

① 曹亦萍，《社会信息化与隐私权保护》，载《政治论坛》，1998（1），第70—71页。

inalienably owned by me. Only I have them. In the second sense, only I have access to my mental phenomena. They are incommunicable. Only I am in a position to know or to feel that I am in pain. This idea leads to skepticism about other minds, for one can never know whether another person is in pain or not. It also leads to solipsism, for if all experiences must be interpreted through my private experience, the world can only be my world."[①]（隐私：传统的二元论认为，任何"心智"都是私人的，如个人经验、感知数据、表象、理念等。这有两种涵义，一是心智现象专属自己（"自我"的一部分）；二是心智之事自我得知，不可他传——心痛与否，唯己感知。这也容易导致对他人的怀疑论，因他人痛痒永远不得而知。同时也产生了自我论，因若所有经验都须亲历而释，则世界便成为自我世界。）当然，privacy 的涵义也有了进一步的引申。由此看来，"隐私"与 privacy/private 并不完全相等，前者在某种意义上大于后者。如上所述，personal 也有 in a private way 之义："Let's talk about this difficult matter personally."（咱们私下聊聊这件棘手的事吧。）secret 强调的是 is not told or shown to anyone else："They actually met at a secret meeting."（他们竟然私下里见了面。）而 selfish 虽有"私"义，但唯私而为，似有过之；然而，在"自私"与"隐私"相比较的语境下，其"私"义又可成立，如："In a civilized society, one should be clear about the nuance between 'selfishness' and 'privacy'."（在一

[①] 布宁、余纪元（编著），《西方哲学英汉对照辞典》，北京：人民出版社，2001 年，第 811 页。

个文明社会里，人们应该清楚地界定"私"的细微涵义。）此外，还有 intimacy，如："Perhaps, he should also know that the intimacy of what staff get up to in their bathrooms is outside the remit of managers."（他大概还应知道，员工在洗手间做的私事，不属经理职权范围之内。）另有 intimity，如："The design of the environment reminds people of their desire for intimity, protection, trust and safety."（这种环境设计使人想到人们对隐私、保护、信任和安全的渴望。）

同样在［3］中，"隐私观念"一般译成 privacy concept、the idea of privacy、considerations over privacy、attitude towards privacy 等，但就本文而言，考虑到其文化及法律传统，以 value（来组合 privacy）似乎更为确切，该词的本义为 the moral principles and beliefs that people think are important，特别是结合上下文，译为 … privacy as a value and as a right… 更切语境，也更通顺。关于"隐私权"，如前所述，这是中国法律传统中所空缺、后来引进的现代法律概念，通常为 right of privacy、privacy right 等。其实，该概念还可细分。根据《布莱克法律辞典》（*Black's Law Dictionary*）[①]，至少有这样三种涵义：a. the right to be alone（个人独处的权利）；b. the right of a person to be free from unwarranted publicity（未经授权，免于公开的权利）；c. The right of live without unwarranted interference by the public in matters with which the public is not necessarily concerned（在与公众无关的事务上不受公众无端干涉的

---

① Bryan A. Garner (ed.). *Black's Law Dictionary* (8th ed). St. Pall, MN: Thomson West, 2004.

权利）。特别是对于"私密领域"（intimate sphere）的研究，又包括：自我领域（Eigen sphere）、隐秘领域（Geheim sphere）、个人领域（individual sphere）、私生活领域（private sphere）、人格领域（personal sphere）等。①

［6］中涉及的"私人空间"，是西方隐私权研究领域的一个重要课题。特别是霍尔（Edward T. Hall）提出的"人际距离学"（Proxemics）理论，按亲近关系，将人与人之间的关系分为亲密距离（intimate distance）、个人距离（personal distance）、社会距离（social distance）和公共距离（public distance）等。②也有学者将其划分为不同的区域：a. 身体区域（Body Territory），即维持其生存的活动空间（"bubble" that one maintains around their person）；b. 初级区域（Primary Territory），即个人居所、车辆及其他生活空间（one's home, vehicle or other living space）；c. 中级区域（Secondary Territory），即为个人特殊目的所建造的场所，如学校、办公室、教会等（a structured place where entry is reserved for special purposes of individuals, such as school, office or church）；d. 公共区域（Public Territory），即人人可去的公开场所，如公园、商场等（an open space where anyone can come and go, such as a park

---

① 简荣宗，《网路上资讯隐私权保障问题之研究》，台湾：东吴大学法律学研究所，硕士学位论文，2000年。

② Edward T. Hall *The Hidden Dimension*, New York: Anchor Books Edition. 1990, pp.116-126.

or shopping mall）。① 就此处"私人空间"的翻译而言，一般可用private space，但在"隐私权"（right of privacy）的语境下，为有所区分，亦可译为personal space。

[7]中的"个性"很容易译成individuality、character、personality、selfhood、selfdom等，其中除了personality（[8]）外，其他都不是法律用语，故不妨考虑personhood，该词的本义为the condition of being a person who is an individual with inalienable rights，用在这里是从法律角度考量人的个性，也有法律人格之意。例如："The very same moment will be the end of his body, the end of his existence, and the end of his personhood."（那一刻便是他形体的灭亡，存在的停止，个性的消失。）"Modern medical treatment requires communication skills, empathy, self-awareness, judgment, professionalism as well as mastering the social and cultural context of personhood, illness and health care."（现代医疗需要沟通技巧，同情心，自我意识，专业判断，专业背景，以及掌握社会文化背景下的人的个性，疾病情况和保健护理。）"It's not just medical questions raised by personhood laws."（法律人格争论不仅仅提出了一个医学问题。）

[8]中的"人格权"（personality），根据《牛津法律大辞典》（*The Oxford Companion to Law*）的解释：In law, personality is the legal quality of being a legal person, i.e. a unit capable of sustaining and exercising legal rights and being subject to legal duties

---

① 见http://www.communicationstudies.com/communication-theories/proxemics。

and liabilities.(在法律上，人格权是法人的实体，使其能够具有和行使法律责任和义务。)同时，也指出其特殊性：It is for each legal system to prescribe whether and in what circumstances it will attribute legal personality to particular kinds of persons, groups, entities, institutions and the like.[①]（对某一具体个人、团体、实体、机构等的法律人格的界定，取决于不同的法律制度。）可谓经典。

此外，[10]中的"无隐私便无自由"未译成 Whenever there is no privacy there will be no freedom，而是与"隐私得不到保护的社会"的意思相结合，整合为"in a society where no privacy is protected and consequently freedom is out of the question"。"自信"也未必总是 confidence、assurance 等，亦可用 strength，如"这次事件反而使我们充满了勇气和自信"（On the contrary, this incident fills us with courage and strength.），特别是融合于句式"as part of its strength in the system, belief and culture"中，更显平实。

综上所述，翻译诸如"隐私"及其相关的法律概念时，对于法律语言的透彻理解，显然离不开比较法学的研究成果，特别是比较法律文化学、传统比较法学及法律移植学等。唯其如此，才不致囿于语言本身。

---

① David M. Walker (ed.). *The Oxford Companion to Law*. New York: Oxford University Press, 1980, p. 931.

独处是一种能力

随着科技的迅猛发展，人们的交往、信息的传递变得异常便利，这固然是社会的进步。但也有副作用，那便是使独处似乎越来越难了。[1]

电脑、电视等，特别是手机已经成为现代人须臾不可离开的工具，它们简直革命化了人们之间的交往形式。离开了这些，有的人会发慌，不知道该做什么。人们曾经渴望独立，但现在又怕被孤立。过去认为，人的社交是一种能力，可如今发现独处其实需要更强的能力。[2]

试想，一个人现在要想完全地静下来，需要克服多少来自各方信息的干扰！说"干扰"并不准确，因为它们好像又确实有用。这就需要能力——判断、平衡、处理、自制的能力。[3]

作为社会的人，交往和独处是两种不可或缺的生活方式。正如身体需要不断摄取能量，人的精神层面也需要不断补充新的信息；但信息不等于知识、思想和情感，它需要沉淀下来，慢慢地被转化和整合，而这些不是在乱哄哄的社交而是在静静的独处中完成的。在西方，人们相信"灵魂在寂静中成长"；在中国，孔子"吾日三省吾身"方成圣人。[4]

这种转化和整合的过程，是在已有的与未有的知识和情感之间建立起联结，形成增长。故在这个意义上讲，一个人的独处能力，也决定了其能否有所长进。[5]

世界三大宗教的创立，都是在独处中完成的：释迦牟尼独自离家后，在尼连禅河畔的菩提树下数日冥想，然后大彻成佛；耶稣一人在旷野里思索了四十天，然后向世人宣布了救世的好消息；穆罕默德每年斋月期间，都要去洞窟里隐居。同样，许多艺术上的杰作也是在孤独中诞生的。[6]

在西方，独处又往往是与亲近大自然联系在一起的。例如，"真正的英国不在喧闹的城市而在僻静的乡村"。[7]

独处并不等于孤独，这是两个性质不同的概念。一个人可以在看似热闹的社交中很孤独，也可以在平静的独处中很丰富——从各个方面丰富和充实自己。"孤独的丰富"是一种理想的高尚境界。[8]

其实，无论中西方，"德不孤，必有邻"（孔子语），"善思者虽独不孤"（英文谚语），他们自有内在的人格魅力。而且，两个丰富、充实的灵魂之间的交流，才会是更有质量的交往。[9]

所以，要不断体验深层次的阅读、思索与感受，就不能不培养和提高自己的独处能力。[10]

译　文

Practising Solitude Requires Special Ability

The rapid advance of technology has made communication and

transmission of data among people extremely convenient. But social progression of this kind nevertheless has a "side-effect" – solitude is increasingly becoming something that is hard to attain. [1]

Computers, television and especially smart phones have revolutionized the way people communicate, becoming their most intimate companions. Some may panic when they are deprived of these things. People used to long for independence but now deeply fear alienation; social intercourse was regarded as a special competence, which has now been overshadowed by the ability to be alone. [2]

Just think how hard it is now for a person to settle down completely – he or she has to surmount interruptions from all sorts of information emitted from various sources. "Interruption" as used here may not be the right word, since the information it brings in may sometimes be useful. Judgment, a balanced approach, appropriate handling and self-control are thus sorely needed. [3]

As a social being, humans need both social intercourse and solitude, just as the body and mind require physical as well as spiritual energies and inputs. In terms of mentality, however, for information to be transformed and integrated into knowledge, thoughts and feelings as something of one's own, serenity instead of bustle seems to be the right condition. In the Western tradition, it is believed that "the soul grows in tranquility"; in China, Confucius' "repeated introspection on a daily basis" made him a saint. [4]

The process of transformation and integration is achieved by establishing connections between the knowledge and sentiments one already acquired with those newly received, which results in growth. In this sense, the capacity for solitude determines how well one can continuously mature in society. [5]

The three largest world religions were actually all established in solitude: Sakyamuni left home alone and meditated several days under banyan trees by the Nairanjana before his great awakening produced Buddhism; Jesus contemplated in the wilderness for forty days and then declared the good news of salvation for the world; Mohammed lived in seclusion in caves during his Ramadan. Similarly, many artistic masterpieces of the world were produced in solitude. [6]

In the West, solitude is also deemed to put people in contact with nature. For example, as the saying goes, "The real character of England lies not in the flamboyant cities but in its quiet countryside". [7]

Being alone doesn't have to be lonely – these are two different things. One may feel lonely in boisterous social contexts, or be fulfilled in isolated serenity. Thus, being enable to enrich oneself calmly and live in "solitary richness" is a noble state one can only dream of. [8]

In today's overcrowded world (both in China and in the West), "Virtue does not remain isolated" (Confucius), "He is never alone who is accompanied by noble thoughts" (English proverb) – personal charisma ultimately radiates out to attract others, and interactions between two abundant minds usually breed something more meaningful. [9]

In this way, anyone wishing to enjoy in-depth reading, insightful thinking and a meaningful sense of feeling, certain kind of competence in practising solitude has to be nurtured and exercised. [10]

深度解析

微妙之处寻等值

"等值"(equivalence)、"等值翻译"(equivalent translation)是译界的著名概念,学者们进行了多方面的研究,提出过各种学说和见解,然而在翻译实践中每次又会有新的发现。

就实质而言,仍源于美国翻译理论家雅各布森(Jakobson)的著名论断,即"不同之中觅等值"(equivalence in difference),而"代码单位之间通常不存在完全的对等"(There is ordinarily no full equivalence between code-units)[1],于是其中便大有文章,因为这个"不同"可指种类、性质、层面、维度等方面,对此有学者将其分为音位、词素、词汇、词组、句子、话语等多个方面进行等值分析[2]。然而,有一个问题横跨这些领域,那便是关于

---

① Roman Jakobson. "On Linguistic Aspects of Translation". In L. Venuti (ed.), *The Translation Studies Reader*. London and New York: Routledge, 2000, p.139.

② 见方梦之(主编),《中国译学大辞典》,上海:上海外语教育出版社,2011年,第74页。

"微妙"等值的处理。

在翻译实践中，科勒（Koller）将翻译对等分为五种情况，而笔者认为其中三种最为实用，即形式对等（formal equivalence），内涵对等（connotative equivalence），语用对等（pragmatic equivalence）①。

该篇的核心词语是"独"——独处、孤独、独立、孤立等，就形式对应（formal equivalence）而言，大致可有 alone、lonely、loneness、single、sole、only、unique、solitary、solitude、isolate、isolation 等，但在理论上讲，这些还都是"可能传达性"，而"本质上，语言间的差异在其必须传达什么，而不在其可能传达什么"（Languages differ essentially in what they must convey and not in what they may convey.）②。

进一步细化到内涵对等（connotative equivalence），可发现涵义最集中的两个词汇是 solitude 和 loneliness，其中的微妙所指，须不只从定义而更要从语境中详加辨析。具体而言，solitude 本义为 "the state of being alone, especially when you find this pleasant"（*The New Oxford English Dictionary of English*, 2001），"when you are alone, especially when this is what you enjoy"（《朗文当代高级英语词典》第 4 版，2009），其特性是 pleasant 和 enjoy。此类的表达，可以说都代表了这种心情。

---

① 见 Koller, W. "Equivalence in translation theory". In A. Chesterman (ed.), *Readings in Translation Theory*. Helsinki: Finn Lectura, 1989, pp.186-191.

② Roman Jakobson. "On Linguistic Aspects of Translation". In L. Venuti (ed.), *The Translation Studies Reader*. London and New York: Routledge, 2000, p.116.

例如："Carl spent the morning in solitude."（那天早上卡尔一个人很清静。）"the solitude of her house on the lake"（她湖边那所房子的清静）"He likes solitude; he doesn't like big cities."（他喜欢离群索居，不喜欢大城市。）"Reading well is one of the great pleasures that solitude can afford you."（阅读是孤独能给你的快乐之一。）"Do not like noise, to be willing to enjoy the solitude of the mind alone."（不喜欢喧嚣，才会愿意享受独自寂寥的心境。）"She longed for peace and solitude."（她渴望安宁，渴望独享清静。）还可涉及相关的能力，如："Be able to be alone. Lose not the advantage of solitude."（要有单独自处的能力，不要放过孤寂的好处）"People need a chance to reflect on spiritual matters in solitude."（人们需要独处的机会来反思精神上的事情。）与此相关的便是 solitary，其义为 "a state of social isolation; a solitary a disposition toward being alone"，亦含有喜欢或惯于独居的意思，如："The house is in a solitary spot several kilometers from city."（那房子距城里几公里，是个僻静的好地方。）"She loved these solitary interludes."（她喜欢这些独处的空闲间歇。）"The old man usually has a solitary walk."（那老人常在那儿散散步。）故在［8］中的"孤独的丰富"用了 solitary richness，其义由 solitude 而来。loneliness（lonely）的基本特点，则是 unhappy because you are alone or do not have anyone to talk to，如："Don't you get lonely being on your own all day?"（你整天独自一人不感到孤单吗？）"He lives a lonely life with few friends."（他孤单地生活着，朋友很少。）

那么，solitude 与 loneliness 的根本区别何在？也许在这些句子中可见端倪："The motif of the book is that 'solitude is the richness of the soul, loneliness is its poverty'."（该书的主题是"孤独是灵魂的财富，寂寞是灵魂的贫瘠"。）"Solitude is sometimes the best society."（独处有时是最好的状态。）
"Solitude restores body and mind. Loneliness depletes them."（独处滋养身心，孤独则消耗殆尽。）这些都颇显褒贬色彩。对此，美国心理学家马拉诺（Hara Estroff Marano）有过深入研究，做出这样的论断：There is a world of difference between solitude and loneliness, though the two terms are often used interchangeably. From the outside, solitude and loneliness look a lot alike. Both are characterized by solitariness. But all resemblance ends at the surface. Loneliness is marked by a sense of isolation. Solitude, on the other hand, is a state of being alone without being lonely and can lead to self-awareness. Solitude is the state of being alone without being lonely. It is a positive and constructive state of engagement with oneself. Solitude is desirable, a state of being alone where you provide yourself wonderful and sufficient company. Solitude is a time that can be used for reflection, inner searching or growth or enjoyment of some kind. Deep reading requires solitude, so does experiencing the beauty of nature. Thinking and creativity usually do too.（在 solitude 和 loneliness 之间有着天壤之别，尽管二者常会混用。外人看来两个词很相像，都以独处为特性，但这种相似只是表面的。loneliness 是一种孤独感，而 solitude 则是一种虽处独自状态，但

并不孤单而是充满自我意识，是一种积极性、建设性的自我整合阶段。独处是一种理想状态。独处时可有大量美妙的事可做——反省、自悟，不断成长，或品味事物；深度阅读、体验自然之美、思考、创作等，同样需要独处。）可谓在词义层面对二者的区别做了较为清晰的辨析。

进而，是对其性质方面的探讨：Solitude suggests peacefulness stemming from a state of inner richness. It is a means of enjoying the quiet and whatever it brings that is satisfying and from which we draw sustenance. It is something we cultivate. Solitude is refreshing; an opportunity to renew ourselves. In other words, it replenishes us. Loneliness is a negative state, marked by a sense of isolation. One feels that something is missing. It is possible to be with people and still feel lonely – perhaps the most bitter form of loneliness. Loneliness is harsh, punishment, a deficiency state, a state of discontent marked by a sense of estrangement, an awareness of excess aloneness. Solitude is something you choose. Loneliness is imposed on you by others.（solitude 是从内在丰富状态里外溢出的平静，是享受平静的一种方法，使我们从中得到满足，继续下去。solitude 需要培养，它也是一种更新，一种自我增值的机会，或称之为"自我充电"。而 loneliness 则是一种具有孤独感的消极状态，令人若有所失；而最让人痛苦的事，可能莫过于和人们在一起时仍然感到孤独。loneliness 是严厉的、具有惩罚性、有缺陷的状态，让人感到因被疏离和极度孤单而不安。独处是自愿的，而孤独则是被迫的。）

原来这是人的正常生活所需要的：We all need periods of solitude, although temperamentally we probably differ in the amount of solitude we need. Some solitude is essential; it gives us time to explore and know ourselves. It is the necessary counterpoint to intimacy, what allows us to have a self worthy of sharing. Solitude gives us a chance to regain perspective. It renews us for the challenges of life. It allows us to get (back) into the position of driving our own lives, rather than having them run by schedules and demands from without.[①]（我们都需要"独处期"，尽管因个人气质不同，所需独处的时间亦有不同。有些独处是必需的，因为可使我们有时间去深思自己。我们同样需要抗拒亲密，只与他人部分地分享。独处可使我们重获视野，打起精神迎接生活的挑战，把命运重新掌握在自己手里，而不至于总是让外部的计划、要求牵着走。）

故在[8]中，对于"独处并不等于孤独，这是两个性质不同的概念"译为："Being alone doesn't have to be lonely – these are two different things." 此处的 lonely 显然是有贬义的，若描述客观状态则完全可以用 alone，即只是自己过活（having no one else present; on one's own），如《圣经》写道："And the Lord God said, it is not good that the man should be alone: I will make him a help meet for him."（Genesis 2:18）（单独生活不好，我要为他造一个合适的伴侣，做他的内助。）对于接下来的"一个人可以在看似热闹的社交中很孤独，也可以在平静的独处中很丰

---

① Hara Estroff Marano. *A Nation of Wimps: The High Cost of Invasive Parenting*. New York: Broadway Books, 2008, p. 125.

富"，其中的"社交"一般用 social intercourse，但这里不应仅求形式对称，而应考虑到在 solitude 和 loneliness 之间的语用对等（pragmatic equivalence），以更显其褒贬对比色彩，故用了 social context，其本义为 the immediate physical and social setting in which people live or in which something happens or develops。接下来"孤独的丰富"中的"孤独"实则亦有褒义，虽并未用 solitude（而是用了 solitary richness），如前所述；而亚里士多德的名言"Solitary man is either a beast or an angel."（离群索居者，或凶如野兽，或善如天使。），此处可做一注脚。而［9］中的英文谚语"He is never alone who is accompanied by noble thoughts."（善思者虽独不孤），也可显出 alone 微妙的褒贬色彩。

　　［9］中的"德不孤，必有邻"此处的"孤"可理解为与外界隔离，对他人无影响，故未用上述词语，而是用了 isolate，其义主要为"to separate somebody or something physically or socially from other people or things" "put someone or something in isolation"等。例如："His phenomenal early success isolated him from his friends."（他年纪轻轻就为成功人士了，这使他在朋友中陷入了孤立。）"Retirement can often cause feelings of isolation."（退休生活常让人感到孤独。）"Elderly people living in social isolation."（生活在与社会隔绝状态中的老人。）；"Do not isolate yourself from others."（不要把自己孤立起来。）"We should never isolate ourselves from the masses."（我们永远不能脱离群众。）"It is impossible to isolate political responsibility from moral responsibility."（政治和道德责任是不可分割的。）故将该

句译为"Virtue does not remain isolated"。

与该词紧密连用的是 alienate (alienated, alienation)，其本义为"to make somebody less friendly or sympathetic towards you; alienate somebody (from something/somebody) to make somebody feel that they do not belong in a particular group"（*The New Oxford English Dictionary of English*, 2001），如："His comments have alienated a lot of young voters."（他的言论使许多年轻选民远离了他。）"Very talented children may feel alienated from the others in their class."（非常天才的儿童可能觉得被班里其他同学疏远了。）故在［2］中"（人们曾经渴望独立）但现在又怕被孤立"，用了 alienation。与此相关，age of alienation（孤独时代），即指现代社会一方面人们之间的沟通日益便利，一方面人们变得愈加孤独、疏离、异化。该术语被广泛运用于哲学、心理学、社会学、宗教学、经济学等，形成了一种个人感觉中的"疏离状态"（an objective state of estrangement or separation; the state or feeling of the estranged personality）等。美国著名心理学家弗洛姆（Eric Fromm）有此论断：The disease of a modern human being, who is estranged from herself, from her feelings, from her fellow men and from nature: alienation from both inside and outside ourselves.（这是一种现代人的病态，把自己与自我感觉、与同伴、与自然分离开来，即与内外的自我统统隔离开来。）此外，在［6］中，又将其变通为 in seclusion。

就语用等值（pragmatic equivalence）而言，如著名翻译理论家图里（Toury）指出的，"Every translation as a concrete act of performance"①(每一翻译都是具体行为),而"Substituting messages in one language not for separate code-units but for entire messages in some other language."②(替代另一种语言中的信息,不是孤立的代码单位,而是完整的意思。)进而言之,"Translation involves far more than replacement of lexical and grammatical items between languages… Once the translator moves away from close linguistic equivalence, the problems of determining the exact nature of the level of equivalence aimed for begin to emerge."③(翻译远不只是语言之间词汇和语法单元的替换,……而一旦译者不再仅仅考虑语言层面的严格对等,那么如何判定期望实现对等层面的确切效果便成了问题。)对此,美国翻译学家兰德斯(Landers)以葡语为例(其实中文亦如是)加以说明。"Nāo vou lá"(我不去那里)可译为:I do not go there / I don't go there / I am not going there / I'm not going there / I shall not go there / I shan't go there / I will not go there / I won't go there / I am not going to there / I'm not going to go there / I ain't going there / I ain't goin't there 等。④ 其中可以体现多种元素,如

---

① Gideon Toury. *In Search of a Theory of Translation*. Tel Aviv: The Porter Institute for Poetics and Semiotics, Tel Aviv University, 1980, p. 28.

② Roman Jakobson. "On Linguistic Aspects of Translation". In L. Venuti (ed.), *The Translation Studies Reader*. London and New York: Routledge, 2000, p. 138.

③ Susan Bassnett. *Translation Studies* (2nd ed.). London and New York: Routledge, 1991, p. 25.

④ Clifford E. Landers. *Literary Translation: A Practical Guide*. Shanghai: Shanghai Foreign Language Education Press, 2008, p. 8.

情感、语气、身份、心境、环境、时间、地域、口音、人际关系等等。

结合中英翻译，林语堂曾以"对他很佩服"一句为例，说明在比较典型的不同语境中至少可以有三种译文。对此不妨稍加改造，理解为——

对他很佩服
I admire him greatly.（通常情况、一般语气）［形式对等］
I admire him profoundly.（相互比较、理性分析）［内涵对等］
I take off my hat to him.（文学表述、感情色彩）［语用对等］

其中的"形式对等"多指语言文字层面的对应性，"内涵对等"更注重词义深层的联结，而"语用对等"则体现更大的灵活性和情感化。

这一点，体现在本文中"能力"的翻译，便有许多微妙之处。如，标题中的"（独处是）一种能力"，在中文里是一般性的，但考虑到其与"社交能力"相比的特殊语境，故用了 special ability；而在［2］中，则又有 special competence 和 ability 等。然而，［3］中的"（这就需要）能力"，是由四部分组成的，不是一个 ability 可以等值的，故须分解开来，由 correct judgment、a balanced approach、appropriate handling and self-control 来共同完成。此外，［3］中"一个人现在要想完全地静下来"，实则指的也是一种能力，但又不适用 ability、capacity、competence 等，因而用了 settle down，以示不易。

此种情况下的对等，在源语与译语之间可以拉开的距离是很大的，而越具中文特色的表述，这一特点便越明显。例如，"自古而今，马在中华民族文化中都是美好寓意的代表，如马到成功、万马奔腾、兵强马壮等等"，若只注重形式和内涵的对等，这些成语便很容易译成这样的模式：to win success immediately upon the arrival of the horses、ten thousand horses gallop forward、strong soldiers and sturdy horses。这样不但啰唆、重复，也与英文的表述形式相拗，故不如变通为："Since ancient times, the horse has been bestowed goodwill implications in Chinese culture. When the word *ma* (horse) is used in an idiom, it usually means <u>instant success</u> and <u>powerful strength</u>."其马之寓意涵盖在后两句之中。又如，翻译著名的禅宗四句格言"教外别传，不立文字；直指人心，见性成佛"，若囿于形式、涵义的对等，便很容易陷入此种句式：outside the scriptures, special transmission; no words are written/no dependence on; pointing straightly to human heart; seeing human nature, becoming Buddha 等。其实，这里不妨将几种对等打通，在完全理解其意的基础上，加以整合：Special transmission, outside the scriptures, with no dependence on words and letters; A direct pointing at the human mind; Seeing into one's own nature and attaining Buddhahood。

这里，没有永远的 1=1，而更多的是 1= n 或 n = 1。典型的，如"南方则吃年前蒸煮好的'陈饭'，名叫'万年余粮'，意思是年年五谷丰登，岁岁有余粮"，其中的"年"和"岁"

实则在英文里没区别，都为 year，故在翻译中便可"合并同类项"，译为 "People in south eat rice cooked before the Spring Festival, which is called 'wan nian yu liang' and suggests good harvest and surplus grains every year"，以求言简意赅。类似的，"美食天堂，异彩平添"，很容易译成 "Delicious heaven, Extraordinary splendor in riotous profusion"，其意实为 Food Paradise；而"热烈欢迎外国朋友来我校参观指导"，循文索句，便是 "Warmly welcome foreign friends come to our school for inspection!"，实意仅为 "Welcome to our school!" 或 "Our school welcomes you!" 当然，不只是"紧缩"，亦可"扩展"，如"酒好不怕巷子深"，若只是译成 "Good wine needs no bush."，似显单薄，不妨补充为：Literally, if your alcoholic beverage is good enough, consumers will not get lost in *hutongs* on their way to your distillery. That is, a really good *baijiu* (fragrant liquor) could lead the most befuddled drinker through the most complex of alleyways, or *xiangzi*, as they are referred to in Shaanxi and Shanxi provinces.

可见，Equivalence is no longer a set of criteria which translations have to live up to, but is rather the group of features (termed the *equivalence postulate*) which characterizes the particular relationships linking each individual TT with its ST: "when considered from TT's point of view, equivalence is not a postulated requirement, but an empirical fact, like TT itself."[①]（"等值"不再是不断更新的一套

---

① Gideon Toury. *In Search of a Theory of Translation*. Tel Aviv: The Porter Institute for Poetics and Semiotics, Tel Aviv University, 1980, p. 39.

标准，而是一种组合特性——可称之为"假设等值"，使得译文与原文之间形成了一种特殊的关系。因而，从译文的角度评判，等值已不是一种规定的要求，而是如其结果本身，是一种经验性的尝试。）

正是由于原文和译文间存在着的"组合特性"（the group of features）及前面所述的"对等层面的确切效果"（the exact nature of the level of equivalence），才使得二者在多种维度上存在着微妙等值关系。除了上文所做的词语分析，在一些具体表述上，亦不乏这种处理。例如，［2］中"过去认为，人的社交是一种能力，可如今发现独处其实需要更强的能力"，其中"需要更强的能力"未译成 which requires stronger capability 等，而是化解为 which has now been overshadowed by the ability to…，更显自然；［5］中，"故在这个意义上讲，一个人的独处能力，也决定了其能否有所长进"，将"有所长进"变通为 mature，并在句尾加上定语 in society，以使其意更加完整；［8］中，"从各个方面丰富、充实自己。'孤独的丰富'是一种理想的高尚境界"，本为两句，译文不但将其整合为一句，而且在最后加上 one can only dream of，以更明其意；［9］中，"其实，无论是在中西方"，未必译成 "In fact, whether in China or in the West"，因这里主要是就孤独涵义而言的，故不妨稍加释意："In today's overcrowded world (both in China and in the West)"；同时，"他们自有内在的人格魅力"，未简单地译成 they have their personal charisma，而是将其展开为 personal charisma ultimately radiates out to attract others，使其更有表现力,而"更有质量的交往"也未译成其书面意思 communication of quality,而为 interactions between two abundant minds usually breed something more meaningful,使其内涵更加饱满;[10]中,"要不断体验深层次的阅读、思索与感受,就不能不培养和提高自己的独处能力",译文为"anyone wishing to enjoy in-depth reading, insightful thinking and a meaningful sense of feeling, certain kind of competence in practising solitude has to be nurtured and exercised",其中将"体验"由 to experience 和 to enjoy 双重译出,但不显余赘,而是强调了一种积极的感受,也是一种 1=n 的模式。

  总之,翻译中的这种微妙等值处理,是在多个层面、维度上进行的;除了形式对等(formal equivalence)、内涵对等(connotative equivalence)之外,在语用对等(pragmatic equivalence)方面尤其变化多端,细致入微,需要额外的功力。

中医：一门人的系统医学

作为一种文化，中医其实不是一般意义上的医学。[1]

以西医为代表的现代医学，把人看作是解剖器官，将疾病与患者的生命相分离；在治疗过程中，检查仪器、西药是主导地位，客观条件决定一切，人处次要地位。在中医里，病症永远不会是局部的；人在治疗过程中占主导地位，药材、疗法为次要，人的因素决定一切。这主要由中医的形成和理念所决定。[2]

在中医看来，人既是自然的产物，又是自然的延伸和精华，因而人与自然服从同一法则——道；人道依存于天道，天道服务于人道。进而，形成了中医独特的整体观念和辨证论治的核心价值及治疗方论。[3]

人们试图以现代学科的分类来界定中医学，但发现很难，因为中医的对象其实不是"病"，而是"人"。然而，人是复杂的综合体，介乎自然科学、社会科学和哲学之间：既是物质的，又是精神的；既是局部的，又是整体的；既是人为的，又是自然的。因而需要多方、综合、辨证地加以考虑。[4]

中医医生眼里的疾病，不是某个器官组织的病变，而是病人整体机制出现了某种失衡。因而，治病的根本在治人。例如，人的情绪对于人的疾病和健康有着非常微妙而深刻的影响，这在西医是不可以也不愿意解释的，但却被越来越多的事实所证明。[5]

本人在国外曾从事自然疗法的研究，对此有着亲身的体会：西医"头痛医头，脚痛医脚"理念和疗法，越来越多地受到了人们的质疑，而中医的头痛医脚、眼病治肝、肾虚补脾等等，令西方人感到惊奇，因而有越来越多的人开始尝试、接受中医，并收到意想不到的疗效。[6]

宇宙本来是一个系统，而作为宇宙一部分的人体，自然应当系统地来医治。科技、设备再先进，也不能解决有关人的所有因素，诚如显微镜下固然可以看到细菌，但却看不到产生病症的心理与情绪。[7]

所以，从这个意义上，中医并不是一门单纯的医学，而是基于自然理念，对人体状况所做的系统判断与诊疗。[8]

Traditional Chinese Medicine: Treating the Human System

As a culture, Traditional Chinese Medicine (TCM) is in fact considered far more than a medical science for people. [1]

Modern medicine, represented by Western Medicine (WM), regards the human body as no more than an assemblage of anatomic organs in which pathological states exist in isolation from the overall well-being of the person who suffers from them. In its treatment, almost everything is dominated by Western medications and instruments and essentially these objects, instead of the "person", are the focus. In TCM, however, there is no such thing as a "partial disease"; instead, the person as a whole is taken into account, and medical materials and therapeutics are subject to specific human conditions based on its traditions and ideas. [2]

In TCM, the human body, as a natural product, is also the quintessence and an extension of nature. In a way, both humans and nature are bound to follow the *Dao* (the rule of the universe) – the heavenly *Dao* begets as well as serves the human *Dao*, resulting in the core values and therapeutics of TCM, its conceptual holism and treatment based on syndrome differentiation. [3]

It is thus difficult to define TCM in modern scientific terms, since what it treats are actually not diseases as such, but rather individual persons. A complex entity synchronizing natural and social sciences and philosophy, both physical and spiritual, objective and subjective, partial and integral, which requires comprehensive, multidimensional and dialectical consideration – that constitutes the kernel of TCM. [4]

For a TCM practitioner, a disease is not merely pathology in certain organs, but a loss of balance in the entire organism, and the root cause lies in the person as a whole. For example, a person's mood has some subtle and profound effects on his or her health and conditions – the phenomenon has increasingly been proved by the facts, but WM finds it hard to accept and explain. [5]

From my experience as a natural therapist researcher abroad, I have witnessed the "stop-gap" and "removal of lesion" approach of WM being increasingly questioned by the public, who have started shifting their attention to TCM, where a headache may be cured from the foot, or an eye complaint treated in the liver, or a kidney deficiency supplemented by the spleen and so on. Fascinated by its remarkable curative effects, more and more people have tried and received TCM treatment. [6]

Given the fact that the system builds in the nature of the universe extended to human bodies it produced, it should naturally be the focus of medicine, not the technology or facilities: no matter how advanced these are, they will never replace human factors. It is true that under a microscope one can find bacteria – but not the mentalities and emotions that may have caused the malady. [7]

In this sense, TCM should never be regarded as "clinical medicine" only, but rather as systematic diagnosis and treatment for people based on a natural understanding of individual human conditions. [8]

深度解析

参照　变通　融合

此文是笔者为首届中医翻译大赛所写的中医普及性文章，看似平浅，但蕴含了中医学的基本属性和特征，既需语言翻译能力,又需相当专业知识。针对参赛译文中的主要问题,拟从以下三个方面加以分析点评。

1. 多维度的参照

在[1]中,"不是一般意义上的医学",参赛者一般译成 "is not considered in a general sense" "is not a common medicine" "is not just common medicine" "as is often referred to, but a kind of culture"等,固然可以接受,但推敲起来,不够准确。纵观历史,西方也有传统医学,主要是由古希腊希波克拉底(Ἱπποκράτης, Hippocrates)奠定的古典西方医学,但从16世纪人体解剖学的建立,到17世纪物理学、化学知识对医学的渗透,医学家通过实际观察和实验来研究人体的疾病问题,从而逐步形成了科学医学体系,一般译为 scientific medicine,以有别于其他医学体系,如之后的"循证医学"(evidence-based medicine)等。

在[5]中,"中医医生"多被译成了 Chinese doctor,其实有误。在西方,西医被称为 orthodox medicine(正统医学),这与其说是医学的分类,不如说是一种社会文化的认知(即为社会大众所认可),而中医属于 alternative medicine(complementary medicine, fringe medicine),即另类医学,或补救医学、替代医学等。《牛津简明英汉医学词典》对此解释如下:the various systems of healing, including homeopathy, herbal remedies, hypnosis, and faith healing, that are not regarded as part of orthodox treatment by the medical profession, especially when offered by unregistered practitioners... The extent to which individual registered practitioners indulge in or spurn these therapies varies enormously but is governed by the overriding principle that shared care is only permitted if the registered practitioner remains in overall control; this is often unacceptable to those practicing alternative medicine.[①]（包括顺势疗法、草药、催眠法及信仰疗法等各种治疗体系，被医学界摒除在正统医学之外，特别是那些未注册的行医者。当正统疗法无效时，慢性病或不治之症患者便去尝试这些大部分未经证实的疗效。……即只有在注册医师主导下，才能进行与另类医学的配合治疗，而另类医学的治疗师对此又往往不能接受。）这段论述，不但界定了西医（正统医学）和中医（一种另类医学），而且可以看到对中医医生的称谓——practitioner 或 medical practitioner；而笔者据在国外的实践，认为在某种情况下，还可称为 doctor of Chinese medicine（下文亦有所涉及）。

同样在［5］中，对于"疾病"，参赛者使用了 illness、sickness、ailment、malady、disease 等，似乎都有道理，但应选择在此种语境中最恰当的那一个。分析起来，illness 主要是指 not feeling well，如"She was tutored at home during her illness."（生病期间，她在家由私人教师辅导。）而 sickness 意为 the state of being ill or unhealthy，与 illness 类似；ailment 则为"小病"（not serious illness），如"The pharmacist can assist

---

① 伊丽莎白·马丁（主编），《牛津简明英汉医学词典》（*Oxford Concise Medical Dictionary*），白永权主译，香港：牛津大学出版社，2000年，第49页。

you with the treatment of common ailments."（药剂师只能帮助你治疗日常小病。）相比之下，malady 则为 any unwholesome or desperate condition，即更严重的疾病，但现在更常用在社会方面，指 a serious problem in society（社会顽疾）等。就（中医医生眼里的）"疾病"而言，不同于上述这些，而是一种 general disorder，即为 disease，《牛津简明英汉医学词典》（第459页）释为：a disorder with a specific cause and recognizable signs and symptoms; any bodily abnormality or failure to function properly, except that resulting directly from physical injury (the latter, however, may open the way for disease)（有某种特定病因、并有可识别的体征和症状的病症，包括任何躯体畸形或不能正常发挥的功能，但不包括物理性损伤［尽管后者可导致疾病］）。故 disease 最为恰当（同样适用于［2］［4］）。但在［7］中，……（产生）"病症"（的心理与情绪），则又不妨为 malady。

第［2］中的（这主要是由中医的）"形成和理念所决定的"，一般翻译成了 "which is mainly determined by its formation and concepts" "which is mainly decided by the development and idea of TCM" "It is attributed to the formation of traditional Chinese medicine as well as its concepts" 等；其实，这里的"形成"是一个历史过程，有的用了 how TCM came into being，比较得要义，或可用 based on its traditions (and ideas)，尽管在字面上好像相距远一些，但比较起来，在内涵上则是最接近的。

实际上，此文处处从一种比较的角度来阐述问题：说中医不是一般意义上的医学（［1］），主要是相对西医而言的；把人看成解剖器官的是西医，而中医则更看重人的因素（［2］）；而试图以现代学科的分类来界定中医学，也是很难的，会得出不同的结论（［4］），也是以西医为标准的；中医对于"病"的理念，西医也是不认同的（［5］［6］［7］）；等等。故相应的翻译也应有对比意识，如用"while… but…" "from the point of view, … however, …" "… regard… , in a way…"等对比式介词、句式等。其中，由比较得鉴别，非类比但有对比，以表示两种不同性质的医学。例如，［5］中的"病变"，中医里并无恰当的对应词，故不妨用西医中的学科术语 pathology 等。同时，在语言、语境层面，还要做出许多变通与融合。

2.合理性的变通

参赛译文中的许多译法，显得比较生硬、僵化或有"字典痕迹"。这既有语言也有理解上的问题，故须在翻译中加以磨合和变通。

就标题"中医：一门人的系统医学"而言，参赛者大都将其中的"人的系统医学"译成了"A Systematic Medicine Concerning Human body" "A Systemic Medicine for Humans" "A Systems Medicine of Human" "A Systemic Medicine for Humans" "A Human-oriented Medical Science" "A Systems Medicine of Human" "A Systematic Medical Science about Human" "A Systematic Medical Science about Human"等，显然是将"人的系统医学"断成了"人的|系统医学"，实则，应理解为"人的系统|医学"，即将人看成是一个系统（即中医的核心理念），而且应当加上"医

治"之意,同时应避免重复词语 medicine。有的参赛译文具有这种意识,如"An All-round Therapy for Human""A Systemic Medicine of Treating Human Diseases""A Therapeutic Approach for People"等,但不妨进一步明确为:"Traditional Chinese Medicine: Treating the Human System"。这种变通虽然在语言层面上看似不对等,但却在实际内涵中更加相符。

在原文中有许多不同的"人""病人""人体""人的因素"等,但其"人"却未必都是同样的英文对应词,须详加辨析,变通处理。例如,[2]中"把人看作是解剖器官",其中的"人"大都被译成了 man、people、human 等,但分析起来,man 与 human 都主要指与自然或其他物种的区别,如:"According to Lao Zi, man and nature are united as one in essence, and man cultivates himself as cultivating the nature in the *Dao*."(在老子看来,天人合一,人成于道。)"Some animals possess the characteristic of man."(有些动物具有人的特征。)"After all, we are human."(毕竟我们都是人。)当然,man 有时也泛指"正常人",如:"No man in his senses would have done so."(没有一个神志清醒的人会这样做。)但是,这些却并不是此处"人"的性质;此处是就解剖学意义上的"人"来讲的,故可用 human body,更具客观性。

至于"人"(处次要地位),参赛译文也以 human、humans 居多。其实,这里强调的是医生眼里活生生的人,即"a human being, considered as someone with their own particular character",故应为 person,既是客观的,也是主观的"人",如:"人

的情绪对于人的疾病和健康有着非常微妙而深刻的影响。"(A person's mood has some subtle and profound effects on his or her health and conditions.)而下面的"人"（在治疗过程中占主导地位），虽性质依然，由于是对中医的治疗理念而言的，故不妨将其扩展为 the person as a whole，以使这一概念更加完整；同样，[5]中的"治病的根本在治人"的"人"，也可比照处理。

"人的因素"，有的译成 man's factors、person as a factor 等，实质可为 human factors、personal factors，但在医疗语境下，更常用的是 human conditions。类似的如："He is in good condition."（他身体健康。）"The doctors describe his condition as serious and say he is very lucky still to be alive."（医生说他病情严重，能活着已经很幸运了。）

在[8]中，"人体状况"更突出了这种性质，不过为强调其具体性，不妨译为 individual human conditions。但是，[7]中的"人的所有因素"，涉及的又不只是医学问题，还有人的心理、情绪等，故不妨又以 human factors 为宜。与此相关，[2]中的"将疾病与患者的生命相分离"，其中的"生命"一般都译成了 patient's life，固然不错，但在医学语境里，不是一般的生命状态，而是一种病人的身心状况，如"医务人员要对病人的生命负责"(Medical staff are responsible for the well-being of their patients.)，故以 well-being 更宜。

然而，[4]中的"既是人为的，又是自然的"，参赛者又多将其译成这样一种关系，如 man-made and natural、man-made factors and nature、artificial or natural、human and nature 等；其实，

这里更多强调的是主观与客观，故不妨用 objective and subjective 等。与此相关，［3］中的"人与自然服从同一法则"，许多参赛者翻译成 obey、rely、abide by、obey to、submit to、comply with 等，但这些词都有 be obedient to authority 之义，用于"人"是可以的，但用于"自然"显然不合适。《老子》中有句名言，"人法地，地法天，天法道，道法自然"，可译为"Man follows the ways of Earth; Earth follows the ways of Heaven; Heaven follows the ways of *Dao*; *Dao* follows its own ways."此中的 follow 用得很自然，其义为 do the same as…，故此处不妨译为"both humans and nature are bound to follow the *Dao* (the rule of the universe)"，其中括号内进一步说明 *Dao* 的性质。

在［5］中，"病人整体机制出现了某种失衡"，其中的"机制"多被译成了 mechanism。但此处应考虑在医学界、生物界更适用的词语，即 organism，其义为 a living thing that has (or can develop) the ability to act or function independently，故不妨译为 a loss of balance in an organism。

一些看似简单的词语，若不加认真考量，也会有偏差。如［7］中"但却看不到产生病症的心理与情绪"，其中的"心理"译成 psychological factors、psychic 等，"情绪"译成 mood、sentiment 等，似乎都欠准确，不如 the mentalities and emotions 更恰当。［8］中的"单纯的医学"译成 pure medical science，固然不能算错，但有更多学术研究的味道，pure medicine 是更符合大众的一种疗法；而［2］中的"（病症永远不会是）局部的"多被译成了 localized、localization 等，而 local

的本义为"existing in or belonging to the area where you live, or to the area that you are talking about",显然用此概念过大。

与此类似,[4]中的"以现代学科的分类来界定中医学",一般译成"to define the Chinese medicine by the classification of modern science""define TCM in accordance with modern classifications of disciplines""to define TCM in line with classification of modern disciplines"等,固然都是不错的;然而,就性质而论,亦可用 in modern scientific terms,即以那种对待科学学科的理解来界定中医。

同时,在词序上也不必过分拘泥于原文,如[3]中"既是自然的产物,又是自然的延伸和精华",其中"延伸"和"精华"的逻辑重要性是中国式的思维,而在英文里顺序则是相反的,如"… as a natural product, is also the quintessence and an extension of nature"等。在[5]中,"这在西医是不可以也不愿意解释的,但却被越来越多的事实所证明",参赛译文一般译成"which is not acceptable and refused to be explained by Western medicine, but has more and more been proved by the facts"等;其实,不妨以英文的思维,变通词序,如"the phenomenon has increasingly been proved by the facts, but WM finds it hard to accept and explain",从而捋顺其轻重缓急。

3.整体观的融合

纵观参赛者的译文,有些句子固然翻译出来了,但比较零碎，不够通畅——主要是指在思维上需要加以整合，从而写出更加地道的句式。

例如，[4]中的"人们试图以现代学科的分类来界定中医学，但发现很难"，被普遍译成"People tried to clarify the modern science to define traditional Chinese medicine, but have found it is very difficult…""People try to define the traditional Chinese medicine with the classification of modern disciplines. However, the process is difficult…""An attempt to dignify TCM as the categorization of modern disciplines is hardly available, since it…"等。这些似乎在字面上很"忠实"，但其实是中文的思维，须在根本上重新组织，不妨改译为："It is thus difficult to define TCM in modern scientific terms, …"。接下来，"人是复杂的综合体，介乎自然科学、社会科学和哲学之间：既是物质的，又是精神的；既是局部的，又是整体的；既是人为的，又是自然的。因而需要多方、综合、辩证地加以考虑"——出于中文"意合"的特点，此段文字中的一些概念和句式在翻译中须加厘清和梳理。具体而言，"复杂的综合体，介乎……之间"，比较典型的译文，如："a complicated combination – it situates somewhere among natural science, social science and philosophy – …""Humans are complex in that they are natural, social and philosophical at the same time"等。其中"综合体"似乎都没有体现出来，应该是一种 entity、synthesis、unity、body 等；"介乎……之间"的实质是"其中有/综合了……这些成分"，显然不是 among、between、in the mist of 之类的，而是 synchronize、combine、coordinate

等;"局部的""整体的"似乎又不完全对应 part and whole、local and general 等;"需要多方、综合、辩证地加以考虑",指的是"构成中医的核心内涵",应体现在kernel、essence、core values 等核心词上。

[3]中的"因而人与自然服从同一法则——道",一般译成"Thus, men and nature observe the same principle – Dao" "so people and nature obey the same law – Tao" "Therefore, both humanity and the nature abide by the same set of rules known as Tao"等,固然都有可取之处,但鉴于通篇所讲的自然与人体的客观规律,这里不妨引申为"to follow the *Dao* (the rule of the universe)",也是一种通融。特别是"人道依存于天道,天道服务于人道",一般容易译得繁杂冗赘,如"the law of humans depends on that of heaven while the latter serves the former" "Human's principle relies on the nature's and the latter one serves the former one" "Human Tao depends on Heaven Tao, while Heaven Tao serves Human Tao"等;其实可不必转换主语,而"一以贯之"为:"the heavenly *Dao* begets as well as serves the human *Dao*"。

回到上文所述[1]中的"不是一般意义上的医学",将其译成"… in fact, not a medicine in its general sense" "not a common medicine" "not a commonly regarded medicine"等,再自然不过;然而,如果通观全文,便会发现,本文所论述的是中医不仅仅是一种医学,而且涉及哲学、文化、人学等,故整句不妨译为:"As a culture, Traditional Chinese Medicine (TCM) is in fact considered far more than medical science for people."所以，原文的第一段，往往宜放到最后翻译，以收统揽全局之效。

此外，一些细节上的问题，如漏译题目、格式混乱、不分段落、标点错误、字体怪异等，亦应引起注意，因这些其实也是专业水平的一部分。

总之，就本届中医翻译大赛而言，参赛者的热情和总体水平都值得肯定。以上问题亦会出现在其他专业的翻译之中——翻译质量的提高永无止境。我们有足够的信心，期待在接续下来的历届大赛中，涌现出更多高水准的译文。

"革命"概念的中国化

现代意义的"革命"概念源于西方，19世纪末以日语为媒介，传入了中国。中国的现代革命观念显然是在西方现代思想影响下形成的，但又有很大区别。[1]

英文里的 revolution（革命）一词出自拉丁文词根 *revolutio* 和 *revolvere*，意为"向后转动"，后逐渐演变为以强制手段推翻政府或改变社会秩序，从而建立新制度。中文里原来也有"汤武革命"，但指的却是"易姓"和"王朝更替"；中国传统文化中的"革命"显然只是由"改朝换代"所塑造的。[2]

1890年之前，revolution 多翻译成贬义的"造反"（"革命"），富于破坏性；如王韬首次使用了"法国革命"，而康有为在提及日本维新所引起的动荡时，也称之为"革命"："及倒幕维新，而革命四起。"可见，作为现代概念的"革命"和 revolution 之间的最早对应，是以法国大革命之类的社会动荡为中介建立起来的。难怪，1895年孙中山到了日本时，发现当地报纸把他的党称为"革命党"而大吃一惊，有受辱之感。[3]

应当说，西方的革命观念，在中国最初是以传统文化中的"改朝换代"为根基而被理解和有选择性地吸收的。大约1900年后，"革命"逐渐被赋予了与以往割裂的新涵义，如《清议报》（1901年10月12日）所论："是故有易姓而非革命者，如汉灭秦、魏灭汉、晋灭魏，驯至乎元灭宋、明灭元、清灭明，皆是也。有革命而不必易姓者，如日本自神武天皇以来，二千余年，皆一姓相传，专制为治；而明治维新之后，由专制政体，改而为立宪政体，是也。欧洲诸国……当其在百余年前，固多专制为治，而未有所谓立宪政体，君民皆治于法律之下者也。自拿波仑第一崛起之后，诸国之民，骚然变动。遂逼其平日之专制政体，改而为立宪政体。而君公贵人，仍多世袭罔替焉，此皆革命而不必易姓者也。"至此，西方的"革命"概念在中国得以较为全面地被审视和接受。[4]

进而，邹容（1885—1905）在其《革命军》中做了充分的发挥："扫除数千年种种之专制政体，脱去数千年种种之奴隶性质，诛绝五百万有奇披毛戴角之满洲种，洗尽二百六十年残惨虐酷之大耻辱，使中国大陆成干净土，黄帝子孙皆华盛顿，则有起死回生，还魂返魄，出十八层地狱，升三十三天堂，郁郁勃勃，莽莽苍苍，至尊极高，独一无二，伟大绝伦之一目的，曰革命。巍巍哉！革命也。皇皇哉！革命也。"至此，中国的革命概念具有了特殊的道德成分，这与西方迥异。[5]

然而，许多中国知识分子对于 revolution 应当翻译成"革命"还是"改革"存有疑虑。典型的，如梁启超在《释革》中所言："'革'也者，含有英语之 Reform 与 Revolution 之二义。Reform 者，因其所固有而损益之以迁于善，如英国国会一千八百三十二年之 Revolution 是也，日本人译之曰改革、曰革新。Revolution 者，若转轮然，从根柢处掀翻之，而别造一新世界，如法国一千七百八十九之 Revolution 是也，日本人译之曰

'革命'。'革命'二字，非确译也。'革命'之名词，始见于中国者，其在《易》曰：'汤武革命，顺乎天而应乎人'；其在《书》曰：'革殷受命'。皆指王朝易姓而言，是不足以当Revo.［省文下仿此］之意也。……Ref. 主渐，Revo. 主顿；Ref. 主部分，Revo. 主全体；Ref. 为累进之比例，Revo. 为反对之比例。……其前者吾欲字之曰'改革'，其后者吾欲字之曰'变革'。"可见翻译在二者间的纠结。然而，随着改革在中国的频频失败，社会普遍倾向革命，于是"革命"的译语渐渐占了上风——政治影响翻译，此为典型一例。此时的革命，已不免更具激进色彩。[6]

中国当代革命观的形成，带来了相当一段时期的暴力的正当化和斗争哲学的主宰。用暴力推翻旧制度、扫除旧势力似乎成了唯一的"正道"，而革命的人生观就是要与天、地、人斗，而且其乐无穷。在此过程中，凡不主张革命的，便被视为历史前进的阻力，于是中文语境里原本中性的"反动"一词，逐渐等同于"反革命"，而且出现了重罪——"反革命罪"。[7]

1954年，"反革命罪"首次写入了我国宪法。1982年修宪，仍将此罪保留。鉴于此罪下的无数冤案和反对此罪的不断呼声，1997年"反革命罪"正式在《刑法》中更名"危害国家安全罪"，标志了我国法制建设的一个划时代的进步。[8]

历史证明，疾风暴雨式的"革命"，带来的往往是破坏和倒退，而脚踏实地、遵循客观规律的改革，才会带来实效和进步。中国以经济建设为核心的崛起，已日益融入全球化，使其在政治、经济、社会制度等层面，远远摆脱了激进式的革命，步入了和谐发展的新常态。然而，在思想、意识、道德层面，如何反省百余年来从西方引进、经中国文化改造、与改革相融合的现代革命观念，进而告别以往，迎接更新，似乎是当下一个值得研究的问题。[9]

译 文

"Revolution": A Sinicized Concept

The concept of "revolution" in a modern sense, originating from the West, was introduced into China through Japanese as a lingua franca in the late-19th century. But the modern Chinese revolutionary idea, though shaped by Western thought, is still quite different from that of the West. [1]

Etymologically, the word "revolution" originated from the Latin *revolutio* (n.) and *revolvere* (v.), meaning "roll back". It gradually evolved into a forcible overthrow of a government or social order, in favor of a new system. In classical Chinese, there were also terms like 汤武革命 (*Tang Wu geming*), or "the revolution of Tang Wu", denoting the alteration of emperors' surnames and the regularity of changing dynasties. Clearly, the connotations of "revolution" (*geming*) in traditional Chinese culture was derived from nothing but a pattern of regime replacement. [2]

Before 1890, the term "revolution" was mostly translated

into Chinese as 造反 (*zaofan*, a synonym of *geming* at that time), or "rebellion" in a derogatory sense, full of destructiveness. For example, Wang Tao, a senior official of the Qing Dynasty (1636-1911), for the first time derogatorily mentioned the "French Revolution" (法国革命) in a document. Also, while mentioning the Meiji Restoration, Kang Youwei wrote in his "memorial to the throne": "When the Restoration started, revolution arose from all directions." In this sense, *geming*, in its modern sense, and "revolution" were initially linked by referring to social chaos (such as the French Revolution). That was why Dr. Sun Yat-sen (1866-1925) was so surprised to find his party was called 革命党 (*geming dang*) or the "Revolutionary Party" when he arrived in Japan in 1895, and felt he was being humiliated. [3]

It may perhaps be put in this way: Initially the Western concept of revolution was understood and selectively taken into the traditional cultural context of "regime-replacement" in China. Around 1900, certain new connotations then emerged concerning "revolution", distinguishingly different from that of the past. As the *China Discussion Daily* (Oct. 12, 1901) commented: "There were events of changing emperors' names of different dynasties devoid of any trace of revolution, such as the Han Dynasty replacing the Qin Dynasty, or the Wei the Han, and the Jin the Wei Dynasties... Even the Yuan replacing the Song, and the Qing the Ming all followed the same pattern. Some revolutions, as they happened, did not have to involve changing emperors' names for different dynasties: in

Japan with their autocracy Emperor Jinmu's name was not changed over a period of two thousand years of several successive dynasties. After the Meiji Restoration, this autocracy was transformed into a constitutional monarchy. Countries in Europe, … a century ago were dominated by autocracy as well (none of them had anything resembling a constitutional monarchy), but both rulers and the ruled were subject to the law. After the rise of Napoleon I, people in these countries initiated their uproar which compelled autocracy to be transformed into constitutionalism, although royal households and hereditary aristocracies remained – which could be called 'revolutions without altering titles.'" Up to now, it was possible for the Chinese to evaluate relatively fairly and take in the Western concept of revolution. [4]

Moreover, Zou Rong, a young revolutionary further elaborated the newly defined concept in his *Revolutionary Army*: "It is to abolish various autocracies that have been rooted for thousands of years as well as to get rid of all sorts of slaveries. The burning shame imposed by the five million or so Manchurians' barbarian colonial rule over the past 260 years has to be completely wiped out and leave China as a Sukhavati (pure land) where every Chinese descendant could be as decent as Washington, resurrecting with a reincarnated spirit from the bottom of hell to the upper level of paradise. In this mood, we will emerge into a new frontier, with lush growth of trees and grasses, full of vigor, heading for a uniquely great and noble goal. How glorious, splendid and magnificent a revolution is!" As an exclusive feature from the West, moral elements had thus been incorporated into the Chinese concept of revolution. [5]

However, doubts remained among the Chinese intellectuals on whether "revolution" should be translated as *geming* (revolution) or *gaige* (reform). Typically, as Liang Qichao pointed out: "The character *ge* in fact contains the meanings of both 'reform' and 'revolution'. The former refers to change for the better by removing existing defects, such as the 'Revolution of the parliament of the United Kingdom' in 1832, which was translated by the Japanese as '改革 (かいかく)' or '革新 (かくしん)' (reform). As for 'Revolution', it is like a rolling wheel, drastically throwing out something old to make way for a new world, such as the 'French Revolution' in 1789, which is translated by the Japanese as '革命 (かくめい)' (revolution). In this context, *geming* was not the right term to translate 'revolution'. The initial appearance of *geming* in Chinese is found in the *Book of Changes*: 'Tang Wu *geming* was guided by the heavenly *Dao* and in line with the populace's wish', as well as in the *Classic Book of History*: 'The Shang Dynasty was overthrown by the mandate of heaven.' – all these denote altering the titles of different dynasties, which is not appropriate for 'Revolution'.... 'Ref.' refers to a movement with the momentum gradually and progressively abolishing most of the obsolete, whereas 'Revo.' means an action capable of radically and absolutely replacing the previous object... In my view, the word derived from the etymon 'Ref-' denotes 'reform', whereas the word stemmed from 'Revo-' signifies 'revolution'. Namely, the former should be rendered as '改革' (*gaige*) and the latter '变革' (*bianqe* – an interchangeable word for *geming*)." Entanglement as such could ever be seen in translation between the two terms. With the constant failure of reforms in China, the public mood increasingly switched to revolution, which inevitably became more radical and, as a result *geming* prevailed, signifying how translation had been influenced by politics in China. [6]

The legitimacy of violence and the dominance of class struggle philosophy characterized the modern Chinese concept of revolution for a quite lengthy period of time, when every old system and tradition had to be wiped out by way of violence – the only legitimate means to take, and fighting with nature and man would bring endless enjoyment. Meanwhile, anyone who dared to slightly disagree with revolution would be deemed "reactionary" – the term, previously a neutral word, was at this time often applied interchangeably with "counter-revolutionary", which ultimately referred to a capital felony – "the crime of counter-revolution." [7]

"The crime of counter-revolution" was stipulated in China's first Constitution (1954), and remained in its revised Constitution (1982). With countless unjust cases revealed and constant public outcries against the crime, however, in 1997 "the crime of counter-revolution" was finally replaced by "the crime of endangering national security" in the Criminal Law, marking an epoch-making progress in perfecting China's legal system.[8]

History has repeatedly proved that revolutions or "violent storms" only bring destruction and setbacks, while following objective laws and carrying out surefooted reforms normally yield progressive effectiveness. China's rise, centering on economic construction and increasing integration into globalization, has long freed itself from the fashion of radical revolution and entered a stage of harmonious "new normal" development in the fields of politics, economics, social systems, and yet a question remains, requiring our serious consideration: How to switch our mindset in terms of ideology and morality, to leave the past and embrace this renewal?[9]

深度解析

在历史沿革语境中"善译"

"善译"理论,是晚清时期著名语言学家马建忠提出来的。他以参据拉丁语系、撰写《马氏文通》(1898年)而闻名,为中文的现代语法结构创立了基本框架,使后人受益至今;殊不知,更早于此的,则是他超前的翻译思想,而这对于翻译诸如"革命"这样具有历史沿革语境的概念,别有深意。马建忠在《拟设翻译书院议》(1894)阐述了他的"善译"观:

夫译之为事难矣，译之将奈何？其平日冥心钩考，必先将所译者与所以译者两国之文字深嗜笃好，字栉句比，以考彼此文字孳生之源，同异之故。所有相当之实义，委曲推究，务审其音声之高下，析其字句之繁简，尽其文体之变态，及其义理精深奥折之所由然。夫如是，则一书到手，经营反覆，确知其意旨之所在，而又摹写其神情，仿佛其语气，然后心悟神解，振笔而书，译成之文，适如其所译而止，而曾无毫发出入于其间，夫而后能使阅者所得之益，与观原文无异，是则为善译也已。

此段涵义丰富，涉及语义学、文法学、修辞学、语用学及文化研究，亦与西方翻译学家奇尔顿（Chilton）的论点相吻合："Language as a social semiotic imposes a structure of values, social and economic in origin, on whatever is represented."[1]（作为社会符号的语言，含有其所代表的社会和经济根源及其价值体系。）"Anything that is said or written about the world is articulated from a particular ideological position."[2]（任何所言所书，都是某一特殊思想意识的表达。）可见，翻译绝不似一般想象那样简单、容易。

首先，对于所翻译的对象，要"经营反覆，确知其意旨之所在"，同时"以考彼此文字孳生之源，异同之故"，即有一

---

[1] Stephen Chilton. *Grounding Political Development*. Boulder, Colorado: Lynne Rienner Publishers, 1991, p. 4.

[2] Stephen Chilton. *Grounding Political Development*. Boulder, Colorado: Lynne Rienner Publishers, 1991, p. 10.

脉络清晰的整体把握。就 revolution 而言，在西方的线索比较清晰，如［2］中所示，源于拉丁文词根 *revolutio* 和 *revolvere*，义为"向后转动"，后逐渐演变为以强制手段推翻政府或改变社会秩序，从而建立新制度等。① 为使译文更加明确，不妨加入 etymologically。"从而建立新制度"固然可译成 in order to establish a new system，但此处有二者比较之意，故用了 in favor of，类似的如："The representative went on to say that EU was determined to carry out the project and strongly in favor of protecting the public domain from re-privatization."（该代表坚持欧盟要落实该项目，以保护公共利益，而不致使之私有化。）故形成 ... originated from... meaning... into... in favor of... 的句式，以求连贯。然而，在中译文里，由于不同的传统文化渊源，则更为复杂，渗透到了几乎各个段落之中。

概括而言，其线索如下：

  改朝换代意义的"革命"（［2］）——具体造反色彩的"革命"（［3］）——赋予新意的"革命"（［4］［5］）——与"改革"相比较的"革命"（［6］）——中国当代革命观及"反革命罪"（［7］［8］）——新常态下的革命观（［9］）

就"革命"在中国传统文化中的主要涵义而言，似可涵盖如下方面：

---

 ① 亦可参见 *The New Oxford Dictionary of English*（《新牛津英语词典》）的 revolution 词条。

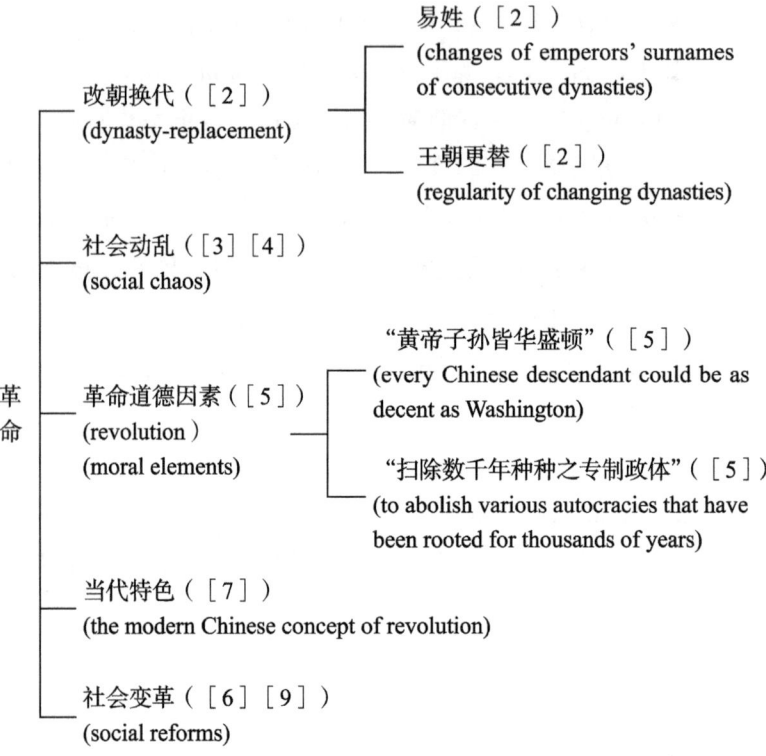

其中，"改朝换代"（具体体现为"易姓"和"王朝更替"）是中国传统文化中"革命"的本义；"社会动荡"是由此引申的负面语义，在翻译 revolution 初期占主导地位；"道德因素"主要由邹容等激进革命青年所倡导，为中国历史语境中的独创；所谓"当代特色"的革命概念，融合了"暴力正当化"和"斗争哲学"的特色；而"社会变革"才回归了其应有的正常语义和语境。

就此，不妨对比西方 revolution 概念的定义：We may use the term "revolution" in at least two senses. One indicates a radical (i.e., comprehensive) change or set of changes. Another is to describe a sudden event that brings about radical change. The liberal revolution should be understood in the former sense, because the radical change Europe underwent did not necessarily occur suddenly or violently, and sometimes took place gradually and (relatively) peacefully. Revolution in the second sense (a sudden series of events bringing radical change), is often the result of the failure to accommodate political institutions to a changing society or set of social values.①（我们所用的"革命"概念，至少有两种涵义：一种是激进、全面或系列的变化；另一种则是对带来剧烈变化的突发事件的陈述。自由主义革命，属于前者，因为欧洲的激进变化，并不一定是突然或暴力的，而有时是渐进的，相对平和的。第二种意义上的革命，即带来一系列激烈变化的突发事件，通常是政治体制未能与变革中的社会或相应价值观做出妥协的结果。）显然，相比西方政治文化中的 revolution，"革命"在中国传统文化中的涵义更为多样、不确定。例如，[3]中"王韬首次使用了'法国革命'"，对此要表述出其贬义的性质，便只有与前面一句"多翻译成贬义的'造反'（'革命'）"联系起来，在括弧中译为"*zaofan*, a synonym of geming at that time"，使之置于当时的历史语境，以便理解。其实，French Revolution 在欧洲革命历史上也是一个特例，如：The "French Revolution" of 1789, perhaps the most striking example of a revolution in this dramatic sense, can

---

① Munroe Eagles, et al. *Politics: An Introduction to Democratic Government*. Broadview Press, 2004, p. 178.

be seen as such an eruption caused by an intolerable tension between the old political order and the new social forces created by economic and cultural change.① （1789 年的法国大革命，也许是这种剧烈变革中最突出的案例，可看作是旧的政治秩序与由经济文化变革所孕育的新生社会势力之间、无法调和的紧张时态的井喷式爆发。）随着中国革命实践的进程，其贬义成分逐渐减少，从而 revolution 的涵义"在中国得以较为全面地被审视和接受"（［4］），而反映在文字上，则是更为准确、恰当地翻译出来，其英译文为"it was possible for the Chinese to evaluate relatively fairly and take in the Western concept of revolution"，而其潜台词实为 as well as to translate it more accurately and adequately，这层涵义在下文中逐渐体现出来。进行历史概念的翻译，对于当时"革命"一词使用的历史沿革背景，亦须有较为量化的了解。根据当时主要媒体上"革命"概念的使用情况，略做如下概述：②

从数据上看，1900 年之前，"革命"的涵义主要集中在本土的"易姓革命"和"汤武革命"上，同时引人注意的还有从西方传来的"法国革命"，该词组在相当一段历史时期内，被中国人用来作为理解西方革命的参照物；当然，如上所述，在此过程中发生了一些历史性的偏颇。自 1898 年戊戌变法失败之后，若干超越

---

① Munroe Eagles, et al. *Politics: An Introduction to Democratic Government*. Broadview Press, 2004, p. 178.
② 参见金观涛、刘青峰，《观念史研究》，北京：法律出版社，2009 年，第 374 页。（略有改动）

"革命"一词使用的历史沿革背景(1896—1911)

年份\类型	1896	1897	1898	1899	1900	1901	1902	1903	1904	1905	1906	1907	1908	1909	1910	1911
易姓革命	4	2	12	1	5	15	9	140	50	29					15	
汤武革命	3		1	2		2	5	4	3						1	3
法国革命	5	20	31	21	29	102	231	161	58	83	104	38	2	42	20	
政治革命		2	15	7	88	70	229	88	41	714	106	35	9	7	5	
经济革命			1	4	1	2	19	4		27	19		4	10	4	
社会革命			2		2		1	1	12	350	71	3	1	3		
无政府革命									2	23	258	289	1	2		
中国革命党			2	2	2	6	8	47	5	10	532	371	183	50	203	93
总计	12	24	64	37	127	197	502	445	171	1236	1090	736	200	114	248	96

其传统涵义的内涵出现了,如"政治革命""经济革命""社会革命""中国革命党"等,从而逐渐形成了现代中国革命观。

同时,善译观还注重将"所有相当之实义,委曲推究,务审其音声之高下,析其字句之繁简,尽其文体之变态,及其义理精深奥折之所由然",其实质是翻译中的语用语言等效问题,其最大特点是重视信息的"接受者",即要求译文在读者中产生的效果与原作相同,而这又是一个无止境的过程。在[1]中,"以日语为媒介",似可译成"through Japanese medium""the Japanese language was used as a medium of communication"等,如"以英语为媒介的中学西渐"可译为 learning into the West through English medium 等;但考虑到中文与日文的特殊关系(相同的汉字、不同的发音与差异的字义),故用了 (through Japanese as a) lingua franca,该词指 a common language used by speakers of different languages,即可理解为"被操汉语、日语者所共同使用的汉字"。从社会语言学的角度,在中国由传统社会向现代社会转型的近代史中,日语充当了独特角色;特别是戊戌变法失败后,梁启超乘日本"大岛"兵舰逃亡日本,办报、著述,将西方的许多现代词语、借助日文传入了英文。仅就政治、法律词语,常用的便有:人权(human right)、公证人(notary)、引渡(extradite)、主权(sovereignty)、上诉(appeal)、出庭(appear in court)、代理(deputy)、民主(democracy)、民法(civil law)、自由(freedom)、共和(republic)、证券(security)、刑法(criminal law)、仲裁(arbitration)、投票(vote)、判决

（judgment）、法人（legal person）、法定（statutory）、法医学（forensic science）、法则（rule）、法律（law）、法学（the science of law）、法庭（court）、社团（mass organization）、社团法人（commonalty）、免除（exemption）、治外法权（extraterritoriality）、制裁（sanction）、取缔（outlaw）、拘留（detention）、所得税（income tax）、所有权（ownership）、政府（government）、政策（policy）、政党（political party）、政治家（politician）、信托（trust）、特权（privilege）、财团法人（incorporated foundation）、时效（prescription）、动产（real estate）、假释（parole）、国际（international）、国际公法（Public International Law）、传票（summon）、债务（debt）、债券（bond）、领土（territory）、领空（territorial sky）、领海（territorial waters）、宪法（constitution）、总理（premier）、警察（police）、议会（parliament）、干部（cadre）、权利（rights）等等。从而大大丰富了中文的现代词语，也在一定意义上拉近了与西方语义的关系。

进而言之，善译应"适如其所译而止，而曾无毫发出入于其间，夫而后能使阅者所得之益，与观原文无异"，是翻译的最高境界。

同时，[7]中的"重罪"，一般很容易译成 most serious crime，但其专业术语为 felony，其基本涵义为 the act of committing a serious crime，而且通常会 "involved either the death penalty or a forfeiture of the felon's land and goods"①，总之是公认的严重犯罪，

---

① 加纳（主编），《牛津现代法律用语词典》（*A Dictionary of Modern Leagal Usage*, 2nd ed.），北京：法律出版社，2003 年，第 353 页。

故此处变通为 capital felony。

在［4］中，"改朝换代"可有多种译法，如 change dynasties/regimes、substitute a new regime for the old、the old dynasty was replaced with a new one 等。纵观中国历史，这已形成了一种特殊规律，同时又应避免一般意义上的重复，故不妨稍加发挥为 a pattern of regime replacement 等。《清议报》是梁启超逃亡日本时在东京与友人所办，"以主持清议、开发民智为主义"，在语言和思想上为中国由传统社会向现代社会的转型，起到了相当的启蒙作用。对于其中所述各个朝代的更替，可不必拘泥于语言形式上的 the Han Dynasty replacing the Qin Dynasty, … the Wei Dynasty replacing the Han, … the Jin Dynasty replacing the Wei Dynasty 等，而可做相应的简化。

在［5］中，所引述邹容的《革命军》，充满着炽烈的革命热情，气势磅礴，振聋发聩，有如一声震撼大地的惊雷，把皇冠震落于地，它的巨大作用和影响，如鲁迅所评："……便是悲壮淋漓的诗文，也不过是纸片上的东西，于后来的武昌起义怕没有什么大关系。倘说影响，则别的千言万语，大概都抵不过浅近直截的'革命军马前卒邹容'所做的《革命军》。"[①] 在翻译中，就其中的激奋之词，既要体现其语势，又要对一些铺张语句做些抒顺、变通和精炼处理，如："郁郁勃勃，莽莽苍苍，至尊极高，独一无二，伟大绝伦之一目的，曰革命。巍巍哉！革命也。皇皇哉！革命也。"其中用了三个"革命"，而译文可做这样的

---

① 鲁迅，《杂忆》，载《鲁迅全集》（第一卷），北京：人民文学出版社，1981年，第226页。

处理: "In this mood, we will emerge into a new frontier, with lush growth of trees and grasses, full of vigor, heading for a uniquely great and noble goal. How glorious, splendid and magnificent a revolution is!" 鉴于该篇的主旨是"革命",故 this mood 自然为其所指,而 noble goal 亦承其脉络,直至最后盛赞之语,和盘托出 How ... a revolution is,三而合一;同时,对其中汪洋恣意的形容也"适如其所译而止",拿捏尺度。

置身于 19 世纪末 20 世纪初的中国历史语境,其实类似的论述并不少见,值得参照。典型的如谭嗣同的《仁学》:"《易》明言:'汤、武革命,顺乎天而应乎人。'而苏轼犹曰:'孔子不称汤武',真诬说也。至于谓汤、武未尽善者,自指家天下者言之,非谓其不当诛独夫也。……志士仁人求为陈涉、杨玄感,以供圣人之驱除,死无憾焉。若其机无可乘,则莫若为任侠,亦足以伸民气,倡勇敢之风,是亦拨乱之具也。"[①]不妨译为:
The Book of Changes claims that "The geming (dynasty-replacement movements) mobilized by Shang Tang and Zhou Wu were in line with the heavenly *Dao* and popular feelings." But Su Shi said, "Confucius did not speak highly of the two leaders", which to me is an insult. Surely, as the populace discussed, Shang and Zhou were not perfect, but that does not mean they should be condemned as tyrants... Men with lofty ideals and integrity are eager to be heroes like Chen She and Yang Xuangan, but even they were expelled and died without

---

① 谭嗣同,《仁学》,郑州:中州古籍出版社,1998 年,第 343—344 页。

regret. Although their opportunities were denied, however, they would rather have been chivalrous swordsmen or to have acted as messengers to bring order out of chaos. In that way, the common good and courageous ethos could have been promoted.

再如，《〈天义报〉启》所论："地球之上邦国环立，然自有人类以来，无一事合于真公。异族之欺凌，君民之悬隔，贫富之差殊，此咸事之属于不公者也。……由是种族革命、政治革命、经济革命遂为人民天赋之权。然环顾世界各邦，其实行种族革命者尚占多数，若政治一端，虽实行共和政治者，犹不能尽人而平等，经济一端更无论矣。试推其原因，则以世界固有之社会，均属于阶级制度，合无量不公不平之习惯相积而成，故无论其迁变之若何，均含有不平之性质。非破坏固有之社会，决不能扫除阶级，使之尽合于公。顾今之论者，所言之革命，仅以经济革命为止。不知世界固有之阶级，以男女阶级为严。……故欲破社会固有之阶级，必自破男女阶级始。……居今日之中国，非男女革命与种族政治经济诸革命并行，亦不得合于真公。"[①]
不妨译为：Since man appeared on the planet, none of the countries around the world have so far achieved true justice – alien invasions, confrontations between the monarch and the people, extreme disparity between the rich and the poor and so on all characterize its nature… People are endowed with natural right to mobilize ethnic revolution, political revolution, economic revolution. Among these nations,

---

[①] 原载《复报》1907年7月第10期，转引自高军等编，《无政府主义在中国》，湖南人民出版社，1984年，第16—17页。

ethnic revolution seems to be a dominant phenomenon. Politically, in countries where a republic has been put in place, that "all men are born equal" is still out of the question, let alone in an economic sense. The root causes, if explored, may be found in their inherent class-based society, where copious injustices have been accumulated. In that case, whatever changes have taken place inequality remains… It is impossible to achieve justice without destroying the inherited society and abolishing classes. "Revolutions", currently discussed, are mostly confined to economic revolution. Among various classes, gender discrepancy is the worst… Therefore, eradicating innate classes must start from the actual inequality between male and female… In today's China, true justice can never be attained unless gender revolution is implemented side by side with ethnic, political and economic revolutions.

在［6］中，梁启超对于 Reform 和 Revolution、Ref. 与 Revo. 之间的辨析，现在看来未必正确。例如，reform 由 re- 和 form 两部分组成。re- 是拉丁文词根，义为 again、back 等，form 为 shape、mould 之义。form 来自拉丁文的 *forma*（a mould 或 form），是许多英文词汇的词素，如：conform（中古英语）表"顺应"；deform（晚期中古英语）表"变形"；reform（中古英语）表"使其成形"；而 formal（晚期中古英语），最初是指与形式（form）有关，至 16 世纪初有了"循规蹈矩、僵化"之义；format（19 世纪中期）源自拉丁文的 *formatus*，经过法文和德文演化为"形成"（书本）。其核心为"make changes in something (typically a social, political, or economic institution or practice) in order to improve it"① （使一些事情，典型的如社会、政治、经济体系或实践，发生变化，以求改善）。在应用中，如"It also demonstrates that swift reform is often more effective than drawn-out and painful adjustments."（这还表明，快速改革往往比拖拖拉拉的痛苦调整更有效。）即便是 swift reform 也不等于 revolution；又如，"It is said that politics must not be allowed to get in the way of reform."（绝不允许政治因素影响改革的进度。）即使 politics 与 reform 在一个语境中，亦与 revolution 不同。

就 revolution 而言，该词由三部分组成：re- (back) + volut (roll) + ion (n. suf.)。拉丁文动词 volvere 义为"转动、摇滚、翻转"，其前加上 re-，便有了"翻回、旋转"之义。revolution（晚期中古英语）在 17 世纪有了"推翻政府"之义，20 世纪早期又演化出词素 rev，用以表示发动马达；revolt（16 世纪中期）起初用于政治领域，到了 18 世纪又有了"使人伪装逃脱"的涵义。其核心为："A fundamental change in political organization or in a government or constitution: the overthrow or renunciation of one government or ruler and the substitution of another by the governed"②（在政治组织、政府或宪法上所发生的根本性的变化，如被统治者推翻或抛弃某一政府或统治者，以取而代之）。在应用中，如："A revolution in the strict sense of the word just means tremendous changes."（严格来说革命是指重大的改

---

① 见 *The New Oxford Dictionary of English*（2001）的 reform 词条。
② 见 *Randome House Merriam-Webster's Unabridged Dictionary*（2001）的 revolution 词条。

变。)"A year earlier, the War of Independence, also known as the American Revolution, began."(更早一年,独立战争,也就是美国革命爆发。)此处的 revolution 都不可与 reform 相混淆。显然,一百余年前梁启超所做的解释是有误差的;然而,对其原文的翻译,仍须尽力做到"无毫发出入于其间",从而"能使阅者所得之益,与观原文无异",了解历史沿革的本来面目。

同时,对梁氏所述关于"革命"与"改革"译语的消长背景的了解,则有助于翻译的客观性。根据数据统计,其变化如下:①

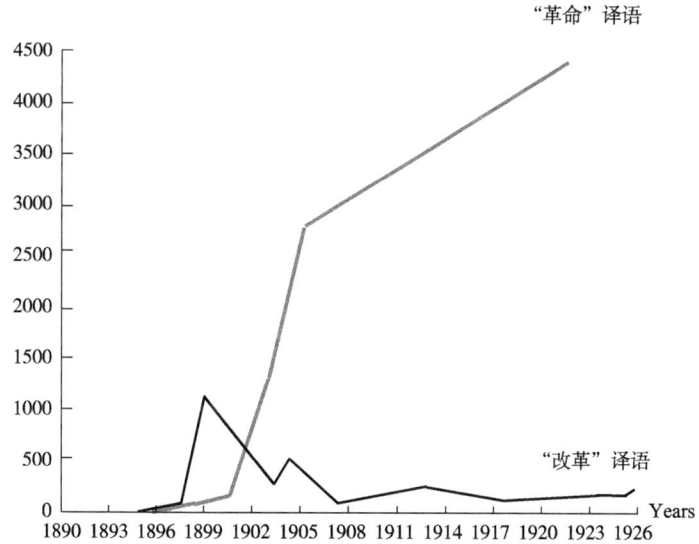

---

① 参见金观涛、刘青峰,《观念史研究》,北京:法律出版社,2009年,第382页。

如图所示，1900年之前，作为译语，"革命"很少使用，如1898年戊戌变法时仅出现了36次，而"改革"则出现了1000余次。变法失败后，1901年"革命"则超过了200余次。随着清政府的腐败无能的暴露，特别是自1900年8月14日八国联军攻占北京后，清政府的合法性受到质疑，从而日益成为革命的对象，致使"革命"译语几乎直线上升。由此，对"政治影响翻译"（how translation had been influenced by politics）的历史沿革背景，做了有力的注脚。

纵观"善译"之道，其要旨在"心悟神解"，从而做到"神似"。以此而论，除了上述词根、词性、词义等语境辨析问题，在句子结构上亦有体现，如［5］中，"至此，中国的革命概念具有了特殊的道德成分，这与西方迥异"，似可译成："Up to now, moral elements had become part of the Chinese revolutionary concept, which is completely different from that of the West." 然而，鉴于该篇论及的是revolution一词在中国历史文化语境中被翻译沿革的过程，此处为强调与西方不同的成分，不妨将其调整并提前："As an exclusive feature from the West, …" 再如，［9］中，"然而，在思想、意识、道德层面，如何反省百余年来从西方引进、经中国文化改造、与改革相融合的现代革命观念，进而告别以往，迎接更新，似乎是当下一个值得研究的问题"，似可译成"However, how to switch our mindset in terms of ideology and morality, leaving the past and embracing the renewal remains a question requiring our serious consideration"，以在语言层面上更贴近原文；然而，译为"… and yet a question remains, requiring our serious consideration: How to switch our mindset in terms of ideology and morality, to leave the past and embrace this renewal?",不但在语势上更加顺达,而且还将问题突出,以画龙点睛。

总之,"一书到手,经营反覆,确知其意旨之所在",对于"无毫发出入于其间"地翻译"革命"一类的概念,自然包括在历史沿革语境的广度和深度上进行探究所需的巨大功夫。

"西法东渐"的启示

自明末清初，随着西方传教士的来华，同时带来了西方的文明与科技，开启了"西学东渐"的进程。特别是 1840 年鸦片战争以后，中国便陷入了"三千年未有之大变局"的种种国内外的冲突之中。在法律方面，传统的律例体系已无法应对，其权威逐步丧失，致使传统的中华体系走向解体，从而令中国在某种程度上被动地进入了以西方制度为标准的近代国家形态。[1]

从清末的修律，到南京临时政府共和宪政的实践、北洋政府时期的法律西化、国民政府时期的"六法体系"，直至香港、澳门的《基本法》，无不受到"西法东渐"的影响。对这样复杂的过程，做一归纳、分析，似可发现某些规律性的东西。[2]

首先，西方法学的输入是以西方知识的传播为前提的，即西方的政法知识依附于对世界一般地理历史知识的介绍。起初，大量依据传教士刊印的中文材料编辑而成的《海国图志》《海国四说》《瀛寰志略》等，都是以介绍世界地理知识为核心的综合性书籍；到了 19 世纪 60 年代后，由于西方国际公法著作的大量翻译及人们对西方社会的深入了解，才有了相对独立的近代西方法学的输入。由此可见，法学必须以社会知识为基础；而今亦然，对西方法学的引进与吸收，仍须以对其社会政治制度等方面的理解为前提，才能收到最佳效果。[3]

其次，法律移植不可避免。对于法律移植历来有否定和肯定两种观点。否定者认为，由于法律与该国的自然状态、社会制度、生活习俗及与其他法律之间的特定关系，一个国家的法律只适合于该国人民；若能适合他国，也纯属偶然。肯定者则认为，各国的基本条件都有相通之处，自古至今法律移植是一种常见的现象，而且是法律发展的源泉。在某种意义上讲，越是民族的东西，越能走向世界。[4]

广义而言，在鉴别、调适、整合的基础上，引进、吸收、同化外国法律中的某些成分，使之成为本国法律体系的有机部分，正是法律移植中最普遍的做法。例如，南京国民政府在正视中国自然经济长期占统治地位、以宗法原则解决民事法律纠纷的社会现实基础上，引进了近代西方资产阶级民法中的私有财产神圣不可侵犯、契约自由和过失责任的原则，较好地做到了中国传统法律文化与西方法律原则的有机结合，从而制定了中国历史上第一部正式的民法典。[5]

再次，在大胆借鉴、吸收外国法律的同时，要保持自身法制的自主性。这主要表现在对外国法的比较、鉴别和选择，同时对外国法进行本土化的改造，使之适应本国的社会条件，并能与本国法相兼容，此后还要对移植法进行不断的修改、补充和完善。例如，清末修律者，在法律移植过程中，注重保持自身法制的自主性，紧扣中国社会实际，为此后中国法律的近代化奠定了相当的基础。这突出体现在《大清新刑律》的制定，该律到了民国初期仍有相当的实效，故南京临时政府决定，除与民主国体抵触部分之外，对此仍予沿用。甚至到了北洋政府时期，对此稍加修改，即成《暂行新刑律》，得以有效实施，从而充分显示了以法制自主原则制定的法律，可以在相当程度上跨越意识形态的羁绊，在不同政府时期具有生命力。这种法制的自主性传统，在当代香港和澳门《基本法》的制定中，表现得尤为突出。[6]

与此同步，要不断地探究中西法律概念之间的对应关系。法律最终要通过语言加以表述，因而语言质量对于建立不同国度法律间的联系与转换，至关重要。在此方面，马礼逊的《华英字典》为早期中英法律概念之间的理解与沟通,做了开拓性的工作。如，最早把"法律"释为 the laws、a law，"原告"为 the accuser or plaintiff，"被告"为 the accused or defendant，"公司"为 the term by which Chinese designate European Companies 等。而麦都思的《英华字典》则将这种对应关系进一步系统化：首先，从固有汉字中寻找直接对应关系，如：adopt —立嗣、立继、继嗣（今译"收养"）；bank —银铺（今译"银行"）；bankruptcy —倒行（今译"破产"）；capital —死罪、问罪（今译"死刑"）；code of Chinese laws —律例（今译"法典"）；police officer —衙役、原差（今译"警察"）等。其次，对于难以用固有中文词语对应的，另造大致类似的汉字组合，如：liberty（not under the control of any one）—自主之理（今译"自由"）；politics —国政之事、衙门之事（今译"政治"）；president（one in authority over others when his proper title is not known, the eye of the head）—头目、长（今译"总统"）；等等。此外，对于"词位空缺"的，做解释性变通。例如：关于 jury，编译者先指出 the Chinese have none，然后指出"乡绅"

（country gentlemen）有时具有类似功能；关于 advocate，编译者先指出中国的衙门（court of justice）里没有 advocates（今译"辩护人"）或 counselors（今译"法律顾问"），而后指出有拟写状纸的"讼师""词讼之师傅"，其作用是"包揽词讼"等。[7]

幸运的是，中文有一个天然的"胞弟"——日文，它在"西法东渐"中的中文与西文之间充当了优质的媒介。据统计，在现代法学词汇里，有近一半来自日文，如：法律、法学、法庭、法人、法则、法医学、法定、公证人、主权、引渡、政党、政府、政治家、权利、主权、人权、债权、债务、刑法、仲裁、出庭、拘留、动产、假释，等等。借助第三语言来鉴别、辨析法律概念，在现实的法律交流、借鉴、翻译、移植中，仍是十分有益的。[8]

从历史的发展来看，正是因为当年有涓涓"西法东渐"的支流，才汇成了当今全球化发展的大趋势。这股洪流将更加强劲，而且是双向性、多维度的，呈现出新的特点与启示。[9]

译 文

Some Revelations of the "Western Jurisprudence Moving towards the East"

With the arrival of missionaries in the late Ming and early Qing Dynasties, Western civilization and science and technology were also brought to China, initiating a process of "Western learning moving towards the East". In particular, after the Opium war of 1840,

China plunged into a period of profound transformation unheralded in China's history of the past three thousand years, that involved various conflicts both domestically and internationally. In terms of law, with its declining authority and collapsing legal system, China was unable to cope with the challenges and was forced to go down the track of moving towards becoming a "modern nation" according to criteria set up by the West. [1]

The influence of "Western learning moving towards the East" was pervasive and profound, as can be seen in various consequential legal practices, such as the constitutional governance of the Nanjing Provisional Government, the Westernization of the legal system of the Northern Warlord Government, the laying down of the legal system of the "six-combined laws" by the Kuomintang Government, and the stipulation of the contemporary *Basic Laws* for Hong Kong and Macao. In summarizing and analyzing the history, certain regularities may be revealed. [2]

First of all, the introduction of Western jurisprudence was premised on the spread of Western knowledge; in other words, the political and legal knowledge of the West was made known following the popularization of information about the geography and history of the world. Initially, comprehensive books centering on the geographical world like the *Overseas Geography*, *A General Introduction of the Overseas Countries* and *An Outline of Abroad* were all compiled from Chinese materials printed by missionaries. Accompanied by a large amount of translation of

Western international public laws and the deepened understanding about the West, it was not until 1860s that Western jurisprudence as a discipline was introduced into China. Clearly, jurisprudence is society-based knowledge, which reminds us of our today's practice in selecting and taking in legal applications from the West – the ideal results come out of a thorough understanding of Western society, political systems and the related aspects. [3]

Second, it is inevitable that legal transplantations emerge from international contacts, and this has long been a controversial issue. Those who oppose it believe that a nation's laws are exclusive (some rare cases are purely accidental) due to special natural conditions, social institutes, cultural customs and unique legal landscape; those who favor it advocate that since conditions are always similar among countries in the world, legal transplantations have not only become a common phenomenon but also a source for development of laws. In a sense, it is easier for things ethical to draw attention of other countries. [4]

In a broad sense, it had become common practice for legal transplantation to introduce, adopt, assimilate and ultimately integrate certain legal elements of foreign countries on the basis of identification, adjustment and confirmation. For example, based on the reality of Chinese society, which had long been dominated by natural economy and where civil disputes were mainly dealt with by patriarchal principles, the Nanjing National Government incorporated principles of the inviolability of private property, freedom of contract and fault liability, as practiced by Western bourgeoisies in civil law, to better combine traditional Chinese legal culture with Western legal principles, in order to formulate the first official *Civil Code* in China's history. [5]

Third, while audaciously drawing on and absorbing foreign laws, one's own autonomy must be maintained in term of developing a legal system by ways of comparison, differentiation and selection. In other words, foreign laws have to be localized before they can be made compatible with the social conditions and laws of the adopted country. Consequently, the transplanted laws have to be constantly revised, complemented and improved. Taking the revision of the law in late Qing Dynasty as an example, during the process of legal transplantation, law makers focused on the reality of Chinese society, laying a solid ground for modernizing the Chinese legal system. The result materialized most fruitfully in the *Qing Criminal Law* (Revision), which was largely valid, with a minor revision concerning its democratic state system, until the early Republic Period. Moreover, the same law was slightly revised and transformed into the *New Provisional Criminal Law* by the Northern Warlord Government and actualized effectively. The practice fully demonstrated that a law enacted with the principle of autonomy could, to a great extent, transcend the hurdle of ideologies and still be legitimate during different periods of government. Surely, the legal tradition of autonomy was most acutely manifested in the stipulation of the *Basic Laws* for Hong Kong and Macao during the transitional period of the 1980s. [6]

In the meantime, a constant exploration of equivalence between Chinese and Western legal concepts is required, since laws are ultimately expressed in language, which quality is crucial in establishing linkage and conversion between the laws of different countries. In this regard, Morrison's *A Dictionary of the Chinese Language* pioneered understanding and communication between Chinese and English legal concepts. For example, *falü* was firstly translated into "the laws", "a law"; *yuangao*, "the accuser or plaintiff"; *beigao*, "the accused or defendant"; and *gongsi*, "the term by which Chinese designate European Companies," amongst others. Medhurst, another pioneering translator, further systematized the correspondence in a number of ways: One, searching for congruent relationship from the existing Chinese characters, such as adopt – *lisi, liji, jisi* (*shouyang* in today's version), bank – *yinpu* (*yinhang* in today's version), bankruptcy – *daohang* (*pochan* in today's version), capital – *sizui, wenzui* (*sixing* in today's version), code of Chinese laws – *lüli* (*fadian* in today's version), police officer – *yayi, yuanchai* (*jingcha* in today's version), etcetera. Two, wherever it was difficult to find the existence of a relationship, two Chinese characters were formed into a phrase to denote the meaning, such as liberty (not under the control of any one) – *zizhu zhi li* (*ziyou* in today's version), politics – *guozheng zhi shi, yamen zhi shi* (*zhengzhi* in today's version), president (one in authority over others when his proper title is not known, the eye of the head) – *tou mu, zhang* (*zongtong* in today's version). Three, whenever there is a vacancy, a paraphrase is made, such as for "jury", the editor first pointed out "the Chinese have gone", and then referred it to *xiangshen* (country gentlemen) which carried similar missions. For "advocate", another example, it was explained that since there were no such things as "advocates" (*bianhuren*) or counselors (*falü guwen*) in a Chinese *yamen* (court of justice), *songshi* and *cisong zhi shifu* were actually undertaking the same task of *baolan cisong* (writing legal documents), and thus performing a similar role to that of advocates. [7]

Fortunately, Chinese has a "natural brother"– Japanese, which acted as an efficient medium between Chinese and Western languages. As it is estimated that almost half of the words in modern legal Chinese are Japanese in terms of the characters shared between the two languages. Examples include law, jurisprudence, court, corporation, rules, forensic science, statutory, notary, sovereignty, extradition, political party, government, politician, right, sovereignty, human rights, creditor's rights, debts, criminal law, arbitration, appear in court, detention, personal property, and parole. In today's legal communication, comparison, translation and transplantation using a third language as reference can still be very beneficial. [8]

Judging from this historical development, countless tributaries like "Western jurisprudence moving towards the East" have eventually merged into the current globalized torrent, which will become even more dynamic, mutually beneficial and multidimensional. Consequently, new features and revelations will continue to emerge. [9]

> 深度解析

着眼于法律文化互动中的动态等值

"动态对等"（dynamic equivalence）是美国著名翻译学家奈达（Nida）于 20 世纪 60 年代提出来的，在以后的翻译理论与实践中产生了深远影响。其主要意思为：译文对于译文接受者所起的作用与原文对原文接受者所起的作用，应大体对等；而为达到动态对等，译者要从各种译法中挑选最接近原文效果的译法。本文所涉及的主要是法律文化互动（legal cultural interaction）方面的内容，故拟从以下三方面，就其最佳翻译效果做一探究。

1. 历史语境

明末清初，出现了"西学东渐"的潮流，从中不可避免地带动了"西法东渐"的进程。鸦片战争以后，中国的社会性质发生了很大的变化，在法律制度层面，中国逐渐失去其法制自主性，这主要体现在一系列不平等条约的签订，使外国列强占据了租借地、香港、澳门，建立了自己的行政机构和法律制度，同时某些国家在中国还具有了"领事裁判权"。于是，使中国面临了"三千年未有之大变局"（[1]）。该语出自清末重臣李鸿章之口，他在《复议制造轮船未可裁撤折》中道："臣窃惟欧洲诸国，百十年来，由印度而南洋，由南洋而中国，闯入边界腹地，凡前史所未载，亘古所未通，无不款关而求互市。我皇上如天之度，概与立约通商，以牢笼之，合地球东西南朔九万里之遥，胥聚于中国，此三千余年一大变局也。"以后该语便流行起来，其实这只是对中国历史性变革的一个笼统说法。[1]中的"大变局"不宜是现在流行的 big deal，而是指 profound change、transformation 等；"种种国内外冲突"，可用动名词 involving 相连接，故"中国便陷入了'三千年未有之大变局'的种种国内外的冲突之中"，可变通为："China plunged into a period of profound transformation unheralded in China's history of the past three thousand years, that involved various conflicts both domestically and internationally."而其背景是"西学东渐"（包括"西法东渐"），一般译成 the Western learning、the New Learning、the External Learning spreading to the East 等，这里不妨变通为 the Western Learning moving towards the East，以更显其动态。

同在[1]中，鉴于法制的效力是以法律的权威为基础的，故对"传统的律例体系已无法应对，其权威逐步丧失，致使传统的中华体系走向解体"这句，可将词序调整，以示强调："with its declining authority and collapsing legal system, China was unable to cope with the challenges"。其中的"律例"是中国古代对法律的称呼，也指法律古抄本的说明或有些特别法律，如"大明律例"等，不过都可通译为 law、code、case law 或相关的 legal system 等。而"令中国在某种程度上被动地进入了以西方制度为标准的近代国家形态"，其中的"以西方……的近代国家形态"似可译成 was shaped into a Western type of country，但考察其历史背景，会发现用 go down the track 更适宜，因可表示其演化过程。

［2］中所叙述的是那一段法律进程的简要概括，即在动荡不安的清朝末世，面对强势的西方法律，中国的律法修订者做出了种种艰难努力，为中国法律的近代化的开启做出了难能可贵的贡献，如清末修律时期制定的部分法典为后来几个时期的政府或直接引用，或成为其立法的基础，而这种法制自主性的民族传统，到了制定港澳《基本法》时，得到了空前的发扬光大。这些历史感都应在译文中得以体现，如"影响"在原文中是宾语，在译文中为强调，可转换成主语，同时对其"影响力"应增加词语，如 pervasive and profound 等，将对不同政府有影响的法律置后，否则不足以表述其内在脉络："The influence of 'Western learning moving towards the East' was pervasive and profound, as can be seen in various consequential legal practices, such as…"。应当在译文中增词的地方还有"国民政府时期的'六法体系'"（增加"制定"义，the laying down of）等，否则句子成分就不完整。

在［9］中，"从历史的发展来看"，应贯穿这种历史眼光，但却不是 look at、foresight、eye 等，宜用更"重"些的词语，如 judging from 等。类似的用法如："Judging from what we have accomplished so far, we are optimistic."（从现在的状况看，是有希望的。）"从领导的讲话看，他们越来越关注空气污染、水污染和受污染影响的健康问题了。"（Judging from their speeches, Chinese leaders are increasingly anxious about foul air, filthy water and unhealthy levels of pollutants.）同时，此处的"支流"和"洪

流"是一种形象的比喻,不宜以其他词语,如contribution 和 merger 等来替代;而"双向性",亦不是简单的mutual,而是有 mutually beneficial 的涵义。

2. 法律语境

步入近代,中国法制受到的挑战,其实质体现在西方法律文化对中国传统法律文化的冲击。从历史上看,西方法律文化与中国传统法律文化之间的第一次交锋发生在戊戌变法时,维新派试图将西方的某些政治、法律制度和法律文化引入中国,而顽固派则力图维持中国传统的政治、法律制度,两派政治力量较量的结果,以维新派的失败而告终。清末的法律改革,可说是西方法律文化与中国传统法律文化的第二次交锋。所不同的是,坚持传统法律文化不可动摇的"礼教派"败下阵来,而主张吸收西方法律文化长处的"法理派"占了上风,因而废除了传统法律制度中的一些原则和制度,同时引进了一些西方法律文化中的法律概念、原则和制度。虽然改革后的法律大都未能付诸实践,但毕竟开启了西方法律文化正式涌入中国法律制度的大门,也预示着中国传统法律文化的衰退。

应当说,西方法律文化的输入,不仅提供了一种在整体功能上优于中国传统法律文化的替代物,而且为中国人提供了一种反观和透视自己传统法律文化的参照系统。之后的法学家们,依据西方法律文化所提供的话语模式和普世价值,开始对中国传统法律文化进行重新诠释,而这一切都是以对西方社会知识的普及和对西方法律典籍的翻译为基础的，正如［3］中所述："西方法学的输入是以西方知识的传播为前提的，即西方的政法知识依附于对世界一般地理历史知识的介绍。"其中的"输入"和"介绍"可互换，且不一定都用 introduction，还可变换为"the popularization of information about..."等。而"到了 19 世纪 60 年代后，由于西方国际公法著作的大量翻译及人们对西方社会的深入了解，才有了相对独立的近代西方法学的输入"，其中的"由于"不一定是 because of、thanks to、due to owing to、as a result of 等，而是指相随相伴的一种历史现象，故可用 accompanied by；"独立的（近代西方法学）"不是 independent，因这里实际指的是一种"学科"（a branch of knowledge），故恰当词语应为 discipline。

［4］中的内容涉及"法律移植"概念，这其实是人类不同文化接触（cultural contact）中的一种，有西方学者使用了 acculturation（文化渗透、适应、同化）一词；但探究起来，该词的原义为 the adoption of the behavior patterns of the surrounding culture，特别是指美国早期人类学家对于美洲印第安人的土著文化如何受白人文化影响所做的研究，通常注重一种文化对另一种文化的单向影响，且颇带文化殖民色彩。因而不妨使用"文化互动"（cultural interaction），即指不同文化由于相互接触而相互影响、相互作用的现象，包括相互交流、沟通、碰撞、竞争、排斥、渗透、融合等；与此相应，法律文化互动则为 legal cultural interaction，而语言恰是这种互动的"触点"（见下节所述）。具体到"（法律）移植"概念，不同学者因研究视角不同，采用

了多种不同的词语，如 transplant（移植）、transfer（转移）、spread（传播）、reception（接受）、introducing（引进）、inoculation（嫁接）、influence（影响）、infiltration（渗透）、imposition（被迫接受）、immigration（移居）、imitation（模仿）、borrowing（借鉴）、assimilation（吸收）、adoption（采纳）、accepting（接受）、grafting（嫁接），等等。这里不妨变通为更为宽泛的 transplantation，而把"法律移植不可避免。对于法律移植历来有否定和肯定两种观点"译为"it is inevitable that legal transplantations emerge from international contacts"，既做了增词，即根据上述语境，增添了加下划线的部分，又将"有否定和肯定两种观点"浓缩为 controversial issue。

就对法律移植所持的两种观点而言，在法律界历来有着两套理论根据。早在 18 世纪，孟德斯鸠就在其名著《论法的精神》中写道："法律应该和国家的自然状态有关系；和寒、热、温的气候有关系；和土地的质量、形势与面积有关系；和农、猎、牧各种人民的生活方式有关系。法律应该和政治所能容忍的自由程度有关系；和居民的宗教、性癖、财富、人口、贸易、风俗、习惯相适应。最后，法律和法律之间也有关系，法律和它们的渊源，和立法者的目的，以及和作为法律建立的基础的事物的秩序也有关系。"①所以，"为某一国人民而制定的法律，应该是非常适合于该国的人民的"②。这历来作为法律移植否定派的经

---

① 孟德斯鸠,《论法的精神》(上)，张雁深译.北京：商务印书馆，1993 年，第 7 页。

② 同上书，第 6 页。

典论据。而肯定派则认为，法律基本上是独立于社会的、政治的、经济的因素而自主发展的，法律与社会没有必然的联系。"私法规则不论其历史起源如何，都可以在任何民族、时间和地域存在，而不受限于特定的时间或特定的地域。"[①]美国比较法学家阿兰·沃森（Alan Watson）通过对法律史的考察进一步验证了这一结论。通过对公元前18世纪的《埃什南纳法典》、公元前17世纪的《汉穆拉比法典》与后来的《出埃及记》有关法律条文进行比较，发现它们在内容和形式上都有明显的相似之处："尽管它们相距遥远，但是它们之间必定存在某种联系。它们在语言风格和实质内容上是如此的相似，排除了法律发展彼此孤立的可能性。或许它们具有共同的起源。"[②] "从最早的有历史记载的时期开始，法律移植，即法律规则或体系从一个国家向另一国家、从一个民族向另一民族的迁移，一直是一种常见的现象。"[③]在此基础上，对[4]中的"一个国家的法律只适合于该国人民"，可不必仅拘泥于文字，译成 a country's laws are only suitable to this country，而放在各民族间法律互动的大背景下（严格讲此处各国的法律应理解为 nation's laws），有排除其他国家之意，故可用 exclusive，其义为 not divided or shared with others；而"若能适合他国，也纯属偶然"（孟德斯鸠的论

[①] Alan Watson. "Legal Transplants and Law Reform". *Law Quarterly Review*, 1976, 92, p. 79.

[②] Alan Watson. *Legal Transplants: An Approach to Comparative Law*. Athens, GA: The University of Georgia Press, 1994, pp. 22-23.

[③] Alan Watson. *Legal Transplants: An Approach to Comparative Law*. Athens, GA: The University of Georgia Press, 1994, p. 95.

据）可作为一种插入语，在括号中表述。"与其他法律之间的特定关系"可理解为一种特定的整体法律模式，不妨用 unique legal landscape；同时将语序前后调整，加以强调："Those who oppose it believe that a nation's laws are exclusive (some rare cases are purely accidental) due to special natural conditions, social institutes, cultural customs and unique legal landscape"。至于"各国的基本条件都有相通之处"，不必拘泥于文字译成"there are similar basic conditions between countries"，而可理解为世界上不同国家之间相同条件的比较，"since conditions are always similar among countries in the world"，以更明确。

3. 翻译语境

如上所述，国际间的法律互动（legal interaction）和法律移植（legal transplantation）都是以法律语言和法律翻译为媒介的。

法律与语言有着一种特殊的关系，因为法律是由语言编织出的实体。正如美国法学家格罗斯费尔德（Grossfeld）指出的，"实在法的概念只有在语言中才能获得其存在"，"那些法律概念在现实的世界中没有对应物，若不借助于语言通常无法加以描述"。[①] 的确，与桌子、椅子等概念不同，所有权、代理权、著作权等法律概念并没有直接对应物，若不借助语言便无法理解。语言的多样性是形成人类法律文明多样性的重要原因，而不同的

[①] Bernhard Grossfeld. *The Strength and Weakness of Comparative Law*. Oxford: Clarendon Press, 1990, p. 92.

语言孕育了不同的法律概念和法律模式。法律文明的传播必以语言为中介，而语言的不同是阻隔其传播的重要障碍。然而，在某种意义上讲，语言又是人类法律文明保持多样性的天然壁垒。根据格罗斯费尔德的解释，英国法之所以能够不受外界干扰而独立发展，在于英国法律学家们像科学家那样敏锐地思考，创造出了一套高度专业化、技术化的词汇，清晰地界定了其概念，而这套专业化的语言阻止了欧洲大陆所发生的那场全盘接受罗马法的运动。①

然而，要突破这种法律之间的壁垒，就得倚仗翻译。在中西的这种最初交往中，翻译的角色是由传教士来承担的，如［7］中的马礼逊（Morrison）和麦都思（Medhurst）。应当说，这种翻译并不顺利，也不是一次完成的。至于法律领域的翻译则更有其特殊性，因法律概念和法律规则在两种语言中有着不同的特指，它们之间的"等值"是经过长时间、多角度的匹配才固定下来的，而一旦固化，对后世又产生了深远影响。典型的，体现在［7］中的"把'法律'释为 the laws、a law，'原告'为 the accuser or plaintiff，'被告'为 the accused or defendant，'公司'为 the term by which Chinese designate European Companies 等"，其中的中文宜用其汉语拼音（尽管与当时的发音不同，因当时还没有制定出《汉语拼音方案》）统一标注，以便于读者接受。对于"探究"，可有 probe into、investigate、delve、make a thorough inquiry 等对等词语，参考译文用了 exploration，

---

① Bernhard Grossfeld. *The Strength and Weakness of Comparative Law.* Oxford: Clarendon Press, 1990, pp. 87-88.

是想表现探索"法律概念之间的对应关系"的不易过程；而其后被动语态的 be 动词，由于间隔了 legal concepts，故很容易用复数 are，实则仍为单数 is；而"开拓性"还可有 groundbreaking、creative、exploitation 等，但鉴于马礼逊在华传教、编字典的首创性，用 pioneer 更恰当，该词的原义为："a person who is the first to study and develop a particular area of knowledge, culture, etc. that other people then continue to develop"。（《牛津高阶英汉双解词典》第 8 版）在表述次序上，对于麦都思创建的三种方法的"首先""其次""此外"，因上一层叙述已有 Firstly、Secondly、Thirdly，故不便再用，以免混乱，而可换为 One、Two、Three 等。

在［8］中，涉及作为中文"天然兄弟"的日文，就语言关系来讲，在古代，日文借用了中文里的汉字，但在融入日本文化、社会、传统过程中，其涵义发生了某些变化，总体来讲，有这样三大类型：第一类，同类词，即日文和中文中都有、意思相同或相似的汉字，如问题、政府、地震、心理、修理、表现等；第二类，中无词，即日语中特有但在中文里无意义的汉字，如人形、切手、我慢、地味、片手、目玉等；第三类，不同词，即日文和中文里都有，但意思不同的汉字，如大丈夫（没关系）、手紙（信）、勉強（学习）、用意（准备）、新聞（报纸）、野菜（蔬菜）等。到了现代，日语则以其独特的吸纳外语的能力，在中文与西文之间起到了桥梁作用，特别是在法律词汇方面，如［8］中所列举的，取得了极高的等值效应，其影响延绵至今；充当了"优质的媒介"，该短语不一定按其字面意思译成 quality intermediary，而可进一步就其作用，变通为 efficient medium between Chinese and Western languages；而该段所引这些汉字，因已经由日文"联姻"而形成了与英文的固定对应，故可不必再标示出其汉字或拼音。

综上所述，涉及法律文化互动内容的翻译，其动态等值离不开对相关历史背景的了解、法律语境的辨析及翻译细节的理解与运用，综合起来，融会贯通，才能取得较好的翻译效果。

哲学意义上的中医

医学是一门特殊的自然科学，因为在生命和疾病过程中，不仅需要健康和病理知识，而且涉及大量的心理、社会和文化因素，所以是一门综合学科。[1]

中西医学的根本属性是相同的，即治病、防病、救死扶伤，保护和增进人类健康，但是在哲学意义上，二者却迥然不同。如果说，当代西医是以"技术科学"为基础和中介的"实证医学"，那么中医就是以中国传统哲学为主导的"道理医学"。[2]

正如著名中医学家任旭所指出的，"我国古代医学无论从思想上还是方法上，都紧紧依赖于哲学，甚至用哲学的语言和规律来解释人体的生理、病理现象。中医理论可以不受解剖形态学发展的束缚而独立发展"。[3]

应当说，文化涵盖了哲学，哲学是文化的重要组成部分。[4]

中医典籍认为："从阴阳则生，逆之则死；从之则治，逆之则乱。反顺为逆，是谓内格。是故圣人不治已病，治未病，不治已乱，治未乱，此之谓也。夫病已成而后药之，乱已成而后治之，譬犹渴而穿井，斗而铸锥，不亦晚乎？"此段论述，与其说是医学，在某种意义上，不如说是哲学或安邦治国之道。[5]

类似的还有"釜底抽薪""如丧神守""阴阳交感""阴阳互根""孤阳不生""孤阴不长""重阴必阳""重阳必阴"

等,若不在中医的语境里,这些词汇、术语、警句完全可以作为哲学或文学用语加以诠释。[6]

就"五脏"而言,中西医里都有,但其"心""肝""脾""肺""肾"的概念并不是对等的,因为在中医里这些"脏腑"不单是解剖学概念,还包括了人体系统的生理、病理和精神上的多种功能,具有"象"的意义,是"脏象"。[7]

以"心"为例,西医认为,心是空心的圆锥形肌性器官,位于两肺之间,尖端向左前下方;心脏约有握拳大小,心壁大体上由心肌、心内膜及心脏外面的心包组成。显然,这是一个非常精确、可触摸的器官。然而,在中医里,除此之外,还有下述功能:君主之官,主血脉、藏神;在液为汗,开窍于舌,舌为心之苗,映心之病变。[8]

中医里大量概念又是西医所没有的。如"命门",其意为"生命的门户,先天精气蕴藏之处,为人体生化的来源,生命的根本,其主要功能是为元气所系,是人体生命活动的原动力,藏精舍神,与生殖机能有密切关系;为水火之宅,内寓真火;为人身阳气之根本"。这是一种典型的中医哲学理念。[9]

习近平主席最近指出:"中医药学是中国古代科学的瑰宝,也是打开中华文明宝库的钥匙。"其中自然包括了理解中医里的哲学思想。[10]

Traditional Chinese Medicine: A Philosophical Aspect

Medicine is regarded as a special type of physical science since understanding the life process and the progression of disease, requires much more than just knowledge of health and pathology. Meanwhile, a multitude of psychological, social and cultural factors are also involved, which necessitates that medicine must be an interdisciplinary practice. [1]

Fundamentally, both Traditional Chinese Medicine (TCM) and Western Medicine (WM) aim at preventing and curing diseases, protecting and improving people's health. Philosophically, however, the two medicines are quite different. While modern WM is defined as "evidence-based" one supported and mediated by scientific technology, TCM can be called the "reason-based" oriented by traditional Chinese philosophy. [2]

As well-known scholar of TCM Ren Xu points out, "Relying heavily on philosophy, TCM explains physiological and pathological phenomena of the human body in philosophical language and conceptualization. Its theory has been developed independently of the confines of anatomical morphology." [3]

It is believed that culture includes philosophy, and philosophy constitutes an important part of culture. [4]

For example, TCM classics states that "Obedience to the principle of *yin-yang* cultivates life and resistance to it speeds up death. Patients acting in compliance with the principle can be cured while those who prefer the other way might end up as a worsening case. Resistance, instead of obedience, to the principle of *yin-yang* means killing oneself from within. That shows the reason why wise people give priority to the prevention rather than curing of diseases. They take precautions to nip the first signs of illness in the bud rather than sit on them until illness has become a reality. Medication after the contraction of illness, comparable to drilling a well after feeling thirsty and forging weapons after the break-out of war, is therefore too late." What this paragraph expounds is actually not so much medicine as philosophy or a way of governing a state. [5]

Similarly, many other terms or phrases, such as "taking away firewood from under the cauldron", "saving a boat in an adverse current", "loss of mind, unconsciousness, restlessness, delirium and so on caused by excessive internal heat", "interaction of *yin* and *yang*", "mutual rooting of *yin* and *yang*", "solitary *yang* failing to grow, solitary *yin* failing to increase", "extreme *yin* turning into *yang*, extreme *yang* turning into *yin*" and so on, if these were not read in the context of TCM, they could be well elaborated as philosophical or literary glossary terms or aphorisms. [6]

Concerning the five internal organs, although there are terms for the heart, liver, spleen, lungs and kidneys in both TCM and WM, they are not mutually translatable between the two medical systems. In TCM, the viscera are not only anatomical concepts but also include various functions of the entire human bodily system, reflected in the meaning of *xiang*, namely the state of the viscera. [7]

Taking "heart" as an example, in WM it is defined as "a hollow muscular cone-shaped organ, lying between the lungs, with the pointed end (apex) directed downwards, forwards, and to the left. The heart is about the size of a closed fist. Its wall consists largely of cardiac muscle (myocardium), lined and surrounded by membranes." which is an accurate description of this physical organ. In TCM, however, apart from its physical nature, the heart also functions as a "monarch", controlling blood vessels and preserving the spirit. Sweat is considered as the fluid of the heart which opens in the tongue, and, as the sprout of the heart, the tongue reflects any pathological change in the heart. [8]

There are also many TCM terms that do not exist in WM, such as *mingmen*, which may be understood as "the place where congenital essence is stored. It is the source of the life processes and the base of life. Its main functions are the root of primordial *qi* acting as the primary motivating force for living activities. It is the source of *yang-qi* and the house of water and fire, storing the kidney-*yang*." The narrative is as much if not more cultural as medical. [9]

President Xi Jinping has recently pointed out that "TCM is the treasure of ancient Chinese science, as well as the key to open the treasure house of Chinese civilization." In this regard, its philosophical ideas are surely included in TCM. [10]

深度解析

特定理解基础上的变通
——第二届世界中医翻译大赛点评

第二届世界中医翻译大赛共收到有效参赛译文近三百份。译文总体质量比上届有所提高。参赛译文由广州医科大学基础部英语教研室教师进行了匿名初评和复评，后由世界中医药学会联合会翻译专业委员会组织的翻译专家评出了各级奖项。本文从"词语变通"和"行文变通"两方面，对参赛译文进行了分析，供广大翻译爱好者参考借鉴。

词语变通

翻译中首先遇到的是词语和词组，在汉英翻译中，则要在"字词"与 word 和 phrase 之间不断转换，而它们多有对等之处。在该文的特定中医语境里，一些看似简单的词语，亦有多种选择，须慎重对待。如，[1]中的"疾病"，参赛者用了 disease、sickness、illness、ailment 等，似都可以，但分析起来，对 disease，《牛津简明英汉医学词典》释为"a disorder with a specific cause and recognizable signs and symptoms; any bodily abnormality or failure to function properly, except that resulting directly from physical injury (the latter, however, may open the way for disease)"[①]（有某种特定病因并有可识别的体征和症状的病症，包括任何躯体畸形或不能正常发挥的功能，但不包括物理性损伤［尽管后者可导致疾病］）；illness 主要是指 not feeling well，如"The apparent cause of his illness was excessive drinking, but the real cause was his deep grief at his wife's death."（他生病的表面原因是饮酒过度，但实际原因是丧妻之痛。）；sickness 义为 the state of being ill or unhealthy，与 illness 类似；ailment 则为"小病"（not serious illness），如"Her other sibling don't seem to be able to overlook the sickness and see their sister as a person."（她的兄弟姐妹们也无法宽容她的这个病，不把她看作一个普通人。）；相比之下，malady 则为 any unwholesome or desperate condition，即更严重的疾病，但现在更常用在社会方面，指 serious problem in society（社会顽疾）等。然而，此处的"疾病"与前面的"生命"是一个动态过程，就"医学"（包括中西医）而言，实则是"治病"的过程，故宜为 treating sickness/diseases 等。

同样在［1］中，"自然科学"一般都译成 natural science，固然不错，但在学术表述上更多地译为 physical science，如

[①] 伊丽莎白·马丁（主编），《牛津简明英汉医学词典》（*Oxford Concise Medical Dictionary*），白永权主译，香港：牛津大学出版社，2000年，第459页。

"I admit that the first sentence of this passage points to certain differences between social and physical science."（我承认这段话的第一句，是针对社会科学和自然科学之间的某些区别而言的。）"Mathematics broke away from philosophy and became tied to physical science."（数学从哲学中分出来而且和自然科学联系在一起。）"Joule's work led to one of the basic laws of physical science."（焦耳的工作引导出自然科学的一个基本定律。）对于"一门综合学科"，有的参赛者意识到了其特殊性，故用了 the whole area of life and health、a special discipline、a distinct subject in the academic field、a complete medical science、a total composite subject 等，显然又过于"复杂化"了，不如简化为 an interdisciplinary practice 等。

[2]中的"实证医学"和"道理医学"是另一问题集中点，前者是西医已有术语，后者因中医性质而造。可参赛者对于前者亦多有不知，如译成 empirical medicine、technical science、demonstrated medicine 等，实属不该。对于后者，则可仁者见仁，但也应尽量符合其语境和表述形式，有的如 philosophical medicine、Taoist medicine、rational medicine 等，在语境上固然"有道理"，但鉴于前面西医的 evidence-based (medicine)，此处不妨相应译为 reason-based (medicine) 等。

对于[3]中的"中医学家"许多参赛者用了 the scholar/expert of Chinese doctor，其实在西方，西医被称为 orthodox medicine（正统医学），这与其说是医学的分类，不如说是一种社会文化的认知（即为社会大众所认可），而中医属于

alternative medicine (complementary medicine, fringe medicine),即另类医学或补救医学、替代医学等。《牛津简明英汉医学词典》(第49页)对此解释如下: the various systems of healing, including homeopathy, herbal remedies, hypnosis, and faith healing, that are not regarded as part of orthodox treatment by the medical profession, especially when offered by unregistered practitioners... The extent to which individual registered practitioners indulge in or spurn these therapies varies enormously but is governed by the overriding principle that shared care is only permitted if the registered practitioner remains in overall control; this is often unacceptable to those practicing alternative medicine.(包括顺势疗法、草药、催眠法及信仰疗法等各种治疗体系,被医学界摒除在正统医学之外,特别是那些未注册的行医者。当正统疗法无效时,慢性病或不治之症患者便去尝试这些大部分未经证实的疗效。……即只有在注册医师主导下,才能进行与另类医学的配合治疗,而另类医学的治疗师对此又往往不能接受。)这段论述,不但界定了西医(正统医学)和中医(一种另类医学),而且可以看到对中医医生的称谓—— practitioner 或 medical practitioner。笔者据在国外的实践,认为在某种情况下,还可称为 doctor of Chinese medicine,而此处更确切的应为 scholar of TCM。

　　同段,对于"甚至用哲学的语言和<u>规律</u>来解释人体的生理、病理现象",参赛者大都译成"Even we use philosophical language and <u>laws</u> to explain physiological and pathological appearances of body" "It even interprets physiological and pathological phenomena of human body with language and rules used in philosophical ideas" "We explained the physiological and pathological phenomena of human body with the language and guidance of philosophy"等，其中都把"规律"与 laws、rules、guidance 等自然联系起来，其实要做具体分析。此处主要指中医是一种哲学性很强的传统医学，其概念充斥着哲学的因素，故不妨以"TCM explains physiological and pathological phenomena of the human body in philosophical language and conceptualization"来表述。

[5][6]中，多处涉及"阴阳"概念，这可说是中医哲学理念的基石。《黄帝内经·素问》述："人生有形，不离阴阳"，"善诊者，察色按脉，先别阴阳"。因而阴阳是对自然界和事物发展规律中相互对立又相辅相成两方面的高度概括，这已为英语世界所广泛熟知，如《朗文当代高级英语辞典》（2009，第2682、2677页）所释："*yin* and *yang*: the ancient Chinese philosophy which is based on the idea that everything in the universe is formed and influenced by the combination of two forces called *yin* and *yang*" "*yin*: the female principle in Chinese philosophy which is inactive, dark, and negative, and which combines with *yang* (= the male principle) to influence everything in the world" "*yang*: the male principle in Chinese philosophy which is active, light, and positive, and which combines with *yin* (=the female principle) to influence everything in the world"。从阴阳这一基本性质出发，翻译中所做出的相应变通，尽管各异，但应不致相去甚远。较为典型的参赛译文，如将"从阴阳则生，逆之则死"，译成"If you follow

yin and *yang* you will be alive; otherwise you will die" "following *yin* and *yang* leads you to life; opposing *yin* and *yang* results in death"等，固然较为贴近原文，但还可稍加变通，如所"从"的其实不只是 *yin* and *yang*，而是其法则（principle）。然而，有的译成 "Human will be alive if complying with the natural laws, or will die" "Men will survive when they are compliant the law of nature, or they are doomed to die"等，则似乎又变通得"过"了，因 *yin* and *yang* 与 natural laws、law of nature 毕竟不是一回事。同时，此处的"生"和"死"也可做些变通，如不妨译为 "Obedience to the principle of *yin-yang* cultivates life and resistance to it speeds up death."等。以此类推，[6]中的"阴阳交感""阴阳互根""孤阳不生""孤阴不长""重阴必阳""重阳必阴"等，其翻译可能在细节上各有不同（如将"交感"译成 communicating，将"互根"译成 as mutual foundation，将"不生"译成 not to breed，将"不长"译成 not to grow，将"必阳"译成 must be *yang*，将"必阴"译成 has to be *yin*，等等），但整体意思仍为 "interaction of *yin* and *yang*" "mutual rooting of *yin* and *yang*" "solitary *yang* failing to grow, solitary *yin* failing to increase" "extreme *yin* turning into *yang*, extreme *yang* turning into *yin*"等，故均属可接受范畴。

同时，[5]中的"夫病已成而后药之"的"药"不是名词（medicine、remedy、drug），而是动词，即 curing...with medicine，但在此处，顺其句式，又不妨将其变通为名词 medication，将该句译为 "Medication after the contraction of illness"。

[7]中的"五脏"属中医用语，有的译成 wu zang、five zang-organs 等，其实也未尝不可，但须有说明或注释接续，如："The general name of the heart, liver, spleen, lung and kidney. Each of five zang organs functions to transform and store essence and qi, but also has its own responsibility and connects with the corresponding limb and sense organ."而若依此体例，后面的"心""肝""脾""肺""肾"，亦应先标出 xin、gan、pi、fei、shen，因这些毕竟是中医里的概念，而后再对应其西医概念 heart、liver、spleen、lungs、kidneys，因二者之间并不完全相等。同时，此处的"对等"，也未必是 equivalence、equivalent、reciprocity、reciprocal、equity 等。考虑到是两种医学系统间的概念转换，不妨用 mutually translatable between the two medical systems。

同理，[9]中的"命门"则更是一个典型的中医概念，还未在英语世界广为人知，故最好先以其中文形式（拼音 mingmen）出现，然后再做释译，如 which may be understood as "the place where congenital essence is stored, ..."，以收既变且通之效。

同时，对于该段中的"元气"，有的译成 yuan qi、innate energy、essential qi、the primordial energy 等，似都可接受，但参照相关的汉英中医词典，以 primordial qi 为宜。至于"真火"，许多人按其字面意思译成 the true fire、the real fire、living energy 等，显然没有了解其中医里的特定涵义— kidney-yang、the energy of kidney-yang。类似的，还有"真水"（kidney-yin、 the energy of kidney-*yin*）、"真气"（the vital *qi*）、"真喘"（dyspnea of excess type）、"真意"（pure thoughts）等。

至于［8］中对"心脏"的客观描述，则属西医范畴，应严格遵循其已有英文术语，特别是"心壁""心肌""心内膜""心包"等，不可臆造。

行文变通

文章是包括题目的，这个简单的事实似乎并未被每个参赛者意识或重视，直接体现在对于标题的漏译和误译上。没有标题，不成其为完整的文章，所以通常在初评环节即被淘汰；而标题翻译的质量之所以重要，因其直接反映译者对于原文的理解，并影响全文。很多人将标题译成"Traditional Chinese Medicine Philosophy""The Philosophy of Chinese Medicine""On the Philosophy of Traditional Chinese Medicine"等，若回译过去，便是"中医的哲学"，显然与原文的"哲学意义上的中医"有误差；而"A philosophical Chinese Doctor"则相去甚远，"Philosophically Traditional Chinese Medicine"则有语法问题，"On Traditional Chinese Medicine from an Aspect of Philosophical Significance"则不够简练。所以，较为适宜的为"The Philosophical Aspect of Traditional Chinese Medicine""Traditional Chinese Medicine: A Philosophical Aspect""Traditional Chinese Medicine in Its Philosophical Sense"等。

在［1］中，"因为在生命和疾病过程中，不仅需要健康和病理知识，而且涉及大量的心理、社会和文化因素，所以是一门综合学科"，许多参赛译文采用了这样的句式："Because in the process of both life and disease, not only healthy and pathology knowledge are needed, but also refer to a quantity of psychological, social and cultural factors, medicine is a comprehensive discipline." "In the process of life and disease, it not only needs health and pathological knowledge, but also involves a large number of psychological, social and cultural factors. As a result, medicine is also a comprehensive subject."等，且不论其中的语法错误，就其行文来讲，有些过于"零碎"。须知，与中文的"意合"不同，英文重"形合"，即是将句子成分之间用语言形式手段（如连词、介词、代词等）连接起来，形成完整逻辑关系，英文定义为：The dependent or subordinate construction or relationship of clauses with connective, for example, "I shall despair if you don't come."。故对此须有形合的意识，要着眼整句，甚至整段，如译为"Medicine is regarded as a special type of physical science since understanding the life process and the progression of disease, requires much more than just knowledge of health and pathology. Meanwhile, a multitude of psychological, social and cultural factors are also involved, which necessitates that medicine must be an interdisciplinary practice."，从而将原意加以整合。

在［2］中，"中西医学的根本属性是相同的，即治病、防病、救死扶伤，保护和增进人类健康，但是<u>在哲学意义上</u>，二者却迥然不同"，一般参赛译文，如："<u>The basic attribute</u>

of traditional Chinese and Western Medicine is the same, namely the treatment and prevention of disease, life-saving, protection and promotion of human health, but <u>in the sense of philosophy</u>, the two are very different." "<u>Both traditional Chinese medicine and Western medicine</u> origin from the same root, which is curing diseases, preventing diseases, healing the wounded and rescuing the dying, coupled with protecting and enhancing human's health. However, <u>in terms of philosophy</u> meanings, traditional Chinese medicine possesses huge differences with Western medicine"等。分析起来，原文强调两种医学在"根本属性"和"哲学意义上"的不同，但这些译文却将此重点埋没了。对此，不妨采用"Fundamentally, …; Philosophically, …"的句式，以突出主题，如："<u>Fundamentally</u>, both Traditional Chinese Medicine (TCM) and Western Medicine (WM) aim at preventing and curing diseases, protecting and improving people's health. <u>Philosophically</u>, however, the two medicines are quite different."同时，值得说明的是，当 Traditional Chinese Medicine 和 Western Medicine 首次出现时，应在后面括弧中加上简称 TCM 和 WM，以便下次出现时使用，从而避免整篇使用全称。

在同段，"如果说，当代西医是以'技术科学'<u>为基础和中介</u>的'实证医学'，那么中医就是以中国传统哲学<u>为主导</u>的'道理医学'"，对于其中的衔接部分（带下划线文字），很多参赛译文处理欠佳，例如，"If we say contemporary WM is evidence-based, <u>builds on</u> technology and science and <u>using</u>

them as a medium, then categorically TCM is a 'reason medicine' that develops its doctrines on the bedrock of Chinese traditional philosophy.""Contemporary Western medicine is an empirical medicine that taking technical science as basis and intermediary, while TCM is a theoretical medicine which is dominated by traditional Chinese philosophy."等，不免显得冗赘。其实，不妨使用过去分词短语"While modern WM is defined as 'evidence-based' one supported and mediated by scientific technology, TCM can be called the 'reason-based' oriented by traditional Chinese philosophy."，从而使句子简化、通畅。

在［3］中，"我国古代医学无论从思想上还是方法上，都紧紧依赖于哲学"，其中，对于"依赖于哲学"参赛者大都顺从原文，译成"whose tenets and methods are highly dependent on philosophy""Ancient Chinese Medicine relies closely on philosophy for thoughts and methodology""our ancient medicine was based closely on philosophy no matter on thoughts or measures"等。其实我们不妨使用动名词形式，将状语提前"Relying heavily on philosophy in terms of thought and methodology"，以使句子更加平衡。

在［4］中，对于"应当说，文化涵盖了哲学，哲学是文化的重要组成部分"，一般译成"It should be said that culture contains philosophy and philosophy is a significant component part of culture.""It should be mentioned that culture covers philosophy and philosophy is the significant component of culture.""It goes without saying that culture covers everything, including philosophy, which reversely stands as an essential part of culture."等。应当说这些都是可接受的，但整个句式，特别是对"覆盖""是"等词语可有更多推敲，如"We can posit that culture embodies philosophy, which is in fact part of any culture and constitutes one of its essential components."等。

［5］的"此段论述，与其说是医学，在某种意义上，不如说是哲学或安邦治国之道"，对于其中的"与其说……不如说……"，参赛者一般用了不同的表述，如："This treatise relatively shows the way of philosophy and administration rather than medicine." "It is more like a discussion about philosophy or the way to govern a country rather than medicine in a sense." "… which would be viewed more as philosophical discourse strategies for national governance than merely explanations in medical science."等。这些都有一定效果，亦有缺陷。其实，不妨采用… is not so much… as… or… 句式，译为："What this paragraph expounds is actually not so much medicine as philosophy or a way of governing a state."

［6］中，"若不在中医的语境里"，较为典型的译文，如"If takes out of the context of TCM" "… if not used in Chinese Traditional Medicine language environment" "If they are separated from the TCM context"等，显然是动词上出了问题。我们不妨使用 read 的被动语态"if these were not read in the context of TCM"，以更确切。

[8]中的"尖端向左前下方",有个词序的问题,很多参赛译文未能很好把握,如"with its small end pointing to front bottom-left""with the tip pointing to the lower front-left""with its tip toward the front lower left side"等。其实,中英文里表示方向的词序,许多情况下是相反的,故不妨译为"with the pointed end (apex) directed downwards, forwards, and to the left"。同时,"开窍于舌",被许多人译成"tongue is the sense organ of it""the tongue is acting as the window of the heart""it has an orifice which is the tongue"等,似乎都有一定道理,但在目前流行的汉英中医教材里,一般译为 opens in(to)/at the tongue 等。探究起来,五脏开窍之说,源自《黄帝内经》,指五脏与人体官窍有着相对应的关系,即:肝开窍于目,心开窍于舌,脾开窍于口,肺开窍于鼻,肾开窍于耳及二阴。在英语翻译实践中,逐渐形成了比较稳定的表述,故可跟从。同时,还应参照一些中医翻译专家的通常表述,如李照国、方廷钰、谢竹藩、朱忠宝等学者的译著。

其实,翻译中这种词语和行文的变通,即为某种意义上的 translation shifts,其核心仍是万变不离其宗:Most frequently, however, translation from one language into another substitutes messages in one language not for separate code-units but for entire messages in some other language. Such a translation is a reported speech; the translator recodes and transmits a message received from another source. Thus translation involves two equivalent messages in two different codes.① (然而，从一种语言翻译到另一种语言的信息常常不是孤立的代码单位，而是整体意思，恰如间接引语、译者的再述及从其他来源转述的信息。因而翻译涉及的是两种不同编码系统的等值信息。)

中医翻译，作为一种特定的医学翻译，涉及许多相关的文化、哲学和社会知识，因而体现出特殊的性质，并且要求高超的技巧。望有志于中医翻译者不断提高素质与技能，在下次大赛中取得更好成绩。

---

① Roman Jakobson. "On Linguistic Aspect of Translation". In R. Schulte and J. Biguenet (eds.), *Theories of Translation: An Anthology of Essays from Dryden to Derrida*. Chicago and London: The University of Chicago Press, 1992, p. 65.

附录：

家（节选）

周国平

　　家庭是人类一切社会组织中最自然的社会组织，是把人与大地、与生命的源头联结起来的主要纽带。有一个好伴侣，筑一个好窝，生儿育女，恤老抚幼，会给人一种踏实的生命感觉。无家的人倒是一身轻，只怕这轻有时难以承受，容易使人陷入一种在这世上没有根基的虚无感觉之中。[1]

　　人是一种很贪心的动物，他往往想同时得到彼此矛盾的东西。譬如说，他既想要安宁，又想要自由，既想有一个温暖的窝，又想作浪漫的漂流。他很容易这山望着那山高，不满足于既得的这一面而向往未得的那一面，于是便有了进出"围城"的迷乱和折腾。不过，就大多数人而言，是宁愿为了安宁而约束一下自由的。一度以唾弃家庭为时髦的现代人，现在纷纷回归家庭，珍视和谐的婚姻，也正证明了这一点。原因很简单，人终究是一种社会性的动物，而作为社会之细胞的家庭能使人的社会天性得到最经常最切近的满足。[2]

　　家不仅仅是一个场所，而更是一个本身即具有生命的活体。两个生命因相爱而结合为一个家，在共同生活的过程中，他们的生命随岁月的流逝而流逝，流归何处？我敢说，很大一部分流入这个家，转化为这个家的生命了。共同生活的时间愈长，这个家就愈成为一个有生命的东西，其中交织着两人共同的生活经历和命运，无数细小而宝贵的共同记忆，在多数情况下还有共同抚育小生命的辛劳和欢乐。[3]

正因为如此，即使在爱情已经消失的情况下，离异仍然会使当事人感觉到一种撕裂的痛楚。此时不是别的东西，而正是家这个活体，这个由双方生命岁月交织成的生命体在感到疼痛。如果我们时时记住家是一个有生命的东西，它也知道疼，它也畏惧死，我们就会心疼它，更加细心地爱护它了。那么，我们也许就可以避免一些原可避免的家庭破裂的悲剧了。[4]

心疼这个家吧，如同心疼一个默默护佑着也铭记着我们的生命岁月的善良的亲人。[5]

译文

The Family
By Zhou Guoping

The family is the most natural social organization of all kinds among communities, linking up people, earth and source of life. Having a good partner and a nice dwelling place where children are bred and the elderly cared for, provides you with a sense of a real and comforting life. Singles can surely enjoy a burdenless life, free of raising families, but they may also easily be overwhelmed by its nothingness, feeling rootless in the world. [1]

But so greedy is man as a creature that he always wants something contradictory to itself at the same time. For example, he longs for stability as well as liberty; a comfortable nest as well as a romantic venture. Almost all people see greener grass on another hill and they are never satisfied with what they have, but instead always crave for something more. Marriage is compared to a siege where people are busy with coming in and out of it. Most of them, however, would rather have stability by slightly constraining their liberty, which has been proved by some men about town who, for some reason, abandon their families but then return to appreciate harmonious married life. The reason seems to be simple: Man is after all a social being, whose innate nature is constantly and best comforted in the family as a social cell. [2]

A home, in fact, is not merely a dwelling place; it is itself a living body. The years of two loving lives, forming a family and spending time together, flow on to what end? Surely they mostly flow into the family, mingling with the family's life. As time goes by, the integrated family life is transformed into something more meaningful – shared fate and experiences filled with memories of tiny but unforgettable things, and in most cases, the bitterness and joy of bringing up children. [3]

It is precisely for this reason that partners are anguishedly facing divorce even when affection has vanished. It is simply the living body of a family in which different lives have been consummated that can also feel pain. Keeping this in mind – that its living body is equally sensible to hurt and death – we should be aware to nurture and cherish the family more carefully, as well as avoid the tragedy of family-breakdown. [4]

So, love your family wholeheartedly, just like taking care of a kind loved one who quietly guards and memorializes the years that have melted away in our lives. [5]

译 注

[1] 汉语中的"家"语义范围比较广,在英语中可以有不同的对应词,本文中所涉及的主要有 family 和 home,但"家庭(是人类一切社会组织中最自然的社会组织)"显然不是指住所,只能用 family。同样,"无家的人(倒是一身轻)"若译成 those homeless people、those without a home,回译成汉语便成了"无家可归的人"。

[2] 其中的"安宁"与"自由"相对应,将"自由"译为 freedom 固然可以,但"安宁"译成 peace 或 tranquility 的话,显然不妥,因为 peace 的反义词是 war,tranquility 是 peace、peacefulness 的近义词,其反义词是 commotion(吵闹),故用 stability 为宜。同时,"温暖的窝"和"浪漫的漂流"又是一对矛盾。此处的"窝"可直译为 nest、home,但不可是 house,因为会让人感到没有情感;且"漂流"二字不宜译成 nomadic life 或 drifting,因为前者指"游牧生活",后者通常指没有目的、浑浑噩噩的生活。

［4］此处的"心疼",似可译为 love dearly、feel sorry、make their heart ache 等,而 cherish 更雅。

［5］此句似还可译成"Cherish your home as you cherish a kind family member who blesses, protects and remembers our lives silently." "Let's cherish our home, just as we cherish a good relative who has been quietly blessing and guarding us as well as engraving on his/her mind the days and years of our live."等,但 cherish 用法略显重复,且 home 与 family 并用也有待商榷。

古村落："我们的根性文化"

魏青

传统村落是指拥有物质形态和非物质形态文化遗产，具有较高的历史、文化、科学、艺术、社会、经济价值的村落。但近年来，随着城镇化快速推进，以传统村落为代表的传统文化正在淡化，乃至消失。对传统村落历史建筑进行保护性抢救，并对传统街巷和周边环境进行整治，可防止传统村落无人化、空心化。[1]

古村落是历史文化遗存的特有形式之一，是地方历史经济发展水平的象征和民俗文化的集中代表。古村落文化是传统文化的重要组成部分，它直接体现出中华姓氏的血缘文化、聚族文化、伦理观念、祖宗崇拜、典章制度、堪舆风水、建筑艺术、地域特色等。[2]

古村落是传统耕读文化和农业经济的标志，在当前城市化巨大浪潮的冲击之下，古村落不可避免地被急功近利所觊觎和包围。之所以强调保护古村落，不是为了复古，更不是为了倡导过去的宗族居住生活模式，而是为了了解和保留一种久远的文明传统，最终是为了体现现代人的一份历史文化责任感。[3]

古村落与其说是老建筑，倒不如说是一座座承载了历史变迁的活建筑文化遗产，任凭世事变迁，斗转星移，古村落依然岿然不动,用无比顽强的生命力向人们诉说着村落的沧桑变迁,尽管曾经酷暑寒冬,风雪雨霜,但是古老的身躯依然支撑着生命的张力,和生生不息的人并肩生存,从这点上说,沧桑的古村落也是一种无形的精神安慰。[4]

在城市进入现代化的今天,对待古村落的态度也就是我们对待文化的态度。一座古村落的被改造或者消失,也许很多人没有感觉出丢了什么,但是,历史遗产少了一座古老的古村落,就少了些历史文化痕迹,就少了对历史文化的触摸感,也就很容易遗忘历史,遗忘了历史,很难谈文化延承,同时失去的还有附加在古村落上的文化魂灵。看一个地方有没有文化底蕴,有没有文化割裂感,不仅要看辉煌灿烂的文物遗留,还可以从一座座古村落上感受出来,从古村落高大的厅堂、精致的雕饰、上等的用材,古朴浑厚、巧夺天工的建筑造型上感受出来。[5]

台湾作家龙应台曾写过一篇和大树保护有关的文章:一条计划中的道路要穿过一位老人家门口,要砍倒一株老樟树。树小的时候,老人家还是孩子;现在,她人老了,树也大了。如果树能留下,老太太愿意把自己的一部分房子捐出来,经过协调,工程部门同意留树。龙应台感慨道:"人们承认了:树,才是一个地方里真正的原住民,驱赶原住民,你是要三思而行的;不得不挪动时,你是要深刻道歉的。"对于古村落,不得不改造和推倒时,同样需要三思而行。[6]

Ancient Villages: Our Indigenous Culture
By Wei Qing

Traditional villages are endowed with tangible and intangible cultural heritage of historical, cultural, scientific, art, social and economic values. Recently, however, with rapid urbanization, traditional culture exemplified in these villages has somewhat been diminished, or even vanished. "Protective rescue" for historical architectures in these traditional villages, together with effective measures in renovating their street scenes and surroundings are thus called for to avoid being "hollowed out" or becoming ghost towns. [1]

Ancient villages, one of the unique forms of historical and cultural relics, signifies the attainments of local economic development and folk culture. As part of substantial traditional culture, ancient villages in fact manifest Chinese kinship, communal life, ethic ideas, ancestral worship, rules and institutions, *fengshui*, architectural art and local features. [2]

Overwhelmed by the huge wave of current urbanization, ancient villages – a symbol of the farming culture and agricultural economy – are inevitably coveted and besieged by some "shortsighted profit pursuers". It has to be clear that our preservation efforts are not aimed at restoring the ancient way of living, much less advocating patriarchal system, but at appreciating and preserving a time-honored civilization. Eventually, the historical and cultural mission of modern men has to be carried forward. [3]

Instead of encompassing merely old buildings, ancient villages have withstood all the vicissitudes of time – the dog days of summer and the dead of winter, the change of seasons, and yet their antique bodies are still full of inexhaustible vitality, living side by side with people of successive generations. Only by simply existing there, their tattered shapes provide us with a kind of mental comfort. [4]

Confronted with today's urbanization, the way we deal with ancient villages reflects our attitude towards culture. For many, it may not mean much when an ancient village is converted or disappeared, but historically it has lost a cultural trace and a sense of touch of its past. Once it is devoid of its historical connection, cultural inheritance will become an empty word, and the cultural ethos mingled with these villages will also be gone. In evaluating a place's cultural deposits and continuity, therefore, apart from its splendid cultural relics, the grand hall, exquisite engravings, classy materials, primitive simplicity and elegance, and superb craftsmanship of architectural modeling of these ancient villages, also make a lot of sense. [5]

The Taiwanese writer Long Yingtai has written an article concerning protection of trees: A road was planned to build across an old lady's house, where a camphor tree had to be removed. The old lady said, when she was a child the tree was in its sapling stage, now the tree has grown up as she is in her twilight years. If the tree could be spared, she was willing to donate part of her property to make compensation. After negotiation with the project authority, the deal was done. The writer then sighed with emotion: "We have to admit that trees are the 'aborigines' of a place; when you have to remove them you ought to be very cautious and with deep regret!" When it comes to transforming or demolishing ancient villages, we should surely have the same sentiment. [6]

译　注

本文选自《贵州日报》（2014年6月6日），略做改动。

关于"根性文化"，许多人译成 cultural roots，但该短语是在论及文化根源时用到的，如："I believe that the beginnings of an answer lie in the cultural roots of nationalism."（我相信，一个答案的起点在于民族主义的文化之根。）"Because of different cultural roots between Chinese and other foreign culture, different aesthetics produce when speak of pastoral poetry."（由于中外文化根源的不同，中外山水田园诗会产生审美上的较大区别。）而这里的"根性文化"实质指的是本土文化，故不妨用 indigenous culture，如："'China' shows the people of the indigenous culture of recognition and persist in the Central Plains."（"华"展示了国人对

本土中原文化的认可与坚持。）"Protecting indigenous culture and benefiting local people are the foundations of tourism development."（"保护本土文化"和"让当地人受益"是旅游发展的根基。）

在［1］中，"物质形态和非物质形态文化遗产"固定表述为 tangible and intangible cultural heritage；"无人化、空心化"似可译成 depopulated and desolated，或借用《圣经》中的 exodus，该词的原义为"大批或成群地离开或移居国外"，与中国目前因城镇化而居民大量减少的情况有较大出入。这两个"化"其实意义相近，都表示人员剧减、被挖空了，而英文中常以 hollowed-out 或 ghost towns 来形容，如："In time, China became the workshop of the world, although by then America had long hollowed out much of its manufacturing."（于是中国便顺势成了"世界工厂"，尽管那时美国的制造业早已被挖空了。）"Everybody moved away, and these places are ghost towns now, with the wind whistling through the empty houses and shops."（人人都走了，这些地方变成了鬼城，只有阴风吹过空荡荡的房子和商店。）

在［2］中，"典章制度""堪舆风水""风水"等中国文化负载词语，似乎很难找到对等英文术语，查看有关词典，通常是 decrees and regulations、codes and systems、traditional institutions、geomancy 等，用在这里未必确切，所以这里做了进一步的推敲。

在［3］中，"耕读文化"似乎有许多译法，如 traditional farming-reading culture、Chinese traditional studying-while-farming culture、traditional *gengdu* culture and agrarian culture、the scholar-farmer lifestyle 等，但都太拘泥于字面意思。所谓"耕读文化"，

其实质就是农耕文明，既有别于现代工业文明，又有别于游牧文明和航海文明，即 the farming culture，其中都有"读"的成分，无须都加上 farming-reading culture、industrial-reading culture 等。这里的"复古"，不是简单地 return to the ancients，而是指那时的生活方式，故译为 aimed at restoring the ancient way of living；

"体现……责任感"可译为 carry forward the mission，如："Now I will start looking for people with the passion and vision to carry forward my noble mission."（我正在寻找有激情和视野的人把我的正义事业进行下去。）

［4］"尽管曾经酷暑寒冬，风雪雨霜，但是古老的身躯依然支撑着生命的张力，和生生不息的人并肩生存"，似可译成"Defying harsh weather and filled with vitality, they have existed to this day as constant companions to the dauntless Chinese people." "They have survived countless scorching summers and freezing winters, sheltering generations of people despite their growing decrepitude."等，但不够准确与顺达，主要是太拘泥于字面，而"生生不息"等意又未表达出来。"从这点上说"，不宜译成 from this point of view，因这里意为"仅以古村落的存在而言"，故不妨变通为 only by simply existing there，以示强调。

［5］"但是，历史遗产少了一座古老的古村落，就少了些历史文化痕迹，就少了对历史文化的触摸感，也就很容易遗忘历史，遗忘了历史，很难谈文化延承，同时失去的还有附加在古村落上的文化魂灵"，似可根据字面意思译成：… but to historical legacy, losing one traditional village means not only losing the cultural spirits attached to it, but also losing some traces of history and culture and the sense of touch on them, without which history could be easily forgotten and culture succession would become difficult as history has faded into oblivion. 但这样做失去了主语，且有堆积之感。须知，这里是作者连贯思路的流水表述，译成英文时要在用语和句式上做相应调整，以突出其所指。比如，可增添"For many, it may not mean much when…" "Once it is… ethos mingled with these villages"等，从而更加符合原文的语势。

在［6］中，"如果树能留下，老太太愿意把自己的一部分房子捐出来，经过协调，工程部门同意留树"，对其中的"捐"，有人认为不宜用 donate，因为该词是指"向慈善机构或其他组织无偿拿出财物"，而此处是指将自己部分房子拆除，让出空间修公路。其实不然，这里讲的是尊重私人财产。公家修路，绕过私人财产，必然要多出费用，此处的住户愿意为保留大树而捐出自己的部分房产作为修路多出代价的补偿，实则与 donate 无异。关于"协商"有人认为应该用 mediation，而不是 negotiation，因为该词是指"不同利益双方经讨论达成协议"，而这位户主并不代表什么利益一方，也不一定要签什么协议。其实不然——该户主代表自身利益（对她来讲就是最大利益），而且将意愿落实到行动，一定要签写协议。同时，mediation 的本义为 negotiation to resolve differences conducted by some impartial party，而且是由第三方来协调的，而当事人之间的任何商谈、协调等，都是 negotiation，故成此译文。

地名中的传统文化含量

张国刚

中国具有悠久的文明历史，留下了丰富多彩的历史篇章。历史有时间与空间这两个维度，直白地说，历史就是人们在一定的时间和特定空间创造的事件。时间是流动的，"逝者如斯夫，不舍昼夜"。空间却相对的固化，"人生代代无穷已，江月年年只相似"（张若虚《春江花月夜》）。读万卷书，行万里路。书中所见是历史的时间地图；路中所见是历史的空间地理，而空间地理首先是从地名反映出来的。[1]

年轻的时候读书，有机会到河南、陕西、山西、甘肃等地考察，每每见到《史记》《资治通鉴》中常见的历史地名，在现实中就呈现在我走过的这条路旁的界标上，总是感慨万千，油然升起一种穿越历史时空的苍茫感。中国悠久的历史和文化仿佛就在身边，并不那么遥远。地名是故乡的第一记忆。[2]

西晋末年，永嘉南渡，不少北方士民，被战争所驱迫，离乡背井，迁徙到遥远的南方去，他们不知道什么时候能回到故土。于是，设置了很多侨置的州县，沿用北方故土的名字。用地名保留故乡记忆是人类共同的感情。大航海之后的殖民扩张时代，欧洲人到了美洲、澳洲，给自己新的居住地，安上故乡的旧地名，这在美国、加拿大、澳大利亚，可以说是比比皆是，司空见惯。[3]

由此想到，当下的中国，许多地名是否能很好地保留祖先的历史记忆，传导深厚的历史文化底蕴？值得我们反思。比如说，今天许多省域的简称。安徽，境内有皖江，简称皖，自有其道理，其实安徽最深刻的记忆是徽。陕西简称陕，其实陕县在河南，陕之西并不是陕，而"秦"恰恰是陕西最深刻的记忆。又如，县级机构的设立是秦汉创建郡县制国家体制的基础要素之一。而郡县制是中国悠久历史中最具特色的制度。[4]

　　相反，区与市，却是很晚近的行政体制，中国历史上的市不是行政区划，现在作为行政区划的市是从日本移植过来的。可是，随着我国城市化的扩大，县改为市，成为普遍的事情，也许将来有一天，中国最古老的文化符号之一——"县"，就会逐渐消失。[5]

　　人类社会发展过程中，会丢弃一些传统的文化符号，这是正常现象。但是，这种丢弃一定有某种特定原因。否则人们一定是想方设法地保存历史记忆。联合国的非物质遗产申遗，大约就是鼓励这种行为。而地名的历史文化深度和广度，甚至要超过许多被保护的物质文化遗产。究其原因，在一段时期内，与历史和文化虚无主义有关。[6]

　　民国初年，北洋政府甚至禁止中医公开营业，许多中国传统的节日也被取消，包括正旦（俗称过年），代之以阳历新年。后来，大约群众的习惯力量太强大，才改成了春节。现在我们都把过年叫春节。许多地名的更改，改得越没有历史味道，就显得越进步、越新潮，就跟这种思潮有关。[7]

　　近几年来，国家恢复了许多传统节日，把这些传统节日定为法定假日，这是一种提倡，一种态度。过节是人的需求，一种文化和情感的需求。就像节日的问题一样，我觉得有些被历史与文化虚无主义所妄改的地名，也应该正本清源，还其历史面目。对于各地的历史地名，进行一次拨乱反正，也许正当其时。[8]

译 文

Traditional Chinese Culture Embodied in Place Names
By Zhang Guogang

China has a long history of civilization with a rich and colorful historical heritage. Since history encompasses both time and space, any event in the past was actually taking place in a certain juncture of these two dimensions. While time flows "The passage of time is just like the flow of water, which goes on day and night", sighed Confucius. Space, on the other hand, is relatively stable as described by Zhang Ruoxu in his "Night of Flowers and Moonlight by the Spring River": "Ah, generations have come and gone / From year to year the moons look alike, old and new." When people plan to read and travel extensively, they can actually read sequentially a historical map in books and glance over its spatial geography on roads, initially reflected in place names. [1]

When I was young, as a student I had chances to inspect places like Henan, Shaanxi, Shanxi and Gansu. Whenever I saw place names that I had read in *Historical Records* and *History as a Mirror*, I was involuntarily filled with a sense of the infinite, transcending historical time and space, drawing remote Chinese history and culture close to me; place names can in fact ignite the light of memory about one's native place. [2]

Late in the Western Jin Dynasty (266-316), during the years of Yongjia, many northern civilians were forced by the war to leave their hometowns and migrate to the remote south, and did not know when they could return. To preserve the memory of their hometowns, they set up states and counties using the names of these hometowns to hold the ties of common affection. Similarly, in the era of colonial expansion following the great voyages, Europeans ventured to the Americas and Australia, where they named almost every new place of residence with the names of their hometowns. [3]

It is therefore worth reflecting on how best to preserve the historical memory of our ancestors and transmit our profound culture in today's China. In abbreviating provincial areas, for example, Anhui is named as "Wan", a seemingly reasonable title, as there is a Wan River. But in fact the most impressive place in the province is "Hui". Shaanxi has been referred to as Shan, which is a county located in Henan province. The west of Shan is not Shan either, "Qin" instead actually has more symbolic meanings for the local people. Meanwhile, governments at county level (in the system of prefectures and counties) have been the founding blocks of a state set up since the Qin and Han Dynasties (221-206 BC, 202BC-220AD), characterizing the long history of the Chinese political system. [4]

In contrast, districts and cities are alien governances which came rather late to China's administrative systems transformed from Japan. However, with the pace of our country's current urbanization, converting a county into a city has become a common practice. Perhaps the "county" as one of China's oldest cultural symbols will gradually disappear. [5]

During the development of human society, it is not surprising to find some cultural symbols being discarded for particular reasons, while other historical memories deserved to be well preserved. Failure to do so during a certain period of time, is nothing but historical and cultural nihilism. The Protection of Intangible Cultural Heritage, founded by the United Nations, was probably intended to promote this kind of preservation. In this regard, history and culture conserved in places are more meaningful than many protected tangible cultural heritages in terms of their profundity and extent. [6]

In the early years of the Republic of China, the Northern Warlords (1912-1927) even outlawed the practice of Traditional Chinese Medicine and banned the celebrations of many traditional Chinese festivals, including Zheng Dan (commonly known as the Chinese New Year) which was replaced by the Gregorian New Year but later restored as the Spring Festival under pressure from the people's convention. Presently, there seem to be a trend, that the more their historical flavor is stripped out of place names, the more progressive and fashionable they become. [7]

In recent years, the government has recovered many traditional festivals, establishing them as statutory holidays to meet the demand of people's cultural and affective needs. By the same token, it is time to clean up the mess, get to the bottom of things and recuperate the original features of the place names that have been wrongly renamed by historical and cultural nihilism. [8]

译 注

就标题中的"含量"而言，似可用 contented，但 embodied 更富涵义，如《COBUILD英汉双解词典》（2002）所释："to embody an idea or quality means to be a symbol or expression of that idea or quality"。

[1]"两个维度"似可译成 two/double dimensions，但此处 (history) encompasses both time and space 可具体表明历史两个具体方面的涵义。"时间地图"不是 time map，而是就人们阅读而言的，故为 read sequentially a historical map in books。

[2] 所谓"第一记忆"若译成 first memory 略显直白，而"ignite the light of memory about…"更宜。

[4]"文化底蕴"还可译为 cultural deposits 等。

［5］"（市）不是（行政区划）"未直接译成 not、no 等，而是体现在了"… alien governances which came…"句式中，以更合语境。

［7］"跟这种思潮有关"，将其译文提前，以更为通顺。

［8］"正本清源"，此处不是 radically reform、get to the root 等，而是 clean up the mess，以更好保留地名中的文化因素。